ANATOMY
OF THE
SUPERMAN

"The nose of the bloodhound will be ours, and the ears of the snake; ours also will be the navigational abilities of certain flying insects, which use vibrating fibers in place of gyros. We will have adaptations of the sonar of the bat and the porpoise.

"The eye of the eagle may present problems, since its function must presumably be combined with normal human appearance; yet the betting man would have to guess that superman's sight will be better than the eagle's at any range . . ."

R. C. W. Ettinger

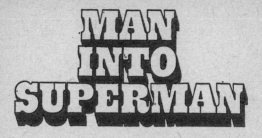

MAN INTO SUPERMAN

R.C.W. ETTINGER

THE STARTLING POTENTIAL
OF HUMAN EVOLUTION—
AND HOW TO BE PART OF IT

AVON
PUBLISHERS OF BARD, CAMELOT, DISCUS, EQUINOX AND FLARE BOOKS

AVON BOOKS
A division of
The Hearst Corporation
959 Eighth Avenue
New York, New York 10019

ISBN: 0-380-00047-4

First Avon Printing, June, 1974.

AVON TRADEMARK REG. U.S. PAT. OFF. AND
FOREIGN COUNTRIES, REGISTERED TRADEMARK—
MARCA REGISTRADA, HECHO EN CHICAGO, U.S.A.

Printed in the U.S.A.

CONTENTS

Preface

SUPERMAN IN THE FIRST AND SECOND PERSON

By working hard and saving my money, I intend to become an immortal superman. Naturally, many still question the realism and propriety of such a goal; they see this kind of ambition as both foolish and vulgar. I hope to show that those who are willing to settle for mortality and humanity just do not understand their predicament or their opportunity, how lowly they are and how exalted they may become.

That physical immortality—indefinitely extended life—is indeed within the grasp of us now living was the main theme of a previous book. Since then, a vigorous *cryonics* program has come into being; "dead" people are being frozen and stored in hope of eventual rescue—revival, repair, rejuvenation and *improvement*.

Practicing immortals are still exceptional, however. (Many are cold, but few are frozen.) There is little support for research to cure old age, despite the efforts and prestige of the Gerontological Society. One reason is a failure of motivation, which depends in part on the feasibility and desirability of improving people—of changing ourselves into supermen. Merely to expand time, without expanding the psyche, seems to hold little attraction.

Furthermore, pundits regularly allow that we should *not* aim to become superhuman, for a variety of complicated reasons. For example, "An ape is not just a super-amoeba, a man is not merely a super-ape, and a 'superman' would not represent progress but only the intensification of our traits and shortcomings."

They assert that when we come out of cryonic suspension—after we are thawed, revived and rejuvenated—our efforts to improve our minds and bodies will result only in more cunning and voracious apes, bigger and hungrier amoebae.

The criticisms are vacuous because they are made in a vacuum; very little serious attention has been given to the potentialities of supermen. To the best of my knowledge, this book is the first of its kind—the first to deal in a reasonably systematic way with the varieties and potential of superhumans. These should be of considerable interest, even to those who choose to regard them as mere possibilities for our remote posterity.

I hope not everyone will so regard them. You, personally, and your families have a genuine opportunity to prolong your lives indefinitely and outgrow the human mold; you can really exercise some of the options outlined here, or else better ones after your own heart's desire, remolded with each change of heart. If you apprehend the reality of this opportunity, and if you actually take the necessary steps soon enough, why then, the adventures of the long tomorrow, which I firmly intend shall belong to me and mine, will be yours too.

1

The Sculptor Sculpted

Some have already decided to try for immortality and transhumanity, including the dozen or so chrononauts now lying frozen in their voyage through time. But to most on-lookers their motives remain somewhat obscure and their vision unclear. What do they love in life, that they cling to it so tenaciously? What marvelous future do they foresee, that they are determined to experience it? In that far sea-son, what strange flowerings do they imagine, that they tug so insistently at Heinlein's "door into summer"? And to what mighty works, what soaring projects, do they imagine they can contribute?

Only a few of the answers are quick and easy. For those who can enjoy leisure in traditional lazy and frivo-lous ways, a world of delight opens wide: an open-ended future may mean a month wandering the Canadian wilder-ness, a winter basking on Pacific beaches, a year listening to Bach and Mozart, or Simon and Garfunkel. *La dolce vita* can become cloying or even disgusting, but some things are likely to wear well: soft grass, a fresh breeze, fleecy skies, a cool drink, crisp snow, a warm hand, a familiar voice—can a thousand years of these be too much?

Other likely rewards are just as tangible. Doubtless the day will come when every citizen will receive a basic in-come of $10,000,000 or more a year just for breathing, and millions more for such onerous tasks as jury duty. As

Benjamin Franklin said, "There is no substitute for luxury," and we can look forward with unabashed eagerness to an era when luxury will be taken for granted as the natural prequisite of every superman who wants it.

Unhappily, grateful and graceful acceptance of better things is not commonplace in the present age of confusion and warped personalities. Eleanor Roosevelt was reportedly baffled by the sweepers of India, who worked bent over all day with short-handled brooms, and could not be persuaded to save their backs by putting longer handles on the brooms. Today there are vast segments of the world population that will not concede it is better to be rich than poor, better to be bright than dull, better to be strong than weak, better to be free than regimented, or even that it is better to live than to die.

As for the possibility and necessity of redesigning ourselves and outgrowing our humanity, which ought to be nearly self-evident, one finds on every side the most solemn and long-winded arguments to the contrary. Hence, perhaps we had best begin with some brief reminders that it is indeed possible for people to design better people.

The Possibility of Human Design

On a rudimentary level, the engineering of humanity is as old as humanity. Every time one of our ancestors swallowed a medicinal herb, he was trying to improve the "natural" functioning of his body, attempting in his small and vaguely defined way to "denature" himself and produce something a little more than human. When he deliberately selected a strong and clever woman for his mate, he may have been attempting, through primitive eugenics, to breed bigger and better children. Not only the wish to create supermen, but even the actual effort, has always been there, regardless of disclaimers, and regardless of its minimal effect so far.

On the level of repair work and prostheses there has indeed been notable success, mostly in recent times. With our eyeglasses, gold inlays and birth control pills we *are* substantially superhuman; we *have* transcended the apparent limitations of our design, without even taking into

10

account our vehicles and other machinery. But the basic design has not been noticeably improved.

In biological terms, scholars believe we are scarcely different from our ancestors 50,000 years removed. Humanity has not evolved further apparently, and is not evolving. In addition, natural evolution at perceptible rates is believed to require isolation of new strains of genetic segregation, which does not occur in the modern world; hence some scientists think men will remain merely men indefinitely.

Or so it appeared before the recent convulsive changes in biology and electronics, including the announcement in June of 1970 that Dr. H. Gobind Khorana had succeeded in synthesizing a gene at the University of Wisconsin. Already a Nobel Prize winner, Dr. Khorana was the first to create from scratch a unit of heredity, in this case one realted to the metabolism of yeast cells.[92] But for many years previously scientists had been unraveling the genetic code and tinkering with the DNA molecules that carry it, and talk of "genetic engineering" had been commonplace. Today, few biologists seem to doubt that we will learn— eventually—how to modify human reproductive cells, or even manufacture them, so as to produce children with exactly the desired traits—not only gender to order, and skin color and hair texture and body size and facial features, not only healthier and stronger people, but truly significant improvements in intellect and personality, and if need be, a completely different animal.

The bolder and more perceptive biologists, of course, have long seen the handwriting on the wall. Decades ago, Alexis Carrel wrote, "For the first time since the beginning of its history, humanity has become master of its destiny ... In order to grow fresh, it is forced to make itself anew. And it cannot make itself anew without pain, for it is both the marble and the sculptor. Out of its own substance it must send the splinters flying with great hammer-strokes, in order to recover its true face."[22]

This kind of talk makes us hopeful, but also a little uneasy. Carrel mentioned "pain." Do we really want to hammer ourselves?

Professor Joshua Lederberg, Stanford's Nobel laureate biologist, has given us a refreshingly different definition of disease: it is "any deficit relative to a desired norm."[99] Delightful! Not only is pneumonia a disease, but also our susceptibility to it; not only is schizophrenia a disease, but also stupidity. *In fact, every undesired trait represents disease.* Thus—although Professor Lederberg does not seem to have drawn the obvious conclusion—humanity itself is a disease, of which we must now proceed to cure ourselves.

There are still numerous naysayers, who assert that it is wrong to "play God." Since this objection is seriously proposed by apparently intelligent people, it requires the formality of an explicit answer. At first, let us think primarily of improvement of future generations, although not excluding the question of remodeling living adults.

The first and most obvious comment is that a hands-off policy does not avoid responsibility. Passivity is just one alternative among many, and it also has its consequences. To choose to do nothing is still a choice, with its advantages, disadvantages and probable sequelae. Unless these have actually been weighed, estimated and compared with alternatives, those who choose not to "play God" are choosing, instead, to play ostrich.

Another preliminary remark concerns the curious tacit assumption that human intervention would be "disruptive," that it might wreck the "normal" and "orderly" processes of "nature." Actually, it is hard to imagine that human engineers could be any clumsier or messier than that old slattern Dame Nature. The "normal" processes of evolution are wasteful and cruel in stupefying degree. Dame Nature considers every species and every individual expendable, and has indeed expended them in horrifying numbers. Even an occasional calamitous error in planned development could scarcely match the slaughter, millennium in and millennium out, of fumble-fingered Nature.

This brings us to the third general comment: it would be absurd—insane—to "trust to nature," because *nature's criteria are not the same as ours.* In fact, nature recognized only two criteria of biological success—survival and proliferation. By these disgusting standards, a fungus might ultimately prove superior to man. In the name of humility and decorum, should we allow superfungus to develop before superman?

But the clearest understanding of the inanity of the don't-play-God notion emerges when we try to envision its detailed application. Exactly what do the stand-patters propose we prohibit? Shall we proscribe, say any "artificial" improvement in human resistance to disease? If genetic correction can eliminate susceptibility to all forms of cancer, for example, shall we withhold the correction and foredoom millions to early, painful deaths? Or suppose drug therapy becomes capable of increasing the intelligence of the average living individual; then stupidity will be the result not of chance, but choice. What would impel you to choose relative stupidity for yourself, or prevent others from being relieved of it?

Clearly, each separate choice must be weighed on its own merits. Hasty acceptance of an apparent blessing can indeed be costly, as witness, for example, the thalidomide error, and on a larger scale the air and water pollution of careless industrialization. Agencies analogous to the Food & Drug Administration will doubtless have their place. But the penalties of inaction may also be severe; millions of lives were lost because of the fourteen year delay in the use of penicillin. And even those who like the status quo must recognize the possibility of a sudden change in environment, for which it is well to prepare—such as a new disease, or a general war, or a new tyrant, or a shift in climate, or a naturally mutated strain of men, or intelligent machines. In fact, a rapid change in environment is certain, since it is happening now; our culture is changing so fast that in order to cope with it, men must soon change also. To go forward is to risk disaster, but to stand still is to ensure it.

The only real alternative to the kind of progress we envision is reaction—a drawing back and pulling in, a closing of the eyes and mind, a regime of ossification and repression, where curiosity is a crime and honesty a sin. This would surely be pathological—"unnatural" in the proper sense.

So far, the goal of superhumanity for ourselves—for living individuals of our generation—seems to be shared by scarcely anyone outside of the cryonics societies, by not a single philosopher, scientist, or writer of acknowledged status and immediate influence. For most of the touted "thinkers," even superhumanity for our descendants is viewed ambivalently and erratically. The eminent philosopher, Pierre Teilhard de Chardin, for example, voiced a gloomy and pessimistic view: "It may well be that in its individual capacities and penetrations our brain has reached its organic limits." And, "After the long series of transformations leading to man, has the world stopped? Or if we are still moving, is it not merely in a circle?" He thought future progress might be mainly collective and spiritual.[168] But he also had a higher, if wavering, vision:

> With our knowledge of hormones we appear to be on the eve of having a hand in the development of our bodies and even of our brains. With the discovery of genes it appears that we shall soon be able to control the mechanism of organic heredity. . . . The dream which human research obscurely fosters is . . . by grasping the very mainspring of evolution, seizing the tiller of the world. . . . I salute those who have the courage to admit that their hopes extend that far; they are at the pinnacle of mankind.'. . .[168]

Albert Rosenfeld, the eminent science writer, has a wry metaphor for the risks we face in manipulating the world and ourselves:

> . . . in dealing with so many of the potent new tools and techniques, man is very much in the position of those Japanese gastronomes who are addicted to the fugu fish. The fugu secretes a deadly poison to which there is no known antidote. Yet its flesh is considered so delectable that Japanese aficionados are willing to pay high prices for it and risk the dangers. The risk is somewhat mitigated by the fact that in Japan only licensed chefs, specially trained to know the poisonous parts from the nonpoisonous and to prepare it nontoxically, are permitted to

14

serve it up. No system is foolproof, of course. Despite all precautions, a couple of hundred Japanese die every year of fugu poisoning.

Perhaps we should all take a lesson from the fugu fanciers. To enjoy the pleasures, we must take the risks. But let us by all means see to it that chefs know what they are doing.[145]

To be born human is an affliction. It shouldn't happen to a dog. Yet, the disease is definitely enjoyable, and we must take care that our "cures" really represent improvement. To what extent, and in what way, can man design superman?

To See Beyond the Horizon

Is it possible to see farther than one can see—for example, beyond the horizon? Certainly—our newer radars can do it. Is it possible to remember more than the brain can retain? Of course—our libraries do it. It is impossible by definition to see through an "opaque" object, and yet the x-ray business is booming. And so on: we can often do indirectly, and by stages, what at first seems quite beyond our scope, and this includes a human study of the superhuman.

Certainly one cannot visualize a *unique* superman, even in faintest outline. In the third place, some of the most important elements of the future will be revealed as complete surprises, and thus cannot be taken into account. In the second place, there will be tendencies to diversity and pluralism. And in the first place, one can foresee no completion to the self-directed evolution of the superman; it must be thought of in terms of open-ended development. The present task is only to outline some of the earlier *options* of supermen, with special attention to those heretofore ignored or underemphasized.

To do this, it must first be shown that *homo sapiens* is only a botched beginning; when he clearly sees himself as an error, he may not only be motivated to sculpt himself, but to make at least a few swift and confident strokes.

We must also review the supermen of literature, scant

and flimsy as these are, to consider whether they contribute interesting possibilities.

The bulk of this book will comprise an investigation of superhuman potential, modes of life and thought. Some of it will be mainly for amusement. Some will be exceedingly practical in a direct and obvious way. And some, necessarily if presumptuously, will touch on certain old and profound problems of philosophy, and will finally force us to consider superman in the first and second person.

2

The Deficiencies of Natural Man

What is wrong with Man? Nothing much, really, say the apologists. In their view, God or Nature has designed mankind perfectly, with imperfections found only in *individual* men, attributable to defects of character or training, or to some variety of sin, or to luck.

Some say further that the human *potential*, with the existing genetic basis, is virtually unlimited: man's brain is a treasure chest to which we need only find the right key. After all, they point out, man's biological nature has been almost unchanged for at least fifty thousand years. (There is some disagreement; Sir Peter B. Medawar tells us there is some slight evidence that color vision is younger than humanity, and may even have originated in historic times.)[118] It is likely that if a baby from the caves of Cro-Magnon could somehow be transported forward in time and reared in New York, he would be indistinguishable from a modern child. Although his native culture had, for example, no mathematics or written language, that child was born with the capacity to learn to read and cipher. All the elements of modern technology were already nascent in those simple hunters and gatherers; implicit in their neurology were the electronic computer and the hydrogen bomb; somehow evolution had already prepared them to be astronauts.

Even today, it is said, we use only a small fraction of our brain capacity. Hidden in those convolutions, some believe, are capabilities yet untapped or even unimagined; our task is not to become superhuman, but to become *fully* human. Possibly even our bodies would function optimally, if only we gave them proper treatment.

Out of such ideas have sprung long successions of fads and philosophies, communities and movements. Some of the still active ones include yoga and vegetarianism, general semantics and scientology, dervishism and organic farming. Devotees of these systems find no fault with our nature; incorrect *nurture* is our problem.

If such ideas have much merit, then there are dangerous pitfalls indeed in any attempt to design new men. Fooling around with the circuitry of the brain, for instance, we might build an improved memory, but destroy, all unknowingly, the capacity for mental telepathy. Perhaps, even, our design is aimed at a superculture we have not yet grown up to, and clumsy attempts to improve the short-run lot of the individual will abort this development.

Maybe so—just maybe. There is a need for caution in tampering with what we don't understand. When we have achieved immortality, perhaps we will decide to go very slowly in innovating "improvements." On the other hand, it is difficult to be patient with our cheap bodies, erratic emotions, and feeble mentalities; when we learn how to make improvements with apparent safety, some people will choose to do so, and probably most others will soon follow.

The objections are largely vitiated anyhow by the failure of their two main implicit premises: (1) that the race is more important than the individual; (2) that mistakes are irreversible. Anyone who believes the first is slightly insane: of this, more later. As to reversibility, this would usually be a question of time and money, and immortals would tend to have both.

It is still necessary to clarify the need for superman by making explicit some of the defects of man, especially his racial insanity, his built-in psychoses. To see our mental defectiveness in a biological frame of reference, it is useful first to look at the crudities and contradictions of our physical construction; and it is helpful to precede this, in turn, by a glance at the lower orders.

"History is more or less bunk," said Henry Ford I, and nearly everybody seems to believe it. Not only written history, but paleontology and natural history hold lessons which are regularly ignored.

The second lesson of paleontology (discussion of the first being deferred as too personal and painful) is that Nature does slipshod work in designing her creatures, whose adaptations to environment are always partial and temporary. Life on earth spans at least two billion years and millions of species; of all those species, 99.9% have become extinct, and both the coming and the going of a species is a torment. In our own times, as one small example, the marsupial wolf has died out in Australia, owing to the competition of the dingoes which are superior hunters. The poor, great, clumsy marsupials slowly starved, together with their young, as the dingoes usurped the game.

Was there ever a marsupial Camelot? Was there one brief, shining geological era in which the marsupial wolves waxed fat and happy and lived in harmony with their environment? Hardly—unless "harmony" includes internal and external parasites from ticks and ringworms to bacteria and viruses; unless it includes bullying and being bullied in establishing a ranking order; and unless it includes the frequent loss of young to sly predators; etc.

Even during the heyday of a species, its "success" generally represents the most pyrrhic of victories. Mosquitoes and frogs do splendidly as species—at the expense of the individual, who has only a minute chance of surviving the larval or tadpole stage respectively; the majority meet their destinies very quickly as fish food. The drone bee has a short life *and* a very small chance to mate; the queens and workers seem hardly more enviable, although we know nothing of their subjective life. In some kinds of spiders, the female eats the male *during* the act of copulation. (This doesn't prove anything, but it gives us some perspective on what is "natural.") Neanderthal man may have done fairly well for a while, but if he survived to middle age, he usually wound up with arthritis or some

19

other chronic ailment, as studies of his remains have shown.

By no means are all the miseries of a species the unavoidable result of competition and predation in any simple sense; some represent plain goofs of nature, or costly compromises. Some insects will fly into flames; horses are said sometimes to run back into burning barns. While these traits may be related to others that do have survival value, they are certainly maladaptive in themselves. Indeed, most traits show up maladaptive in some circumstances; certain cichlid fish, which normally vent their aggression on hostile neighbors, will rend their mates if there is nothing else to attack.[104]

With almost complete generality, the lower orders are flawed and botched, and we can expect the same to be true of man.

The Aching Ape

The purely physical shortcomings of the human animal are legion, and we need only tick off a few, most of them well known.

The worst weakness of all, of course, we share with every other large animal: the susceptibility to degenerative disease, senile debility, and death from old age. A less critical, but still serious, defect is our manner of gestating and bearing children, which represents not only inconvenience but danger to the mothers. If some of us temporarily choose to regard these as "natural," there are plenty of others that are clearly pathological.

Our skeletons and internal organs are only partly adapted to our relatively recent upright posture, as our backaches and fallen arches often attest. Our responses to sickness and injury are only sometimes appropriate, e.g., fever, which is a nearly universal response to infection, is an effective defense against only a few diseases, and is usually harmful, which is why we take aspirin. There appears to be no useful basis for the shock syndrome that usually accompanies trauma, one of its main features being dangerously or fatally reduced blood pressure. (It might conceivably be helpful in some bleeding cases, but not usually.) And everyone knows that the vermiform appendix is not only useless, but a dangerous locus of potential infection.

Again, consider the body's response to foreign protein. In the words of Dr. Medawar:

> Vertebrate animals evolved into the possession of immunological defenses long before the coming of mammals. Mammals are viviparous: the young are nourished for some time within the body of the mother and this (in some ways) admirable device raised for the first time in evolution the possiblity that a mother might react immunologically upon her unborn children—might treat them as foreign bodies or as foreign grafts. The haemolytic disease that occurs in about one new-born child in 150 is an error of judgment of just this kind: it is, in effect, an immunological repudiation by the mother of her unborn child. Thus the existence of immunological reactions has not been fully reconciled with viviparity; and this is a blunder—the kind of blunder which, in human affairs, calls forth a question in the House, or even a strongly worded letter to *The Times*.[118]

Anaphylactic shock, allergy, and hypersensitivity are other aberrations of the immunological process. Now, it might be argued that not *everyone* shows these bad reactions, hence the ideal man exists at least *potentially* in present-day humanity, perhaps even actually (in very small numbers); but this is a poor argument, and not only for reasons already given.

Does it seem unfair to look on susceptibility to infectious disease as a racial defect? A better perspective on this question, and on the statement in the preceding paragraph, is given by considering the devilish phenomenon of sickle-cell anemia. This is a disease which usually causes early death in one quarter of the children of parents of a certain blood type—a blood type that confers high resistance to malaria. This is the devilish part: *either* you (or your wife) are vulnerable to malaria, *or* one fourth of your children will probably die of anemia.[118]

The apologist maintains that, in every deplorable case, either the individual or the local environment is "abnormal." Well, it might be possible, after a number of generations, by purely eugenic methods to breed a race from present stock which will be free of disease (other than senile degenerative disease) in some carefully chosen environment. But most of us would have no part in this, and even then, viability would depend on continuance of the special environment. There is really no evading the fact: our species is in many respects, and possibly in most respects, physically abnormal.

Life in the Garbage Can

Life—as we used to say erroneously about nature—abhors a vacuum; it will creep into every nook and cranny that offers the least hospitality. Let the smallest ecological niche appear, and presto—some form of life has adapted to it and claimed it, moved in bag and baggage. This is all very clever and enterprising, but not much fun for the organisms involved; adaptation is grim business.

We don't know anything about the feelings, if any, of the common house fly, so we can't truly say whether they enjoy their early lives as larvae in the garbage cans they inhabit. Neither can we say whether tapeworms or body lice are thankful for their existence. But we can be fairly sure that the ancestors of the woolly mammoths were pretty uncomfortable in their adaptation to the advancing ice; and the woolly mammoths themselves were even more uncomfortable when the ice receded, since they became extinct.

Many humans also have adapted to "life in the garbage can," although we cannot yet be sure how much of the adaptation is genetic and how much cultural. Aggressiveness pays off for conquerors, but for the conquered, the needed trait is submissiveness. One *might* speculate, for example, as to the genetic nature of the Untouchable class in India, who for many generations have had to live off the leavings, and accept the abuse, of the higher castes. Have they become a genuine biological sub-species or variety, servants bred and born? One is tempted to guess this, based on our experience, for example, with breeding varieties of dog, which certainly differ in temperament.

22

There is much danger and uncertainty in attributing hereditary character traits to human groups. For instance, British historian E. R. Bevan, writing about the stormy and aggressive nature of the ancient Hebrews, remarks, "We must not indeed conceive the Jews of those days as like the Jews of Medieval Europe, an unwarlike people given to sedentary pursuits and the handling of money. It was the policy of the Christian Roman Empire which barred to the Jews the profession of arms, and produced the type commonly regarded in later times as Jewish. . . . To picture the bands of Judas Maccabeus we should not think of the Jews of Medieval and modern times, but of people more like the fierce monotheistic *ghazis* of the Indian frontier—Afghans and Pathans."[13] He apparently thought centuries of losing had bred warrior aptitudes out of the Jews, and would have been astonished to see the Jews of modern Israel, despite great disadvantages in numbers and equipment, kicking the tar out of all comers. Conceivably the Untouchables also have such latent resources, although there are important differences: in particular, the Indians apparently *accepted* their lot, while the Jews always believed in their own superiority and never dammed up their aggressiveness but only diverted it, when necessary, into different channels. (This also exacted its price, however, and the adjustments were very abrasive.)

Regardless of the validity of particular examples, it is obvious that there must exist species and varieties which are abnormal and miserable. Growth and population pressures tend to force life into every available niche, and while the adapting life form *tries* to make a virtue of necessity, success is usually very incomplete. Biological "success" does not require happiness, or comfort, or even the absence of the most wretched misery, if the primitive drives are strong enough. The process of adaptation can be excruciating for an entire species—and after all that struggle, when one is well settled in the garbage can, something is likely to move the can or start throwing in the wrong kind of garbage, and it has all to be done over again.

To some degree, we all live in the garbage can, and the

lesson, once again, is that we must never be complacent about accepting the "natural order" of things.

The Four F's and the Motivational Jungle

We are trying to dispel the superstition that man's psyche is "normal" in some important sense, that it would blossom in beauty if only we could find the right milieu of spiritual sun and soil. There is no such milieu, and cannot be, as long as man remains himself. It is easy to show that man's instincts, emotions and motivations are not only accidental, but mutually inconsistent.

Our first impulses are to feed, fornicate, and flee at need or opportunity. Some scholars would add a fourth—"fight;" they believe a generalized aggressive impulse is part of our basic nature. Professor Konrad Lorenz, director of the Max Planck Institute for behavioral physiology, thinks that aggression, in man and other species, is a true instinct, that it represents "appetitive" behavior—we hunger to fight other people, just as we hunger for food, because intraspecific aggression (within the species) had evolutionary forces working for it. He writes:

> (Man has) in his heart the aggression drive inherited from his anthropoid ancestors . . . the aggression drive is a true, primarily species-preserving instinct . . . it is the spontaneity of the instinct that makes it so dangerous. . . . The completely erroneous view that animal and human behavior is predominantly reactive and that, even if it contains any innate elements at all, it can be altered, to an unlimited extent, by learning, comes from a radical misunderstanding of certain democratic principles. . . . The fact that the central nervous system does not need to wait for stimuli, like an electric bell with a push-button, before it can respond, but that it can itself produce stimuli which give a natural, physiological explanation for the "spontaneous" behavior of animals and humans, has found recognition only in the last decades. . . .[104]

Dr. Lorenz' interpretations of his fascinating observations are not always convincing, and are vigorously disputed by many scientists. Not all of us will accept as rep-

24

resentative the dictum of Genghis Khan: "The greatest pleasure in life is to see your enemy in the dust before you, and to put your foot on his neck." But it *cannot* be reasonably disputed that we have strong and strongly inherited tendencies that are equivalent, in sum, to a headful of violent and frequently antagonistic instincts and emotions. That some of our instincts are derivative and relatively newly risen does *not* weaken their force nor change the fact that they can often override the supposedly more basic drives.

A minor but convincing example of an autonomous instinct is that of sucking in infants. It is obviously related to the feeding instinct, in its origin, but it is *not* the same; it has acquired a separate, independent status. The baby needs to suck, and wants to suck, and if its stomach is filled too quickly, will continue sucking motions until its appetite for sucking—distinct from its appetite for food—has been temporarily satisfied.

One of the most important and troublesome of our latter instincts, or endogenous drives, is the tendency to idealism or zealotry or fanaticism, or what Lorenz calls "militant enthusiasm," of which he writes:

Like the triumph ceremony of the greylag goose, militant enthusiasm in man is a true autonomous instinct: it has its own appetitive behavior, its own releasing mechanisms, and, like the sexual urge or any other strong instinct, it engenders a specific feeling of intense satisfaction. The strength of its seductive lure explains why intelligent men may behave as irrationally and immorally in their political as in their sexual lives.[104]

Of course, ideas of what is "irrational" or "immoral" in this context need to be made explicit, as they have not been by Lorenz. We shall discuss similar ideas, from a slightly different point of view, in Chapters 6 and 7. But it should be very clear that we are full of warring impulses, with no fixed ranking of priority, and that Lorenz' "parliament of instincts" can by no means be depended upon to produce a satisfactory compromise.

The idealists, humanists, *et al.* may insist that, regardless of instinctual elements in our psyches, it is possible to rise

25

above them by an effort of will, or by appropriate early training. Besides other shortcomings, such notions exaggerate the importance of nurture vs. nature.

It is a very strong presumption that there are rather sharp limits on what can be done by purely educational and training techniques. Certain "progressive" educators have claimed that they can make almost any child into virtually anything, if they catch him early enough. Still, one doubts that even the most skillful teacher can train a dog to do calculus (although a colleague of mine at Highland Park College claims he has taught his German Shepherd to do quadratic equations), and probably few children, however devotedly coached, could become competent mathematicians, or generals, or surgeons, or bankers. As for purely moral and emotional aspects of training, these probably represent problems that are more difficult, not less.

A pig cannot fly, and however conscientiously he may diet, however he may direct his mind to lofty thoughts, he just isn't going to get off the ground—as long as he remains a pig; and neither is his swinish temperament going to become angelic, or even human, however firmly or tenderly we teach him. Man, also, is both limited and confused in his fundamental nature; the confusion of poorly reconciled instincts and emotions amounts to racial psychosis, a kind of built-in schizophrenia. The evidence is very strong that there is no cure—as long as we remain human.

The Mutilated Beggar

By now it should be clear that man is an accident, not only his body but his psyche a patchwork of makeshift adaptive compromises. His attributes do not fit any apparent grand design or rational blueprint, but represent only the current, tentative result of the endless tugging and hauling of evolutionary forces, including random elements and self-contradictions.

It is said that in eighteenth-century France—and in twentieth-century India—beggar parents sometimes put out the eyes of their children, or cut off their hands, to

26

make them more effective as alms-seekers. Possibly these child-mutilators were "right;" perhaps their chances of life, or the family's, were improved by these cruel "adaptations." But it is only in the same sense that Mother Nature was "right" in designing our insanities and inconsistencies; we, or our ancestors, were thereby made "fit," as individuals or communities, to survive in the savage and merciless world of nature—for a while. Among our psychic mutilations, it is reasonably clear, are our tendencies to servility and submissiveness, which have their uses but nevertheless oppose and degrade the more basic traits of self-assertion and aggression; and our tendencies to zealotry and self-sacrifice, similarly opposed to the rationally preferable inclinations toward self-interest and self-preservation.

In sum, then, man—along with every other creature—can be considered only a beginning and a dubious compromise, in both mind and body. In the course of "natural" development, he might or might not eventually attain a higher and more harmonious state; but the race cannot depend on that, and the individual cannot wait for it. We must remake ourselves, and in planning for this we might begin by looking at previous speculations, the supermen of literature.

3

From Gilgamesh to Olaf Stapledon

I will break the door of Hell, and smash the bolts;
I will bring up the dead to eat food with the living,
and the living shall be outnumbered by the host of them.
                                    —The Epic of Gilgamesh

A sampling of legend and literature will show us some curious—and curiously distorted—supermen. They provide some positive clues as to what may be, and also reveal crucial limitations in previous speculation and aspiration.

Gilgamesh

The oldest of all mythical supermen seems to be Gilgamesh the hero-king; he apparently dates from Sumer, 5,000 years ago, although the epic has been put together from Babylonian clay tablets of about 650 B.C.[60] Already we see the central contrast and conflict between men and gods, viz., men are mortal and the gods jealously reserve unending life to themselves.

Although two-thirds divine, powerful and cunning, Gilgamesh cannot wrest from the gods their ultimate treasure. At first he is full of arrogance and resolution (see quotation above), and he even succeeds briefly in stealing a plant from the bottom of the sea which confers immortality; but this is stolen from him by a serpent. (To this day, serpents can renew themselves by shedding their skins.) At last he is forced to accept the common human fate and the advice of an admonishing goddess:

> *The life thou seekest thou wilt not find.*
> *When the gods created mankind they determined death*
> *for mankind; Life they kept in their own hands.*
> *Thou, O Gilgamesh, fill thy belly; Day and night be thou*
> *merry; Day and night be joyous and content!*
> *... Regard the little one who takes hold of thy hand;*
> *Enjoy the wife in thy bosom.*

Thus the very earliest literature already confronts the principal problem of humanity to date—mortality—and exhibits both modes of response: resignation and rebellion, apologism and prolongevitism. (The latter term, coined by Professor Gerald J. Gruman, refers to the will to prolong life by human effort.)[60]

Nietzsche & Orwell

Friedrich Nietzsche was the man who popularized the term "superman" (*übermensch*,) and who became a patron saint of the Nazis; he was a creature of many contradictions in his person and in his writing. It is as easy to demolish his illogic as to admire his literary bravura, but this is not our primary interest, which rather concerns any new or constructive ideas he may have had concerning the purpose of life and the quality of the superman.

The Nazi version of the Master Race was indeed close to Nietzsche's take-off point in delineating superman; he spoke of "... blond beasts of prey, a race of conquerors and masters...." It is interesting to note, however, from our place in history, that he regarded not the Germans but the *Russians* as the archetypical blond beasts of Europe, and said, "A thinker who has at heart the future of Europe will in all his perspectives concerning the future calculate upon the Jews and the Russians as above all the surest and likeliest factors in the great play and battle of forces."[131]

The superman has first of all the will to power:

> What is good? . . . To be brave is good. . . . What is good? All that increases the feeling of power, the will to power, power itself, in man. What is bad? All that comes from weakness.[181]

The superman is strong, and his appropriate morality is a *Herren-moral*, a morality of the master, rather than the prevailing *Heerden-moral*, the morality of the herd. In the "slave morality" of the Jews and Christians, good and evil are reckoned from the standpoint of those affected by an action, while superman views good and evil from the standpoint of one who *effects* the action.

Superman is an aristocrat, and although in some writings Nietzsche seems to be postulating a new species of Homo Superior replacing mankind, for the most part he appears to regard superman as an occasional individual among humankind (although he said none had yet been born), and his superman seems to *require* lesser beings to lord it over. Superman's habitual mien is said to be one of poise, self-containment, and aloofness—*aloofness*, apparently, from the inferior masses.

All this sounds downright un-American, but it contains some nuggets of truth—specifically that the individual must serve himself, the "Ego whole and holy," following his own instincts, rather than serve society. So far, so good: Judaeo-Christian morality does indeed have some peculiar inversions of values. But his failure comes not only in his self-contradictions—we should *want* to sacrifice ourselves for superman!—but in his simplism, his massive inadequacy in analyzing motivation and the individual-societal interaction.

George Orwell's oligarchs in *1984* are not called "supermen," but they are disconcertingly like Nietzsche's heroes—they exalt *power* above all else, and they are the spiritual descendants of the Stalinists, who in turn represent Nietzsche's blond beasts of Europe. One of Orwell's characters gives us the ultimate extension of the glorification of one kind of power, in his imaginary totalitarian state:

> The Party seeks power entirely for its own sake. We are not interested in the good of others; we are interested

30

solely in power. Not wealth or luxury or long life or happiness; only power, pure power ... Power is not a means, it is an end.... The object of persecution is persecution. The object of torture is torture. The object of power is power.... How does one man assert his power over another?... By making him suffer. Obedience is not enough. Unless he is suffering, how can you be sure that he is obeying your will and not his own? Power is in inflicting pain and humiliation ... If you want a picture of the future, imagine a boot stamping on a human face—forever.[133]

In the grotesqueness of this *reductio ad absurdum* we find the measure of Nietzche's shortcoming: he saw only a small facet of the truth. Nevertheless, the best of Nietzsche is very good, and he made an important contribution toward exposing the illusions of the altruists.

Most supermen of history or legend fall into two general categories (each with many subdivisions): the meliorists and the apologists, those who try to subdue or outwit nature, and those who submit or try to accommodate to oppressive conditions. Among the Orientals, these are exemplified respectively by the Taoist *hsien* and the ascetics of India.

As Professor Gruman tells us, the Taoist alchemists of China consciously aspired to become supermen in an essentially modern sense—by using science to master the forces of nature. To quote one commentary:

How, then, can he (man) stand co-equal with Heaven and Earth? If he seize for himself the secret forces of Heaven and Earth, in order thereby to compound for himself the great elixir of the golden fluid, he will then exist coeval with Heaven and Earth from beginning to end. Such a one is called the True Man.[60]

The *hsien* (the word is both singular and plural) was neither beautiful, athletic nor solemn, as is common in Western tradition: he was a shrewd, gnarled fellow, often earthy and humorous. But he supposedly had superhuman—although not supernatural—powers. He could control the weather, travel at enormous speeds, change his appearance, or make himself invisible; and to cap it all he had tremendous longevity, if not immortality. The Taoists did not merely daydream; they sought to discover, and in some cases claimed to have found, practical methods of medicine and discipline to attain their goals. Unfortunately, the claims appear to have been somewhat exaggerated.

In various Indian systems, on the other hand, the emphasis was not on satisfying wants but eliminating them, subduing oneself rather than the world, leaching the soul of all restless humors and vain desires.

The best known of the Indian saints is the legendary Siddhartha Gautama, the Buddha. His religion ignored questions of deity and concentrated on achieving serenity through self-discipline; he preached that by attaining Nirvana, the extinction of selfish desire if not of the self, one could escape from the "wheel" of reincarnation and become nothing—or perhaps everything—by an unclear kind of union with the universe.

Such ideas still exert enormous influence in India, although often in perverted form: where Gautama counseled self-discipline, many of the derivshes and yogis following him have advocated mortification of the flesh—sleeping on beds of nails, crouching on the same rock for forty years, etc. Warped and even psychotic as these notions seem to us, they do lead sometimes to extraordinary feats and remarkable control of the body, which can almost be called superhuman.

George Bernard Shaw

For fairly tenuous reasons, one of Shaw's comedies of manners is called *Man and Superman*.[154] The only really clear trait he attributes to superman is one we have already noted in myth and legend: pride and aspiration. As Shaw says in his preface, "What attracts and impresses us ... is ... the heroism of daring to be the enemy of God. From Prometheus to my own Devil's Disciple, such enemies have always been popular."

The protagonist in *The Devil's Disciple*, in his turn, says,

... I knew from the first that the Devil was my natural master and captain and friend. I saw that he was in the right, and that the world cringed to his conqueror only through fear. I prayed secretly to him; and he comforted me, and saved me from having my spirit broken. . . .

This is slightly misleading, of course: the operative words are "captain" and "friend," not "master" except in an archaic sense. Superman welcomes a comrade in arms, and even a temporary leader, but not a substitute divinity, not just a new tyranny for the old. In essence, from this point of view, superman is not the devil's disciple, but is the devil himself, *i.e.*, the proud and determined spirit who will endure no shackles and accept no limits to his ambition, who will submit to no reins and willingly serve no purpose but his own. As Don Juan says in the dream scene of *Man and Superman*, ". . . to be in hell is to drift: to be in heaven is to steer."

As to other qualities of superman, Shaw is mostly vague or negative. For example, in *The Revolutionist's Handbook and Pocket Companion* (an appendix to the play *Man and Superman*), he says:

> That the real Superman will snap his superfingers at all Man's present trumpery ideals of right, duty, honor, justice, religion, even decency, and accept moral obligations beyond present human endurance, is a thing that contemporary Man does not foresee ... he will imagine them, not as true Supermen, but as himself endowed with infinite brains, infinite courage, and infinite money.

Well, brains, courage, and money are all excellent commodities, and for that matter, no one who acquires a large increment of any of these can remain himself. As for the "moral obligations beyond present human endurance," these seem in Shaw's imagination to be merely the same old trumpery ideals, the central one being martyrdom for humanity. There are several references to the "Life Force," and in the preface to *Man and Superman* Shaw writes:

> This is the true joy in life, the being used for a purpose recognized by yourself as a mighty one; the being thor-

33

oughly worn out before you are thrown on the scrap heap; the being a force of Nature instead of a feverish selfish little clod. . . .

The last quotation above is probably closest to Shaw's personal view. How do we know? For one thing, there are various warnings about trying to attain superhumanity; in the play, the Devil remarks about ". . . the fool who pursues the better before he has secured the good;" also, "Beware of the pursuit of the Superhuman: it leads to an indiscriminate contempt for the Human." Furthermore, Shaw's superman is admittedly desired mainly to perfect our social and political organization, and the author plainly thinks that all this demands is a lot of Fabian-Shavians.

In fact, G. B. S. explicitly says in his preface to *Man and Superman:*

> . . . it is a common practice with romancers to announce their hero as a man of extraordinary genius, and then leave his works entirely to the reader's imagination. . . . You cannot accuse me of this pitiable barrenness, this feeble evasion. I not only tell you that my hero wrote a revolutionist's handbook: I give you the handbook at full length for your edification if you care to read it.

In other words, as we might have anticipated, Shaw's superman is Shaw himself. This is quite a letdown, but we had no right to expect anything of the play except entertainment.

The Star-Begotten of H. G. Wells

The greatest speculative writer of his era tackled the superman theme at least three times—in *The Food of the Gods, Men Like Gods,* and finally in *Star-Begotten.* Each time he served up a very thin soup, with nevertheless a flavor worth tasting.

As needs must, he acknowledged the near-paradox of man trying to foresee superman:

"Let us admit," said Keppel, "that this is attempting the most impossible of tasks. The hypothesis is that these coming supermen are stronger-witted, better-balanced, and altogether wiser than we are. How can we begin to put our imaginations into their minds and figure out what they will think or do? If our intelligences were as tall as theirs, we should be making their world now . . . You make me feel like the sculptor's dog trying to explain his master's life to the musician's cat."[178]

He also took a few roundhouse swings at the vulgarity and simplism of most attempts to read the future:

> . . . what do you find in all these Utopias and Visions of the Future of yours? . . . First of all caricatures of current novelties—skyscrapers five thousand feet high, aeroplanes at two thousand miles an hour, radio receivers on your wrist-watch . . . attempts to be startling in artistic matters . . . odd little fancies about sex relations . . . But these people of the future are invariably represented as being—I put it mildly—prigs and damned fools . . . They are collectively up to nothing . . . They have apparently made no advances whatever in subtlety, delicacy, simplicity . . . They never say a witty thing; they never do a charming act. The general effect is of very pink, rather absurdly dressed celluloid dolls living on tabloids in a glass lavatory.

He was wrong to sneer at gadgetry, which is an essential part of our salvation. We already have the two-thousand-mile-per-hour planes, and will soon have the wrist radio; they are not just toys or status symbols. But he was right in calling for more subtlety and delicacy in postulating superman, and made an effort at least to hint at some possible transhuman traits: "(They will move) easily and gracefully, as one does who has no conflicting nervous impulses . . . They will be much more *alive to things* . . . immensely amused . . . They will be busy, laughing people."

Rather frail hints, yes, but not completely empty. And in at least one passage Wells gives us a little thrill of wonder with an explicit bit. The protagonist is talking with his wife, a "Martian," *i.e.* someone mutated by cosmic rays directed on earth by an alien intelligence:

At first that "fey" was a fantastic exaggeration and then it became more and more an observation ...
She did not want to go (to the concert).
"You used to like music."
"But I have *heard* music, dearest."
"*Heard* music! My dear, what a queer way to put things!"
"... I've a feeling that I've done with music ... If one has taken music in—hasn't one taken it in?" ...
Even with friendship, even with love, she had that same flash of interest, that rapid appreciation, and then she turned away. To what?

To what, indeed? And why should turning to something new necessarily imply the turning away from the old, even if the new is in some sense greater? An acrobat can enjoy a simple stroll; a French chef can savor simple foods. Even this one tiny vision Wells offers is probably illusion. Yet clumsy as his hints may be, he does evoke exciting feelings; he does bring superman a trifle closer to emotional reality.

Olaf Stapledon

The Epic of Gilgamesh comes to us from the relatively recent past, and while some of its concepts are on a scale of cosmic grandeur, it is generally earthbound. The epics of Olaf Stapledon span galaxies of space and giga-years of time, his novels comprising "future histories" that are in some ways unmatched in scope.

Written from 1930 to 1950, Stapledon's efforts by the calendar belong to the modern era of science fiction (dating from the old *Amazing Stories* magazine of Hugo Gernsback, beginning in 1926), but Stapledon does not convey a modern flavor; there is something distinctly quaint and old-fashioned in his writing, in both the approach and the particulars. None the less, he may have contributed more than any other single writer to concepts of superman.

To begin with, besides conveying a sense of wonder and awe with unusual effectiveness, he tried repeatedly to remind us of the open-endedness of life and the mounting magnitude of future challenges, as opposed to the stagnant utopias of many authors: "The mental and spiritual advances which, in your day, mind in the solar system has still to attempt, are overwhelmingly more complex, more precarious and dangerous, than those which have already been achieved ... Out of every victory shall come that which makes a greater struggle necessary."[161]

Like many others, he tended to emphasize ethical and emotional aspects of superman; but unlike most others, he sometimes managed to pin down a few particulars, if not in full, at least in hints. One of his stories concerns a superdog—as capable as man intellectually, but trapped by his still canine nature. His "Second Men"—the first in a chain of successors of homo sapiens—have a generalized emotional and aesthetic sexuality and other differences: ". . . the lusty admiration which at first directs itself solely on the opposite sex is the appropriate attitude to all the beauties of flesh and spirit in beast and bird and plant." Parental interest is also universalized, and there is a ". . . passionate spontaneous altruism . . . wars were so hampered by impulses of kindliness toward the enemy that they were apt to degenerate into rather violent athletic contests, leading to an orgy of fraternization."

Occasionally he managed a strikingly concrete example of alien attitudes, as when he mirrored our sexual neuroses in those of another society, one in which the act of eating is both sacramental and shameful, something to be performed only in private and never mentioned in polite society:

He saw with the mind's eye an early Neptunian couple engaged upon an act which to them was one of shocking licentiousness and excruciating delight, but to the Terrestrial eye was merely ridiculous. This guilty pair stood facing one another, their mouth-aprons removed. From mouth to crimson mouth there stretched a curious fruit, not unlike a much-elongated banana. With mobile lips both he and she were drawing the object into the mouth, and eating it progressively. They gazed into each other's kindled eyes, their cheeks aflame. Clearly they were both enwrapped in that exquisite sweet horror which is afforded only the fruit that is forbidden.[161]

37

While this has serious flaws, it has the inestimable virtue of being definite. Elsewhere, he often presents his suggested superhuman traits in name only, with nothing of detail or consequence. His "Fourth Men" are great brains forty feet in diameter, who nevertheless do not seem very bright. His "Fifth Men" are built of improved bone, muscle, and nerve tissue, but of unspecified capabilities; much worse than this, their faculty of telepathy is almost totally unexplored in its implications. (Later writers, to be sure, have not done much better; this is an immensely rich lode for someone willing to do some real work.)

In general, Stapledon is very weak in technology, gadgetry, biology, and psychology. As a writer, he can neither plot nor characterize. In short, he is little more than an amateur philosopher. Yet he grappled manfully with themes that intimidated those better qualified; he forged ahead where the professional hung back or turned aside. He insisted that there is a Big Picture, and he took it seriously. If there is something slightly Quixotic about the mismatching of his goals and capabilities, still he deserves our respect and gratitude.

Sherlock Holmes & Nero Wolfe

Detective stories have given us many supermen. Lately they tend to be superhuman mostly in the hardness of their skulls (being knocked unconscious at least once in every adventure, with nary a concussion) and in their ability to handle alcohol and women. A few, however, have shown talent that is not clearly bogus; probably the best known is the eccentric genius of Baker Street.

Of Holmes' personality traits, the outstanding is vanity; he is always posturing and soliciting flattery, as Dr. Watson frankly concedes. In fact, we get the impression that Holmes has chosen his tawdry and ill-paying profession because it gives him endless opportunity to strut and to humiliate others, both colleagues and criminals. We may again dubiously reflect: Does the superman require a foil? If a legitimate foil (the criminal) were lacking, would he seek victims elsewhere? Could he tolerate a world full of peers?

As to Holmes himself, it is doubtful; still, vanity is not his only motivation—another is the legitimate one of self-actualization, the employment of his powers and skills. These stem mostly from *memory, perceptivity, and deductive reasoning.*

His memory is amazing, but selective: he knows the characteristic appearance of the ash from every brand of cigar, but nothing of literature or astronomy. "You see, I consider that man's brain originally is like a little empty attic, and you have to stock it with such furniture as you choose . . . It is a mistake to think that that little room has elastic walls and can distend to any extent . . . there comes a time when for every addition of knowledge you forget something that you knew before."[38]

Holmes' *perceptivity* never comes across very clearly. It is partly training; the detective has schooled himself to notice such things as a man's fingernails, coat-sleeves, boots, trouser-knees, shirt-cuffs, the callosities of his forefinger and thumb. He even makes a practice of counting the stairs in every staircase he climbs, and twits Dr. Watson for overlooking this! (There is some pretty queer furniture in that little attic.) But the perceptivity also depends on natural talent, and is largely unexplained. Holmes can ". . . by a momentary expression, a twitch of a muscle or a glance of an eye, fathom a man's inmost thoughts." Unexplained, but fair enough. In 1970, a book appeared called *Body Language*, which attempts to make explicit some of the ways in which we can "read" people; it isn't easy.[50]

As to Holmes' famous faculty of "deduction," this is the core of Doyle's writing success: in each story he bravely spells out the workings of the detective's genius for the reader to admire. Naturally, these chains of inference are ridiculous, for example:

I *knew* you came from Afghanistan . . . . Here is a gentleman of a medical type, but with the air of a military man. Clearly an army doctor, then. He had just come from the tropics, for his face is dark, and that is not the natural tint of his skin, for his wrists are fair. He has undergone hardship and sickness, as his haggard face says clearly. His left arm has been injured. He holds it in a stiff and unnatural manner. Where in the tropics could an English army doctor have seen much hardship and got his arm wounded? Clearly in Afghanistan. The whole train of thought did not occupy a second. I then remarked that you came from Afghanistan, and you were astonished.[38]

Although the links of logic in Holmes' chains of reasoning have the strength of limp spaghetti, the principle is correct: a keen sense of relatedness, and the confidence to use it will be an important part of the intellect of any respectable superman.

Rex Stout's super-detective, Nero Wolfe, is a little more convincing than Sherlock Holmes, and more amusing, although there are many points of similarity or analogy. Wolfe is fat rather than lean, and addicted to orchids rather than cocaine; Holmes tends to asceticism, Wolfe to self-indulgence; both are misogynists, probably to simplify the storytelling. Wolfe's vanity is equally momumental; his assistant, Archie Goodwin, tells him. "You regard anything and everything beyond your control as an insult," which is really a very impressive comment, in a lowkeyed way.

Wolfe's memory is even more phenomenal than Holmes', and with no nonsense about overcrowding the attic. The fat man can recall long conversations verbatim. On one occasion he found it necessary to know a telephone number that had been dialed in his office; although he had paid no particular attention at the time, he was able to recall the occasion to mind, *remember the sounds of dialing,* and reconstruct the number from the remembered sounds! This is delightful, and the author must have a bit of genius himself to imagine such a thing.

Of course, the reader is convinced of Wolfe's genius more by intimidation than persuasion: witticisms, ten-dollar words, bits of arcane information concerning French cuisine—these tend to overpower us. As for hard-core performance, instead of Holmes' chains of inference we have flashes of insight, associations of ideas more tenuous or more remote than a non-genius would entertain. In one story, for example, he was led to the identification of a culprit by a slight similarity between the true and assumed names.[162] This is fair enough, even if particular examples are dubious; this is a proper attribute of superior man.

Modern Science Fiction

Sorting out the supermen of modern science fiction is a staggering task, and there is no pretense here of fairness, let alone completeness; only a very few that are useful and accessible are touched on. There is endless duplication, often with trivial variations; who has priority or who is most innovative is difficult to decide.

We must remember also that superman is not the only theme in science fiction, and some of the best writers have had indifferent success with it. Robert Heinlein, for example—in my opinion the best of living science fiction writers—has never produced any notable supermen, except for the very modest extrapolations in *Beyond This Horizon*.[73] His most ambitious effort, the human Martian in *Stranger in a Strange Land,* was an absurd hodge-podge of mysticism and occult powers.[74]

In 1939 *The New Adam* by the late Stanley G. Weinbaum was published, and by his own account intended to produce a classic which would avoid the error, which he attributes to Nietzsche and Wells, of merely accentuating human qualities.[175] The product is nearly a total catastrophe, the one touch of originality being the double mind of the superman: he can follow two trains of thought at once, see both sides of a question simultaneously—although he has a single identity—and can engage his two minds separately or in conjunction. This is somewhat intriguing in potential, but the theme is only stated and never developed. (Something vaguely like Weinbaum's superman has actually been created, by surgically splitting the brain of a monkey, which then can carry on two different tasks at once.[171] The surgical fusion or separation of identity—of consciousness—remains one of the most important problems of biology and philosophy.)

In the forties, A. E. van Vogt gave us *Slan!,* one of the grand-daddies or godfathers of a huge and still proliferating clan of supermen, whom we might characterize as the white-hat cowboys of the space age in fiction. They are all-American boys, Tom Swift types with a few biological improvements and a paranormal power or two. He also wrote *The World of Null-A*. under the influence of Korzybski's *General Semantics Seminar;* null-A stands for non-Aristotelian, the idea being that human minds are inferior because they are enslaved to Aristotelian or single-valued logic, whereas the real world is many-valued and there are many alternatives besides "A" or "not A" in a given proposition. Van Vogt's contribution was real, but it was not the actual delineation of supermen; rather, it was a kind of intricate and fast-paced adventure which, in spite of all the silliness, evoked a formidable feeling, the mood of wonder and marvel that leaves the reader just a little changed.

Arthur C. Clarke has produced brilliant and enchanting visions, at least three of his stories involving supermen. Yet, ungrateful and ungracious as it may seem to say so, his creations also lack substance; their merit is chiefly in mood and sense of adventure.

The main transhuman element in one of his books, *The City and the Stars*, centers on the storage of personalities in electronic data banks; since the personality patterns can be impressed onto new bodies at will or stored indefinitely, this constitutes immortality. This is a good idea, if not an original one, but badly flawed. Clarke seems to think it more or less self-evident that identity resides in the *patterns* of the personality and memory, so that if my pattern is impressed on a robot, the robot becomes I. However, this is definitely not self-evident, and probably not even true. See, for example, reference 45.

Clarke's most ambitious super-race of mutated men occurs in *Childhood's End*. In this story, the children of a century or so hence, suddenly show paranormal powers (clairvoyance, telekinesis, etc.) and, even more important, merge into a kind of hive mind to form a single transcendental entity, which leaves earth and the parent generation without a backward glance.[24] Yet, powerful as the story is, everything is done with mirrors; we are not given even semi-explicit reasons for either the strengths or the weaknesses of the new entity.

Alfred Bester's *The Demolished Man*, finally, is notable

for its attempt to flesh out the concept of mental telepathy. The "peepers" or mind-readers of the story interact with ordinary people and with each other in ways that are emotionally and socially interesting, even if the developments are often halting and unconvincing.[12] At least he has tried to come to grips with some specifics. Imagine, for example, the poignancy of unrequited love when the parties can read each other's thoughts. Imagine the challenge of a group conversation of peepers, in which skeins of thought are interwoven in patterns involving space dimensions as well as time, visual constructs as well as auditory. Bester has made these, at least to some degree, explicit, and has shown the way for more ambitious efforts.

Summary

Toting up the score, and paying some attention also to examples not specifically mentioned here, we seem to have something like this:

Ethical aspects of superman have often been stressed, and the types described usually fall into one of two classes: the *social* superman, who is a paragon of altruistic virtues, and the *amoral* superman, who is generally pictured as cold and calculating.

Intellectual qualities are primarily limited to *memory* and capabilities of *computation*.

Emotional aspects are infrequently investigated, except for the common trait of *pride* or arrogance; when they are, an emphasis on *warmth* and empathy is sometimes shown, more often *coolness* and serenity.

Emergent traits, those which are more characteristically superhuman, are often fantasies of the paranormal, extrasensory perception and "psi" powers.

Development of superman is usually through biological evolution, natural or technologically assisted.

All this is fairly useful, as far as it goes, but much is missing. Some of the apparently overlooked or under-emphasized aspects will be discussed in subsequent chapters.

43

Probably the most striking weaknesses in the literature center on *time scales, euthenics, and immortality.*

Natural evolution, even assisted by eugenics (planned breeding), is generally slow. Stapledon imagined billions of years were required to produce his Last Men, and modern science-fiction writers blithely create galactic societies with only slightly modified people in them. But it is clear that genetic engineering will produce radical alterations in a very few centuries at most. Change will not be gradual, but explosive; we are on the verge of a sharp discontinuity in history.

"Euthenics" refers to improvements in the current generation, in existing—even mature or elderly—individuals. There is reason to believe that unlimited change and development is possible even for you and me (see Appendix), and this opens vistas that hardly anyone has looked into; heretofore it has been almost universally assumed that each generation, and every species, has an inexorable and limited destiny fixed by its hereditary character. The possibility of correcting errors—both of nature and our own blundering—changes the ground rules and the viewpoint completely. Most especially, we must consider the feedback or bootstrap process by which our instincts, drives and motivations can be consciously modified by successive iteration.

Finally, few writers have tried to deal with indefinitely extended life, and those few have missed many of the implications. The chief implications concern the sanity and outlook of the individual, which will be among our main concerns.

4

Changes in the Chassis

The word "superman" is laden with emotional freight, clouded with semantic confusion and distorted by childish romanticism. To some, it immediately conjures up specters of the Master Race and the Nazis, a connotation of arrogance and coldness, if not brutality. To others, the word is objectionable because it suggests accentuation, rather than transcendence, of human qualities.

I will retain the word in spite of these handicaps, and indeed partly because of its shock value. I want to take by the scruff of the neck the dainty, the timid and the supercilious, and rub their noses in it; we must aspire to be, and intend to become, superior to mankind and to all its past heroes, individually and collectively, and in all aspects—physical, intellectual, emotional and moral.

The most difficult and disturbing questions concern superman's mentality and personality, and these are deferred to later chapters. Less frightening—if often startling—are the physical options, those of anatomy and physiology in the narrow sense, which will now be investigated.

I shall not attempt to conceptualize superman as a single, integrated entity; not only would that be beyond the scope of this essay and the skill of the writer, but it would be false to the spirit of the immortalist, who sees everything as open-ended, tentative and incomplete. Rather, I shall select certain traits for attention, without implying that these are necessarily the best or most important, and

45

without fixing the date at which their implementation might become feasible. I am dealing here only in conjectures and suggestions, although it is hoped that the guesses are shrewd and the suggestions reasonable.

Assembly vs. Invention

Superman does not have to be invented. We reject, as a trivial example, the "Superman" of the comics, the "man of steel" who is "more powerful than a locomotive" and "can leap tall buildings at a single bound." We reject not his banality but his dishonesty; barring super-flatulence, for example, there is no apparent way for him to alter course or maintain thrust in midair.

We likewise reject the super-powers of most heroes of science fiction, who have the magical ability to exert direct control over other minds, over matter, or over space and time—the dealers in telepathy, psychokinesis, teleportation, precognition, etc., who beat the game by changing the rules. It is true that we don't yet know all the rules, and we are probably mistaken about some we think we know; nevertheless, it is more honest, and will probably be more fruitful, if we give our superman chiefly those powers that are extensions of reasonably well-established phenomena. As we shall see, this will still provide immense scope for quantitative and qualitative improvement.

Instead of inventing superman, we can assemble him. We already have examples of all the traits and abilities required for a very respectable superman indeed. New ideas will undoubtedly occur, but we need postulate no more than already exist, their sources being: (1) rare human talents, (2) talents of other species, and (3) machine talents. After this, we can build speculation on flimsier hints and clues—in fact, we must, since long-range development will surely dwarf our boldest imaginings.

In the first category, there are several subdivisions. First, there is the obvious lode of *variance* among men. Most races need warm beds, but the Indians of Tierra del Fuego sleep nude in a climate worse than Chicago's. Most of us just want to lie down, but now and then we notice a Jim Ryun or a Dick Fosbury. And by far the majority of men can function in bed at most once a day, but Dr. Kinsey assures us there are those who can jump in and out like jackrabbits, several times a day, week in and week out. (Or so they say.)[93] Since such capacities are known to exist, they must have some anatomical and physiological basis, which can be discovered and (eventually) duplicated by various means, including not only genetic manipulation but also treatment of the mature individual by chemistry, surgery, special virus inoculations, and other means. This is not exactly self-evident, and it is conceivable that certain traits tend to be mutually exclusive, making it difficult for a single individual to embrace them all, even if desired; but the overriding presumption is that, once we thoroughly understand something, we can duplicate its effects sooner or later, and even improve on them. As supermen, *all* of us will have the important talents of the *best* of us, and anyone who doesn't like the monotony can choose to remain inferior.

In the category of "rare human talents" I include not only the fairly constant talents of exceptional people, but also the occasional creative successes of more ordinary people. All of us, at times, have performed "over our heads," reaching a peak not matched before or after. There was some reason why we could do it, and it should be possible to make such ability routinely available. Again, children have certain capacities that are often gradually lost as they grow older; in particular, the young have acute senses—their hearing everything is not just nosiness, but sharp ears; their finickiness about food is not just temperament, but sensitive taste. Still again, systems such as yoga and hypnosis seem able to unlock hidden stores of perception and control, stores which will inevitably be made public.

A little more difficult, perhaps, will be the appropriation of the skills of other species, because of the greater likelihood of incompatibility. Nevertheless, the hybridization of animals, including man, through artificial means has been predicted by competent biologists, based on work already in progress.[44] If some animal is doing it, then it can be done; and if it can be done, it can scarcely be doubted

47

that we will do it, if we wish. It is only and always a question of effort, money and time.

The third category is really blue-sky, because in principle a machine can be made to do anything that is physically possible; and if we envision the human brain coupled to a machine or complex of machines—so that the machines are extensions of the person—then, with only modest reservations to be noted later, *we* can do anything, which means we can be anything.

Feasibility and Credibility

Before jumping into the jam-pot, a further word is in order about how serious the ensuing suggestions may be, and how much evidence exists that such things will be possible.

Specific references to current art will be sprinkled lightly throughout, but most of the book avoids technology and addresses itself to the lay reader. An *Appendix* is provided with selected references to and excerpts from the technical literature, providing some specific support for some of the conjectures.

But useful as particular detailed hints may be, a mere generalized optimism, a hopeful reading of history, is even more useful. From the amount and rate of recent progress, surely it is pikestaff-plain that, *at the very least,* we shall eventually be able to imitate nearly every existing life process.

For example, suppose we want to give our superman the ability to hibernate (and we do). It isn't necessary to know anything whatever about the mechanism of hibernation in order to predict a hibernating superman; it is only necessary to know that hibernation exists—for instance, in bears. Since it exists, it can be studied, understood and imitated or improved upon. It is not self-evident that hibernation can be made compatible with the totality of other physiological processes in man, but presumptively it can. At the worst, the ability to hibernate will require the sacrifice of some other ability, or some loss of efficiency in other capacities, or a larger body size.

At this point it is also necessary to beat a little on a

horse that not everyone realizes is dead. There are still too few who appreciate how far the facts have outrun the judgment and imagination of experts and seers. Consider that Vannevar Bush—a brilliant, creative scientist—testified that an intercontinental missile was far in the future; and this virtually while the Russians were building one. Add that H. G. Wells, in reaching for an example of the ridiculous, cast his scorn on the "2,000 mile an hour airplane."[178] And that Britain's Astronomer Royal called space travel "utter bilge" in 1956, one year before the first sputnik.[58] Consider that Auguste Comte in 1835 said that man could *never* know anything about the chemical composition of the stars—just a couple of decades before Kirchhoff invented the spectroscope, which told us more about the chemistry of stars than we knew about the chemistry of the earth ... the list could be extended almost indefinitely. (See also Chapter 11.)

It is unimportant that optimists have also been wrong, because the failures of optimism pertain mainly—perhaps entirely—to details and time scales. Sometimes a particular means has proven impractical (think of the dirigible), but the end (in this case, comfortable air travel) has nevertheless been attained. Often a road proves much longer than expected, full of twists and obstacles; but superman's development is not dependent on any timetable.

If we think of superman as our remote descendant, then time scales are unimportant. If we think of superhumanity as our own condition, after freezing and resuscitation, then again we have plenty of time; no one gets impatient in the freezer. In either case, the usual "practical" considerations dwindle to almost nothing, and we can focus chiefly on what is possible *in principle*.

Energy and Success

One definition of a superman would be "someone with more than human potential for success." We cannot say, with any confidence, what constitutes success until we know much more about ourselves and the universe, but we can tentatively assume that "success" refers to survival and security, and possibly dominion, along with the learning, growth and development that make these possible, and such subjective criteria as comfort and joy.

Possibly, then, we can get some notions about superman by looking at unusually successful humans and analyzing their virtues.

As a first approximation, by general agreement, the main factors in personal success, under present conditions, are energy, talent and luck—in that order, if we are speaking of moderate success. Energy is by far the most important requirement, if you hope to become moderately rich or gain fairly rapid advancement in your vocation or employment. What counts is the *marginal* or *extra* performance you can turn in, above that required to get by or to satisfy standard demands. Every "premium" increment becomes very important: if your output, by some appropriate measure, rises from 110% of standard to 120% of standard, then your *premium* output has doubled.

If we measure success by the crassest but readiest criterion—money—then the picture is plain. If you increase your earnings, by overtime or moonlighting, from 110% of your living cost to 120%, your savings are doubled. (Better yet, reduce expenditures 10%; because of the income tax, a penny saved is more than a penny earned.)

At this point, someone may object impatiently: What do these hum-drum, workaday notions have to do with superman? Surely a superman is not just someone who can work a little harder! Besides, if everyone had this capacity, the competitive edge would be lost! Furthermore, has the number of supermen increased markedly since the use of stimulants became common—coffee in seventeenth-century Europe, amphetamines in twentieth-century America, etc.?

The last question is complex, and as far as I know the correlation has not been studied extensively. As for the rest, bear with me a while.

Explicitly, if you were a plumber in 1968, earning $4 per hour, and you doubled your savings by increasing your output from 110% to 120% of standard, this would mean a yearly added saving of perhaps $800; if for simplicity we disregard advances in earning power and inflation, and compound this at 6% for 40 years, it would come to a grand total extra saving of over $130,000.

If you are an academic, the results are nearly as obvious. If you work 10% longer or faster each day and double your output of pedestrian scholarly papers (or committee reports, etc.) you will have a high probability of tangible reward. In business management, the situation is similar.

In fact, a hypothesis suggests itself about the remarkable correlation between scientific achievement and youth. (Most of the important advances in physics and mathematics have been made by young men.) Perhaps it is not originality or creativity or insight which diminishes with age, but just energy and available time. The older man has less physical strength and more family and administrative responsibilities; he just can't devote long hours to taxing work of his own choice. It may be partly a matter of energy in the literal, physical sense, a question of body metabolism; and there may also be an alteration of "physic" energy, of motivation and life style.

Needless to say, this hypothesis cannot be the *complete* explanation of the correlation of genius with youth, since it does not readily interpret the variations with different professions; but if it has any validity, it offers another very striking instance of the way in which modest quantitative differences can become critically important qualitative differences. In order for the potential genius to *function* as a genius, *i.e.* to produce works of genius, he requires that little extra strength and drive. Since major works are rare, a slightly reduced store of energy is likely to mean not just fewer works, but none at all. In other words, there is a kind of threshold effect, a small gain in energy being translated into a quantum jump in productivity.

As introduction to a slightly different view of the same phenomenon, consider the effect of a slight increase in the intelligence of a population. The distribution of intelligence in a population seems to follow nearly the bell-shaped "normal" curve, with the greatest number of individuals near average, and smaller numbers above and below.

Let us suppose that for a certain sub-population the average IQ is 100, and about 2% are "gifted", having an IQ greater than 130. (These are more or less typical figures.) Now, if the average could be increased to 110, with the shape of the distribution curve almost unaffected (roughly 10 points added to each individual's IQ), then, the mathematicians tell us, the number of "gifted" people would jump up to about 9%! Keeping the distribution curve, an increase of only 10% in the average intelligence would multiply the number of "gifted" people by about 4½ or 450%. In the "genius" range the effect is even more pronounced.

In general, then, a shift of a few points in the average will sharply affect the number of very bright—and very dull—people. In particular, a modest improvement in the average may result in a startling increase in wheel-horses, those key people whose efforts are most important for quality and progress. (These observations apply irrespective of any reservations one may have about the usefulness of particular tests, and those who dislike the words "bright" and "gifted" may use the word "effective" instead.)

Now, one can also examine the productivity of the individual in the same way. There is—I believe—a similar statistical variation in the individual's productivity, measured against time. We work "over our heads" only occasionally, and we really transcend ourselves only rarely; yet it may be just those times of transcendence on which we rely for exceptional ideas or perceptions. Thus, a relatively small increase in energy may multiply several-fold our times of transcendence and our major works. It follows that a functional superman might result from something so modest and simple as an improvement in the glandular system, producing more energetic people.

Admittedly, energy is only one factor in success, and it depends partly on competition—it is partly a relative rather than an absolute factor. When machines do almost all the physical work and much of the thinking, and when everybody can be optimized, a moderate boost in the individual's energy may count for little. But that time is well in the future, and the early versions of superman may quite possibly center on physical and psychic energy.

. . . or the leopard his spots?" This was Jeremiah's question, and he thought the answer negative. In these latter days, however, skin and other outward changes promise to become relatively trivial, quick, and cheap, and it is of some mild interest to wonder whether the Ethiopians, and the Orientals, as well as the Caucasians, will choose cosmetic changes on any substantial scale.

Before very long, the Negro will be able to whiten his skin if he wishes—or blacken it to ebony, as seems more likely if the "black is beautiful" trend persists. Because moods and fashions change rapidly and with unpredictable vagaries, no one can say with confidence what the trends will be, or what effects, if any, they will have on race relations, but one can, as usual, speculate.

The whole question of race relations is a very minor one in the long view: expanding opportunities and multiplying options will make diversity both inevitable and acceptable, in all areas where choices depend primarily on taste or caprice. In those areas where clear-cut differences in quality or value can be shown, there will be uniformity, since everyone will choose the best. But we will surely encounter some surprises in the revelation of what is arbitrary and what is not.

Aesthetic questions will often be found to have surprising answers. To what extent is beauty truly in the eye of the beholder, and to what extent is it absolute? At present, we can only surmise, but I dare say most people feel there are absolute elements of beauty. It is difficult to imagine a point of view from which a wart hog, say, is lovelier than an antelope. Will there ever be a culture which regards a scaly skin—a blotchy, irregularly scaly skin—as more attractive than a smooth one? And so on. One might be tempted to retort that the wart hog thinks itself more gracious than the antelope, but I do not concede the point. After all, the average is *not* our ideal of beauty, nor are these ideals species-specific. A man might easily decide that a peacock, or a panther, is more beautiful than a woman—not more desirable, of course, but more beautiful. In the same way, it is entirely possible that certain races, in some of their traits, are either more or less beautiful than others, even in their own view.

The fact that, in the past, many American Negroes have tried to lighten their skins and straighten their hair proves nothing, because their psyches may have been twisted by the prevalent culture. The fact that many Caucasians like to darken their skins by exposure to the sun also proves nothing, because the urge to be "different" can take many forms. But careful introspection can provide some clues—however unreliable—to our feelings on these matters.

At risk of being obnoxious as well as wrong, let me make a few guesses. First, I think that skin color has no absolute aesthetic value, although texture and highlights may. Ivory, ruddy, brown, ebony—all can be delightful. Likewise, hair color is equally attractive in all shades; at least much more depends on texture and subtleties of reflectance than on simple hue. But hairiness of body (until and unless we consider actual fur) is a negative factor, and in this the Caucasians are the main losers. Frizzy hair on the head is also a debit, and here the Negroids suffer. The black, straight hair of the Orientals is attractive enough, but as a racial trait it suffers from too much uniformity, lacking variation for interesting individuality.

It may be that even if absolute criteria of beauty do exist, their application may take a variety of forms, depending on the training and sophistication of the viewer; we think, for example, of the different forms and styles of music. In any case, there will be a protracted period of experimentation with hectic flutters of fashion.

At first the new opportunities may evoke defensive psychological reactions in some quarters, some people choosing to leave their appearance alone, or even to accentuate existing traits, merely to prove that they were proud of themselves all along. And there will be, indeed, a tendency to respect the other fellow's appearance more than previously, since it will be a matter of choice: he looks the way he wants to look, not the way his accident of birth forced him to. But very soon, in most quarters, the new cosmetics will become big business and the center of high fashion.

Not only changes in skin and hair color and texture, but even changes in physiognomy, eye color and size, and eventually even bodily contours will become relatively easy to perform and inexpensive matters of choice. One year in London the ideal man may be covered with silky blue fur. The next year in Paris a fashionable woman may have small breasts and no pubic hair. After her trip to the beauty shop, you may actually not recognize your wife. Life, yet once again, will become more complicated, with still more avenues to good or ill. One of the benefits, perhaps, will be easier marital fidelity: with so much spice of variety in one's wife or husband, will not the temptation to wander be reduced? In a life of centuries or millenia, such novelties may become more important.

The Elimination of Elimination

If cleanliness is next to godliness, then a superman must be cleaner than a man, and cleanliness is only partly a matter of money.

In the Middle Ages, one of the distinctions between rich and poor was that the former were not quite so lousy; the poor, often unable to keep themselves, their clothes and their dwellings clean, had to resign themselves to lice and bedbugs. Because of the cost of soap and perfume, people could then say, quite literally, "Poverty stinks."

In fact, it still does. With the possible exception of a Howard Hughes, even the wealthiest of us must sometimes mingle with malodorous crowds and inhale the bad breath of passersby or co-workers, not to mention the grime of the gutter blowing in our faces with every gust of wind. And even Howard Hughes cannot escape the stench and indignity of his own elimination.

In the future, our plumbing (of the thawed as well as the newborn) will be more hygienic and seemly. Those who choose will consume only zero-residue foods, with excess water all evaporating via the pores. Alternatively, modified organs may occasionally expel small, dry, compact residues. In any case, urination and defecation as we know them will be only disgusting footnotes to ancient history, which we will read about (or remember) with remote distaste, as we now read about birds disgorging food for their young.

Is such daintiness normal or necessary? Certainly we get along now with little distress in these areas—but so did our lice-picking ancestors. We are highly adaptable, and can put up with a lot. But lice, nevertheless, are incompatible with the better life, and so is the toilet.

The Graceful Glutton

Gluttony has usually been considered a vice, or even a sin; and indeed it is a sin against oneself to weaken the body with fat, serum cholesterol, and other present consequences of overeating. There are also Freudian allusions often made against those who love to eat, shaming or at least worrying them about hidden motives of guilt, inadequacy, etc. At the very least, there is a tendency to question the strength of character, if not the moral outlook, of one who indulges himself freely in food.

It will certainly become possible to eliminate the unhappy physical consequences of overeating, in many ways. Foods may be produced that will have all the requisite texture, taste, appearance and aroma of natural foods, but no food value whatever; they will go through you quickly and cleanly—no muss, no fuss, no bother. (Perhaps they will even be eliminated by evaporation, with no indignities.) Then again, your own metabolism may be improved so that ordinary foods will be processed more sensibly, extracting only those nutritional elements that are actually needed at the time, and efficiently disposing of the rest. Special groups of enzymes may be designed; or, if necessary, symbiotic organisms may dwell in your gut—something like an improved tapeworm, but perhaps microscopic for aesthetic and other reasons—which will process the food as needed. The Romans, usually referred to as "decadent," were said sometimes to continue banqueting for many hours, renewing their capacities by occasional regurgitation; we will acquire the same capacity without the indelicacy.

But is not such a notion, indeed, decadent? Who knows? Certainly there have been good and even great men who

56

loved their food and drink, and showed it—Winston Churchill, for instance. Huge numbers of people depend on a nervous habit—smoking, or chewing gum—which is hardly more dainty than eating. Surely a normal person will not *need* to glut himself; at the same time, why should he not have the means to do so, if he sometimes wishes? Or even if he often wishes? Why should this be regarded as more than a minor idiosyncrasy, like an addiction to crossword puzzles?

Various retorts suggest themselves. For instance, if someone craves such massive animal satisfaction, why not eliminate the middleman and use electronic stimulation of the brain? To this question, there is a fairly easy answer: one does not desire, for example, sexual orgasm alone, but the whole ritual of lovemaking, with its nuances and subtleties; analogously, one desires not just to slake his thirst, but to clink the goblet and admire the sparkle; and in the case of food, one may well wish not just to achieve satiety, but to eat, or dine, or banquet.

Whether meals will be more or less important in various eras of the future, no one can yet say. But our general rule is to leave our options open, and try to assure that what we want will be there when we want it. We shall grow in many directions, and some of us will grow in gluttony.

Integrated Man

The integration efforts of the future will, of course, not concern anything so trivial as social amalgamation of the human races, but will be of two kinds. First, we must achieve the integration of the individual's own body. Second, we will consider the incorporation of genetic traits of other species into our own heredity.

The human body at present is not so much an entity as a kind of loose alliance or empire. The brain dominates the body, and the conscious center dominates the brain, but very imperfectly. In many locations and functions, the nominal command center has neither communication nor control: the whole muddles through, more or less, through the creaky operation of custom and tradition, but with frequent breakdowns and low general efficiency. Far from the seat of empire, many of our tissues and organs carry on trade with the "outer" world, but have scarcely heard of government, while their individual citizens, the cells, are totally parochial.

The possibility for improvement exists, even prior to genetic tailoring. Unusual individuals and special techniques have long been known to be associated with astonishing powers: we think especially of yoga and hypnotism, as well as congenital talent. The yogis, it is well known, often learn to exercise surprising control over "involuntary" functions, such as heartbeat, slowing or speeding it at will and beyond the ordinary range.

The dentist can use hypnosis—or teach the patient to use autohypnosis—to interfere with normally ungovernable pain signals (or with their interpretation or processing) to eliminate the annoyance. I can wiggle my ears, individually. J. B. S. Haldane claimed he could detect the opening of his pylorus, and the passage of waste materials along his sigmoid flexure—a sensation not unlike a "belly full of snakes."[64]

The afferent nerve supply is especially rich from the skin, special sense organs, joints, and commonly-used muscles—it also exists from the other organs—and there seem to be many possibilities for outbound communication as well.[64] Thus we see the physical basis of these unusual abilities. Why they are so unusual is not easy to say: one is tempted to guess that they have low marginal survival value, and thus low priority in evolutionary selection. However that may be, we are sure to find good uses for all of them.

Turning to the adoption of the talents of other species, the field is even richer. It may not be possible, or at least it may not be practically feasible, to incorporate *every* animal ability into superman's body; it is clear that some functions and capacities may derive from the total organization, or from the interaction of major subsystems that are incompatible with our basic plan. For example, we can hardly expect, by strictly biological means, to acquire the hovering ability of a hummingbird or a bee. But only a small fraction of the possibilities seem even tentatively ruled out.

A simple, but extremely useful improvement, on which animals may provide some clues, concerns muscular coordination. The seal can balance balls on his nose, perhaps the result of fine coordination of the neck muscles useful in catching fish. (Some human acrobats, after training, can do almost as well.) Cats are noted for agility. Bears, clumsy as they look and awkward as their paws are, can scoop fish out of water, a feat few humans seem able to learn easily. All such talents surely depend on relatively small differences in anatomy and physiology, since the animals named are all mammals; hence it seems nearly certain we can incorporate all such abilities into superman. And it goes without saying that every superman will also have the *maximum* talents of every human, including, for example, the finger coordination demanded for concert-caliber piano playing. It seems unlikely that these several talents will prove mutually exclusive to any important extent.

The nose of the bloodhound will be ours, and the ears of the snake; ours also will be the navigational abilities of certain flying insects, which use vibrating fibers in place of gyros. We will have adaptations of the sonar of the bat and the porpoise. The eye of the eagle may present problems, since its function must presumably be combined with normal human appearance; yet a betting man would have to guess that superman's sight will be *better* than the eagle's at any range, since our larger size permits larger lens aperture, hence finer possible resolution.

The advantages of many of these adaptations will not merely concern efficiency; subjective vistas will be opened. For example, the dog has relatively poor vision and is colorblind besides; it seems rather plain, to anyone who has observed dogs that their keen sense of smell affords a rich variety of subjective connotations and appreciations; similar remarks can be made about blind species. When a species finds some of the windows on the world shut or narrowed, it tends to open wider the remaining ones. Superman would have all his windows opened wide, and be able not only to use, but to enjoy the view.

Any self-respecting superman should be able, at the very least, to endure the worst conditions his native planet can threaten. Dandridge Cole pictured an early-model superman as running tirelessly through the snow, virtually naked, disdaining to use a vehicle for trips of a few miles or even a few dozen miles.[26] This would save a good deal on road taxes and car payments, but presumably the main motive would be the sheer fun of it, the joy of exercising one's (super) faculties, just as a healthy person now enjoys a brisk walk in crisp weather. Weather resistance would also, once more, provide an extra margin for survival in emergencies or unusual contingencies.

The first modification could be to speed up the acclimatization that most of us already exhibit. In one test of this adaptability, several city-bred men were subjected to six weeks in the open, sleeping at night with only one army blanket in 37° temperature.[81] Measurable physical changes included metabolic rate and changes in the blood vessels which provided better circulation in the hands and feet. Our first model outdoorsman will be able to make the metabolic change almost instantaneously, and will have variable and controllable vascular parameters.

More striking adaptations are shown by certain aborigines in Australia and by Alacaluf Indians in South America. The Australians can sleep naked in 39° temperatures; their skin and outer body temperatures fall substantially, but they ignore this and sleep without shivering, while the internal organs remain at normal body heat.[81] The Alacalufs of Tierra del Fuego, on the other hand, who also sleep naked in miserable weather—even in sleet or snow—show an increased metabolic rate, and shiver to generate heat, although without awakening.[81]

While no humans can live unprotected in Antarctica, penguins can do so, even enduring a howling wind at 80° below zero; in fact, they can do this for months at a time, without food![151] Part of this capacity depends on a special network of blood vessels in the feet, with arteries close to veins, so that warm outgoing blood in the arteries takes the chill off incoming blood in the veins. As already noted, the outdoorsman will have variable vascular features.

Instead of the penguin's feathers, our snow man may have the hair of the yak or the yeti. Domestic animals, such as some varieties of dogs and horses, grow thicker hair when the weather gets colder, and perhaps superman will be able to grow hair in hours instead of weeks. If it isn't feasible to grow hair that quickly, he might burrow into the snow and hibernate for a few days while the fur is sprouting.

Heat is potentially much more dangerous to life than cold. Living tissue can freeze and live—sometimes even near zero—but it cannot boil and live, even though some microbes can endure many minutes in boiling water, and there are organisms which thrive in hot springs at a temperature not far below boiling. But there are animals, including mammals, that can live in the hottest deserts.

The camel, of course, is the prime example—an amazing animal. Not only is it a mammal, but it is a sweating mammal, yet it can go without water for days in the Sahara. Part of its adaptation is the tolerance of a wide range of blood temperature: in the cold desert night, it cools down to the low nineties, and next day it can slowly warm up to 105°, absorbing a great deal of heat in its massive body, before beginning to sweat. Then when it perspires, water is drawn from the tissue spaces of the body, the blood remaining normal; it can lose more than 30 gallons of water and over 25% of its body weight without harm—and then restore itself with a half hour's drinking![122] (The hump stores fat, not water.) These should be relatively easy tricks to learn, and modified man will wander in comfort, naked, almost anywhere on earth.

Body Armor

The notion of a man with natural armor seems ridiculous at first. We usually associate such armor with the chitinous exoskeletons of insects, or the horny plates or scales of reptiles, and not with mammals. We also have been taught that over-specialization is the biological road to ruin, with the disappearance of the giant reptiles as the prime example; agility is more important than a tough hide. Furthermore, the availability of artificial armor—clothing and vehicles of various kinds—might make it seem rather silly to grow our own. But there are possibilities only recently recognized.

A few years ago a Long Island company reported development of a new nylon body armor for soldiers and police—a one-eighth-inch fabric of special weave that works by "diverting the impact energy from the impact point;" the threads "pull together and tighten up when struck by a bullet, force it to wobble, then actually pucker around the projectile and stop it."[170] A bayonet is said scarcely to dent it.

Perhaps this material did not fulfill its promise or advertising, since I have found no more recent report; but the idea may have some merit. If it does, then a special kind of *hair*, trained to grow in the necessary patterns, might fulfill the function of the nylon. Or there might be a subcutaneous layer, a web of thin, tough ligaments cunningly woven, which would tend to prevent any deep penetrating wounds. After all, many creatures have layers of protective fat under the skin. If the volume and mass requirements of the armor layer and its service tissues are substantial, then our armored man will just have to be a little bigger, but that's no problem.

Imagine the chagrin of a lion who tries to take a bite out of this model of man! The poor beastie would think itself up against Clark Kent in person.

Stinking, Shocking, and Breathing Fire

What about a biological repertory of active defense? As usual, the presumption is that it isn't worth the trouble, but again—who knows? Built-in biological weapons would be relatively puny, but they are also cheap and convenient. There may be periods and philosophies in which the self-contained man is idealized, external appurtenances are scroned, and frontiersmen will have to deal with hostile life-forms on strange planets.

If so, we can design quite a versatile active defense system into a body just a little bigger than present man's, with a few specialized glands and other organs. In this way, we could secrete poisons of many kinds, and deliver them by fang or claw or spray: the formic acid of the ant, the venom of the cobra or black widow, etc. ("Let's get married, Honey." "We can't—you're poisonous and I'm not.")

Chemical active defense is not limited to poisons, but also includes stenches, such as those of skunks and certain beetles. It could also include smoke screens—the cuttlefish uses an inky smoke screen under water—and it should be possible to develop one for use in air.

We could also imitate the electric eel, and acquire the ability to deliver a thousand-volt jolt at will.

An even more delightful trait would be the ability to blow flames, which is actually possible with no great difficulty, even though so far only mythological creatures have done so. The idea occurred to me when I saw some undergraduates display an engaging trick: they would pass gas (flatulence), hold a lighted match near the rear end, and there would be a marvelous puff of flame. (The gas contains combustible hydrocarbons.) For a dragon—or a man—to blow flames, all that is necessary is to belch a similar gas, simultaneously gnashing teeth that are designed to strike sparks, similar to flint and steel. *Viola*—a living blowtorch! (It may take a little practice to avoid singed eyebrows.)

Batman and Dragonfly

The origin of our dreams of flying seems to be in dispute. Some claim these dreams have sexual significance, others that they are related to our ancient fear of falling out of the tree, or still more ancient adjustments to a three-dimensional life in the sea. Or our yearnings may stem prosaically from envy of the birds. However that may be, there is indeed a widespread longing to fly with our own wings, and this longing will assuredly be fulfilled.

Will we really create a race of batmen? Or will Los Angeles one day refer primarily, not to a city, but to a breed of angels, a variety of winged men? The obvious difficulties make an affirmative answer seem absurd; yet bide a wee.

The worst problems of winged men may concern furniture and clothing. To fly is splendid, but to *perch* is ridiculous, and furniture to accommodate wings may require tricky design. But all this is secondary to the feasiblity of flying.

Icarus could never have gotten off the ground. Many studies have shown that man is simply too heavy to fly under his own power. Given earth's gravity and atmosphere, the power and wing surface requirements seem to rule out a flyer the size of a man. The largest flying bird, the condor, has a wing spread of nine feet but a weight of only about twenty-two pounds. The largest animals ever known to have flown, certain pteranodons of the cretaceous, had wing spreads of twenty feet but weights, it is believed, of only about twenty-five pounds; and they were probably soaring creatures primarily, rather than wing flappers.

This is one of the key words: *soar*. It is obvious that men can fly without engines, because they have done so: sailplanes can carry men for hours, if the pilot is skillful in finding updrafts of air to ride. If we add the ability to flap one's wings for added upthrust and forward thrust, then we could have muscle-powered flyers.

However, the use of very large wings to permit soaring, and the ability to flap these wings are not easy to reconcile. What may be needed is a large set of locked wings, plus a smaller subsidiary set that our muscles can flap. This might lead to a man looking like neither an angel nor a bat, but more like a dragonfly—or like the four-inch scarab beetle of Central America, with stiffly spread forwings and beating rear wings.[122]

Recent and current experiments with ornithopters have involved bicycle mechanisms to flap mechanical wings. As far as I know, no one yet has tried the combination of a large fixed wing plus a small powered set. Success with the latter might help pave the way for dragonfly-man.

All this may still sound rather foolish, involving too much effort and too much specialization for a result of very limited value. But the specialization may not be as excessive as it seems, and the result not so limited in application.

Imagine a race with a smallish set of wings, powered by the pectorals and muscles of the back, shoulders and buttocks. Living in the very low-g interior of a hollow asteroid, these people could fly handily, and would be free as birds. In caverns of the moon, where weight is one sixth that on earth, they could attach small auxiliary fixed wings; this dependence on artificial aids might be not much different from our usual reliance on shoes for walking. For those who visit or live on earth, flight would require putting on a large set of soaring wings, and would be almost entirely recreational rather than utilitarian, yet it might seem worthwhile.

There will be myriad complications, some of them unforeseen, but also complications. New sense organs may be needed for navigation, and a balanced body will require patient simulated trials. But the life of the mind, as well as the senses, would be enriched: there could be whole new modes of expression, subjects of fashion and adornment, referents for literature, bases for architecture. At least some of us, for a time, might live in such fairylands.

Aquaman

Oceanography of late has become almost as glamorous as space science, with countless predictions that much of man's technological and economic future lies in the sea; mutual funds have sprung up devoted entirely to speculation in the stocks of ocean-oriented companies. Oil drilling under water is already important, and there are indications that metallic mineral recovery may become so; portions of the ocean floor have been discovered heavily sprinkled with mineral nodules containing substantial amounts of manganese, copper, and cobalt.[179] More sophisticated fisheries and deep-sea "farming" may mitigate the world food shortage.

All these predictions and speculations deserve considerable skepticism; they may or may not prove out. But one thing is sure: there is a lot of ocean—the seas cover more than seventy per cent of the planet. The ocean is much more habitable for man than any of the known extraterrestrial planets. The temperature of seawater is more or less tolerable, and although the stuff isn't quite right either for drinking or breathing, accommodations can be made.

Is it possible to breathe water? Yes—even for a mammal! In a remarkable series of experiments a few years ago, it was found that dogs could live underwater for hours, inhaling and exhaling water instead of air. The main trick required was to keep more oxygen than normal dissolved in the water, under pressure; the small amount in solution at ordinary pressure is not enough for a mammal. While this type of experiment has no direct application, it does show that we are not as far removed from sea adaptation as might be thought.

A full-fledged aquaman must be able to breathe under water, and not just hold his breath while making long dives, as the seals and whales do. Whether our lungs can be modified to breathe both air and water is uncertain. Possibly a set of gills will have to be added, with either lungs or gills hooked into the circulatory system, depending on need. Once again, all these spare parts and alternate systems will need more space—a larger person—unless we can increase the efficiency of other parts.

The usual predictions for life in the sea center on domed cities, with excursions requiring submarines, scuba gear, or something of the sort. But freedom, fun, and safety will be magnified when water becomes one of our natural elements. Making the adaptation will not be easy; there are countless problems in addition to breathing: problems involving the skin, the eyes, the ears and many other considerations. Yet when they are solved, "freedom of the seas" will have an entirely new meaning.

The Way Before the Omnivore

One of man's natural competitive advantages has been his willingness to eat almost anything that doesn't bite him back, and many things that do. It can be wiggly like a rotgrub, squiggly like an earthworm, stinking like limburger, or full of offal like a fresh intestine—a hungry man will eat it, if civilization hasn't queered him to the point of suicide. (Some anthropologists believe that early man was not primarily a predator, but a gatherer and scavenger; he found his dinner under a rotten log, or if he were lucky, he stole some carrion before the hyenas got to it.) He has some digestive peers, including the pigs, and some superiors, including the cockroaches, but not many. By and large, man is a good journeyman omnivore.

In the future, the question of digestion is not likely to be a major one; in a century, at the outside, we will probably have solved the problems of space and population, and our wealth and resources could be such that everyone can live exclusively on caviar, truffles, and hummingbird tongues, if he wishes. Even so, it may be thought prudent to design the greatest versatility into ourselves—in case of unforeseen emergencies—as a convenience in exploring and colonizing new planets, or possibly as a way of deflating the mystique of eating. There may be some small value in asking, how far can superman go in becoming the complete omnivore?

As a first step, we can learn to enjoy—and not merely tolerate—those things our bodies now can process. This will be partly a psychological trick, since many of our repugnances derive from cultural or personal bias, e.g. the Japanese like raw fish and Americans do not. Americans like maize and Chinese do not. And so on. But this improvement may also be partly physical, including the provision for some pleasant new sensations and for blocking certain unpleasant sensations, those associated with specific aromatics or other chemicals in certain foods. (By way of analogy, the ear can be trained to enjoy certain sophisticated combinations of sounds, and can also be physically deafened to certain otherwise irritating frequencies.) At present, "taste" is said to be largely a matter of smell, with the actual taste buds sensitive only to sweet, sour, salt, and bitter signals. In the future, we may invent a great many new kinds of taste buds, or increase the range of those we have.

(Sometimes what seems to be just a finicky appetite is based on metabolism. Some varieties of men—such as those in Africa and South America—seem to lose the enzyme needed to digest lactose after they are weaned, and the dried milk that generous Americans send them makes them sick.)

As a second step, we can adopt or adapt the techniques of the mammalian herbivores, so that we can eat salads of grass if we choose. But of course grass is not very nourishing, even for cows and horses—they need a great deal of it to get by—and this will bestow no major benefit, except to the vegetarians.

As a third step, we can study the termites, design suitable symbiotic bacteria, and attain the capacity to digest cellulose (plant fiber generally, even sawdust) into sugar. This would wonderfully improve our survival potential in hostile or stingy environments.

As a fourth step, we can study the small faunas of caves, and design the ability to extract energy from many kinds of mineral ores, even in the absence of oxygen. In emergencies, then, a superman might be able to subsist on a barren, airless planet! Creatures have been found that actually have such capacities. We may become literally able to chew nails and spit rust.

As a fifth step, we can use techniques borrowed from the desert creatures (mentioned earlier) to get by with a minimum of water, e.g., by allowing a rise in body temperature instead of sweating to keep it low, and by dropping nearly dry feces.

As a sixth step, we can learn the ability—said to be exhibited by some animals, including cattle—to utilize a certain amount of mineral nitrogen as food, rather than requiring all organic nitrogen, thus reducing our need for proteins.

As a seventh step, we might even copy or improve on the performance of the legumes, and fix nitrogen from the air—instead of eating protein, we could inhale its main ingredient.

More generally, we might learn to utilize all the main nutritional elements of air—oxygen, carbon dioxide, water, and nitrogen—so that besides energy, we would need only relatively small amounts of other elements (phosphorus, sulfur, etc.) from other sources to get by. This would be doing *better* than most plants, which require water from the ground and cannot get by with water vapor in the air. The energy could be obtained in a variety of ways, including solar conversion devices of various kinds to utilize the sun's rays; but ultimately, as already indicated, we hope to be able to use a miniature nuclear fusion device (sort of a tiny, controlled-release, hydrogen bomb) that will last, for all practical purposes, indefinitely without refueling, and provide energy for all our bodily purposes, including metabolism and locomotion. A superman of this model, if he chose, could disdain dining altogether. Perhaps cults of asceticism would arise, eating being considered a disgusting display of primitive animalism. And if some of the religions of India maintain their sway, their adherents would welcome the chance to quit being predators of any kind, to live without devouring other living beings. As an outward sign of their moral superiority, such cults might eliminate the mouth from the human (or X-model superhuman) physiognomy, substituting a porous membrane capable of passing only air. For those speaking English, the most obscene four-letter words would be *feed* and *food*.

Among the many possible dimensions of the improvement of man are some simple and obvious ones, such as physical size. Both enlargement and reduction have been recommended at one time or another.

In reduction, there are still ways of looking down on the big guys. For example, one advantage is that little people have little appetites. If human crowding continues to increase, we may prize people who don't take up too much room, or eat too much, or wear too many yards of cloth. Looking at it *durch die Blume,* a little man can live, on the same money, better than a big man.

The best thing about little people is that they are *quicker,* and this for at least two fundamental reasons. First, their nerve-paths, their internal bodily communications, are shorter, thus the signals have less distance to travel (for example, from brain to hand). Second, their limb movements require less time, for mechanical reasons that are a little complex but well established. Thus, smaller humans could accomplish more in a given time, man for man, in most kinds of work—apparently.

The gains in economy and efficiency of mini-men have other aspects too, including military ones. Submarines, airplanes, and especially spaceships have a crying need for small crewmen. Why put a big lard-bottom in the cockpit when only his hands, eyes and brain are useful? Life-support systems—for handling air, water, food, waste, temperature, etc.—are bulky and expensive almost in direct proportion to the size of the crewman.

Even in present-day infantry, the little man has some advantages: he can find cover and concealment more easily, and he makes a smaller target, these being obvious assets, especially in reconnaisance. On the other hand, he hurts more when he does take a hit, and he cannot carry as much armor. On the first hand, again—and this is the main point here: personal strength is not very important in modern warfare. In the days of armor and battle-axe, a big man could demolish a crowd of little men; but today, two little guys with rifles can outshoot a big guy in most circumstances, even if he has a heavier peice.

We hope war between men will die out, but always lurking in the background is the bogey of the ET or BEM—the Extra Terrestrial invader, or the Bug-Eyed Monster. In any case, there are other considerations.

One is the question of vanity. Most of us dislike confronting bigger people. Perhaps this quirk will disappear with improved mental health, which we hope is in store, but I wouldn't count on it. Hence, unless we legislate individual altitude and standardize it, we can probably expect most citizens to buy the "big" option. But how high can we buy?

The tallest man who ever lived may have been Goliath of Gath, before David cut him down. He was perhaps eleven feet, which, interestingly, is approximately the maximum height some scientists estimate to be theoretically possible for a human type skeleton and circulatory system. To go much beyond that would perhaps require a whole new design, and this again might rub our vanity the wrong way. But there is more at stake than vanity: large size does have some absolute advantages.

We need big brains for big jobs. There is, to be sure, no established correlation between human brain size and intelligence; a man with a high-brow or big-dome can be stupid, and a size-six hat can cover a capable mind. It may be that we use only a fraction of our brain cells. Nevertheless, we have to process enormous quantities of data, and this requires a sizable "computer" with billions of storage and switching elements. There is probably no way in which an ant, for instance, could operate at the present human level, because its nervous system just isn't complex enough, and the time will surely come when our present brains aren't big enough either.

This time may be far in the future, to be sure, and there may be answers other than growing bigger brains. Perhaps we will connect the human brain to an electronic computer, by plug-in wires or laser beam, and use this "augmented" brain for heavy work. Then again, it has been suggested that we may "merge" several people *en rapport*, by telepathy or some such, to create a kind of communal brain or hive mind, in order to graduate to higher levels of mentality.

But the last idea is rather fanciful and perhaps distasteful, and living brains are much more compact than computers give promise of becoming, so the bigger brain is the likeliest solution, at least for the relatively near future. How big could our brains—and ourselves—be grown?

The largest animal bodies, and the largest brains, are those of whales, and if we want to go much beyond Goliath we may have to emulate the whale, grow fins and dive back into the ocean. (We may also learn to breathe seawater, which whales cannot do.) Or else, we might colonize small planets, moons, and asteroids, where the reduced gravity would allow a whale of a man to walk around. Earth is restricting, but aquamen or "loonies" might have more freedom. Alternatively, of course, we might become cyborgs; but that is another story.

Cyborgs, Saucer Men, and Extended Bodies

To most people of this era, the prosthesis—artificial replacement for part of the body—is a crutch: ugly, inadequate, and pitiful—a sorry, last-resort substitute for the real thing. And even though it is intellectually obvious that

71

prostheses may become, in many instances, *superior* to the natural limb or organ, they remain repugnant, and the notion of deliberately mechanizing man seems abhorrent, on the aesthetic level if no other. Nevertheless, such attitudes can change, and for at least some people, "progress" will consist of reducing to minimum our dependence on our "natural" bodies. We will be close to ultimate development in this respect when our organic brains are served by "bodies" which are collections of mechanical sensors and effectors—devices for perceiving and manipulating the environment—of variable number and location, not necessarily bound together in a single structural unit.

To show that such a trend exists, and that the goal is technically reasonable, is not difficult. The Russians have reported building artificial arms that respond to the brain's normal signals picked up from the stump of the natural arm; the patient simply attempts to move his arm, as though it were still there, and the prosthesis responds, through a system of electric motors![106] Efforts are also under way to provide artificial arms and hands with tactile sensation, so the patient can actually feel pressures, at least.

Although, to date, mechanical extensions of the body are inferior in sensitivity and facility of manipulation, some of them are greatly superior in raw strength and power. Great walking and handling devices have been designed, operated by a man through servomechanisms: the huge metal arms and legs of the machine imitate and magnify the arm and leg movements of the operator, making the machine a powerful extension of the man.

As for internal organs, everyone knows that there has been some degree of success with artificial hearts, which have sustained life for limited periods in lower animals, such as cattle, and in at least one human patient. Bone and blood vessel replacement by artifacts have become almost commonplace. Some experts believe that, before many decades, there will be artificial stomachs, livers, and kidneys, equal or superior to the originals.[106] Hearing aids are useful in several kinds of hearing impairment. At Western Michigan University, a research program has been reported aimed at nothing less than the development of an artificial eye, which could be connected to the brain of a blind person to provide, not a substitute for sight, but sight itself.

Now, this mention of artificial eyes immediately elicits the question: If we can provide the equivalent of natural sight by artificial means, why not something better than natural sight? A synthetic eye could be made sensitive not only to the "visible" spectrum, but also to a wide range of the ultraviolet and infrared, opening up possiblities which include night vision and qualitatively new aesthetic experiences—colors heretofore impossible and unimagined. (Perhaps we could even "see" radio waves!) The technical problems may well be formidable—in particular, the brain may need extensive training and/or revision to handle the new sensations—but this probably affects just the time scale of development.

A man, part of whose subsystems are mechanical or artificial, has been called a "cyborg." One version of the cyborg envisions all the major organs of the abdomen and thorax replaced by artificial components. At an advanced stage of development, such a cyborg might embody a closed cycle of nutrients and wastes, with no material entering or leaving the body. (Such a closed cycle already exists, in limited form outside the body, in a space capsule.) The gaseous, liquid and solid wastes of the body would be reconverted to oxygen and food; the energy supply might eventually derive from nuclear fusion, scarcely ever requiring refueling. Such a man (the tendency to call him a "creature" should be resisted) would not have to eat, drink, or even breathe, and he would be nearly impervious to changes in environment.

Carrying the notion even further, Dandridge Cole posited "saucer men," people with only their heads—or perhaps only their brains—remaining natural and organic, all other functions being taken over by superior artificial systems, including a "flying saucer" as the vehicle or main body matrix—the saucers providing better mobility—and mechanical senses and manipulators at the individual's service.[26]

One can go even beyond this to the concept of "extended bodies." The brain need not necessarily be mobile; in fact, it might be better protected and served if fixed at home base. The sensors and effectors—eyes, hands, etc—could be far away, and even widely scattered, with communication by appropriate signals (not necessarily radio). Such a person would be a superman indeed. To many his mode of living may be difficult to imagine and unpleasant to consider, but it should not be thought that such a being would be more limited than man or less free—quite the contrary.

In the first place, if our "extended man" wishes, he can retain, and even multiply, the animal pleasures. He can have a variety of remote-control bodies—either organic, or mechanical, or a combination—and he can control and experience these bodies in exactly the same subjective way we control and experience our bodies. The freedom and variety at his command (at *our* command, if we choose this path) will far surpass what ours are now, because his bodies will be greater in number, more varied in location, and far more versatile in capabilities. We cannot easily imagine what it would be like to enjoy such numerous and scattered limbs and organs, but we can be entirely certain of one thing: there will be some personalities, at least, who will enjoy and elect such a style of existence.

For those who find it hard to imagine a largely artificial or mechanized body, there are already some hints that one can, indeed, develop a feeling for it. Consider those pilots who "fly by the seats of their pants," or the operators of bulldozers: they develop great sensitivity to the stresses and states of their machines, which may come to seem as much alive as a horse or even an extension of their body. When the perceptions become direct—when a clash of gears, for instance, produces a physical feeling of heartburn, or a sore elbow—then the machine will be as much a part of the man as any piece of meat.

Since many people still feel a pervasive coldness and bleak utilitarianism in this type of "progress," perhaps I should emphasize further the emotional and aesthetic aspects of these potentialities. If man, or superman, chooses this "extended" type of existence, then he—we, remember—would multiply not only his physical and intellectual powers, but also his capacities and avenues for sensation, appreciation and empathy. For example, we could include animal bodies, suitably modified, in our stock; we could take vacations "in" (in remote control of) the bodies of animals: diving with the otter, frisking with the antelope, stalking with the tiger. (Again, there would be complex problems to overcome, such as integrating a human mind with animal bodies and reflexes; but these are details, as Will Rogers said when he recommended boiling the Atlantic Ocean to destroy German U-boats in World War I.) Endless sexually erotic possibilities are also possible: couples could frolic in diverse forms.

It is not asserted that the cyborg and his extensions are inevitable developments in the main line of human and superhuman progress, nor is it denied that both serious difficulties and grave disadvantages in such developments may exist (although none has been demonstrated, to my knowledge). It may be, for example, that prudence will dictate principal reliance on organic modes, so that small numbers of individuals could carry on in event of a major calamity to a civilization; we may not want to make ourselves completely reliant on sophisticated repair and maintenance services, which might be subject to breakdown. (We remember, ruefully, the dislocations produced by a few inches of snow in New York or a break in a high-tension power line.) Nevertheless, anything that is possible is also likely to become feasible—eventually. These avenues are certain to be explored—they *are* being explored—and it is equally definite that at least a few people sometime will vigorously proceed along this path. The results will be instructive at the very least, and perhaps salvific.

Eternal Life and Giantism

The notion of "extended bodies" can itself be extended to that of the multicorporeal giants, having not only sensors and effectors but even brains distributed over large volumes of space. Such an idea has an interesting relation to the possibility of *infinitely* extended life.

Apparently most scientists assume that infinite life is impossible for fundamental physical and mathematical reasons, which have been made explicit by Professor James S.

Hayes.[72] However, while eternal life is not clearly possible (we don't even know if the future of the *universe* is unlimited), it isn't clearly impossible either.

According to Professor Hayes, if there is any chance at all of accidental death in a given span, in the long run death is certain. He also notes that we would eventually have to cull our memories, since otherwise our brains could not grow fast enough to retain them.

Actually, our information-stuffed brains will eventually have to grow to provide more storage space, and the growth need be controlled; but if available space is infinite, only the annual percentage growth in brain tissue will have to decrease, not the tonnage.

Now, a reader of decent sensibilities will be stunned by the word "tonnage." Tons of brain tissue? Of course: doubtlessly, some irreducible minimum amount of matter, in mass and volume, is required to store a unit of information, and if we jettison no memories, we must become gigantic. Even storing "our" memories in a separate mechanical store or computer, plugged in at will, cannot avoid giantism for several reasons. In any case, we should not *want* to avoid giantism—it is our salvation with respect to the accidental death bogey.

There is a certain risk of catastrophe per year per cubic yard, and we can hardly expect to keep reducing this risk fast enough forever; hence any ordinary individual must expect a fatal accident sooner or later. But a *society,* if it spreads out fast enough, can have a non-zero probability of infinite life. (This will be obvious to mathematicians, and I omit the proof, simple though it is.) Can an individual do the same?

Certainly! To begin with, one may think of himself as located at a point in space, but he is not: each of us occupies an appreciable volume, and can sacrifice considerable material without disaster. For example, rays from radioactive elements constantly damage or kill cells of our bodies—thousands daily—but we replace them and carry on, and in fact do not even notice what is happening.

Of course, we cannot just grow huge, and keep this up indefinitely. Neither can we stomach the notion of submerging ourselves in a "hive" organism—the individual playing the role of a cell in a super-being; we do not want to be reduced to the status of bees or ants or anything similar. The answer is that man could develop a new type of body, the parts of which would not be physically united as they have been heretofore.

It is simply a matter of communication. The hemispheres of a brain, for example, in principle ought to be capable of integration by wires, or even radio, rather than nerves; and the same thing is true of smaller components. We should envisage a race of titans, each multicorporeal, his body divided into myriad components attenuated over a large and increasing volume of space, integrated by something like radio waves. If a star goes nova, only a few planets may be lost—a trifle, a toenail. (We are assuming now that space, as well as time, has no end.)

As always, there will be a price to pay. In particular, the giants will live slowly, of necessity, in Einstein's world: if you are spread over a trillion cubic light-years, and your nervous system signals from one part of you to another at the speed of light, it will take you a long while to think and act. It is interesting to speculate, however, that *this* may explain the mysterious absence of emmissaries from higher civilizations: any culture much beyond the present human stage enters the macrocosmic phase and is more or less out of touch.

In addition to size and slowness, the giants might have another bizarre quality—intermingling of bodies. If the purpose of giantism is immortality, avoiding catastrophe by having one's parts scattered over immense volumes, any small volume (say a planet) would not have to be reserved for a single individual. Thus a galaxy, say, might support billions of individuals, each one scattered onto billions of planets and each planet supporting parts of billions of different people.

People? Beings, rather; they could hardly be much like ourselves, whose psychology and culture are strongly dependent on the physical character of our bodies. Their lives would not necessarily be entirely mental, but they would indeed be strange. They would not stand, sit, walk, talk, or even have a definite location in any easily understood sense. A man could not even perceive the existence of such a being, let alone understand its modes of living.

An obvious nasty conjecture is that the giants are already in our region of space, and we, all unwitting, are their "cells." That the organism's organization, from our point of view, is inefficient and often unpleasant may interest them not at all. An even nastier conjecture is that we are not yet cells, but will shortly be taken over for that purpose, when we reach an appropriate state of development, by already-existing giants evolved from a different form of life. But we can hope that they would not work in such a sloppy manner, or use fully self-conscious cells.

Finally, I am not postulating nor predicting the existence of giants. I think any such development unlikely in the extreme; instead, it seems nearly certain that new discoveries and ways of thinking will appear in the coming centuries which will outmode all such questions. I cannot conceive that we will ever seriously worry about eternal life as contrasted with life "merely" extended for thousands or tens of thousands of years. It is doubtful that the present "limiting" laws of physics—those of relatively and quantum mechanics—will retain their supposed fundamental character forever. The purpose of the little exercise above, other than having some fun, is just to put in their places those who take smug and narrow views concerning what can and cannot happen in the millenial future.

Home Where the Tachyons Roam

Various people have hazarded conjectures as to the "ultimate" development of man or superman. Arthur Clarke has made at least two suggestions: (1) human personalities will be copied and stored electronically, perhaps in several locations, conferring essential immortality and near-invulnerability; (2) the race will graduate to a kind of hive-mind, with individual "people" corresponding to the cells of the super-organism. Neither of these impresses me favorably, the first cavalierly assuming that identity is preserved when this is far from clear, and the second being somewhat distasteful as well as unnecessary.

Professor Gerald Feinberg has speculated that the final

goal of evolution may be universal consciousness—the entire physical universe integrated into a single, fully self-conscious entity, which would then spend its time in varieties of introspection.[53] (Although Dr. Feinberg did not put it this way, one might say our goal is to create, and to become, God.) However, this seems unsatisfactory to me for a variety of reasons. For one thing, it is not yet known whether the universe is finite or infinite; if infinite, it is difficult to see how it could be integrated. More important, this notion seems to make unwarranted assumptions about the nature of consciousness, which in fact is not yet understood. Consciousness is known *not* to reside in our *total* brains (since much can be excised with no noticeable effect), and I doubt that it is possible, even in principle, for *all* of the universe to share consciousness.

In any case, we can hardly talk about *ultimate* development, which is a matter of function, not form, and which is probably many stages beyond our present ability to conceive. Still, it is interesting to project our imaginations as far as we can. The previous section discussed the notion of the multicorporeal giants. Now let us modify and extend this idea to take account of recent developments in physics.

In the last several years, as noted elsewhere, Feinberg, Bilaniuk and others have postulated the existence of particles called *tachyons*, traveling faster than light, and have shown that these are not necessarily inconsistent with Einstein's theory of relativity.[52] Although such particles have not yet been experimentally confirmed, and although they possess some very strange properties, many of which are still unclear, it is assumed that they can interact with ordinary matter and with each other, and can carry signals with any speed *greater* than that of light. (Particles, such as photons and neutrinos, which can exist only at the speed of light are called *luxons*, while ordinary particles which cannot reach or exceed light speed are termed *tardyons*.) If tachyons exist, and possess the properties inferred, what would this mean for our giants?

For a start, it means that the Giants need not be as slow as otherwise persumed; even though their "body" parts are separated by many light-years, "internal" communication could be rapid. (External communication could also, of course.) It is not clear, at least to me, just how fast communication might be. For two observers—or two parts of a giant—not in relative motion, signals can even be instantaneous, the *tachyons* being allowed infinite speed. (A "transcendent," or infinitely fast tachyon, carries no energy, but it does carry momentum, and presumably could transmit a signal; on interaction with a tardyon, the latter would change its direction, although not its speed.) But when the observers—or the parts of a giant—are in relative motion, the problem becomes much stickier, with apparent time anomalies to be interpreted. At any rate, a giant employing tachyons could live much faster than one depending on light-speed signals.

We can indulge in speculations even more tenuous. If the tachyons can interact with the other types of particles and with each other, why should they play only a subordinate or auxiliary role in the functioning of the giants? Why should not a giant, by a gradual process of change and development, *become* a pattern of tachyons? Function is more important than form; perhaps a suitable aggregate of tachyons, with patterns and feedbacks analogous to those in our minds, could be a living entity—ourselves, at a higher stage of development. This would not necessarily solve life's most important problems, but it ought to provide an awesomely powerful means to our ends. The individual would not *become* the universe, as in Feinberg's suggestion, but he could *permeate* the universe; he could exist, perceive and act everywhere simultaneously.

Needless to say, such a notion raises tantalizing questions that we are not prepared to answer. For example, if tachyon-man can think *instantaneously*, then he can complete his life's sequence of thoughts in an instant, and fulfill his destiny, can he not? This is another possible answer to the question, "Where is everybody?" Perhaps advanced races quickly proceed to the level of tachyon-men, and are "finished"—whatever that means.

These reflections also suggest another possibility, without the need for tachyons. Particles of light, electromagnetic radiation—photons—also interact with each other. Could there be such a thing as photon-man—an aggregate

of patterned, interacting photons, collectively constituting a person? Or at least, might the physical parts of a being depend much less heavily on tardyons, and much more on luxons? This also would give rise to startlingly different capacities. All of these possibilities will be actively investigated—perhaps sooner than we think.
think.

Superghost

In many fanciful stories, evolution's goal has been depicted as the development of "pure mind," with the implication that eventually we will become more or less disembodied spirits, freed from the bondage of matter. Sometimes this notion of "pure mind" pictures entities of "pure energy," whatever that means—perhaps beings that are still material, but less grossly material, possibly containing no particles less nimble than electrons. Sometimes, again, there is postulated a being who is built entirely of "force fields," which would be another less grossly physical sort of construct. (Actually, physicists do not usually regard force fields as separable from particles.) But there is also sometimes the bald allusion to superghost, the quite immaterial being of pure mind or pure spirit, which is said to represent our ultimate destiny.

Now, we cannot summarily reject such suggestions merely because they are vague and carry overtones of magic: any speculations about the far future must have these qualities. Neither are we entitled to sneer just because those who suggest the notions become easily confused—which is another way of saying the same thing; it is indeed possible for someone to have a useful idea, or the germ of an idea, without being able to express it clearly or make it hold up in argument.

Neither should we shoot some of the ammunition at hand, for example the false arguments adduced by some of these speculators. Some of the spiritualists are motivated by abhorrence of determinism, whereas in fact this is entirely a separate issue; the arguments for determinism apply with the same force, no more and no less, to a spiritualist world as to a materialist world. Like most people,

81

the spiritualists mix in some bad argument and drag in some irrelevant bogies, but we should be interested in dealing with their best arguments, not their worst.

Further, we should not be swayed by nasty words such as "dualism." Everyone realizes the world must be monistic in the sense that its parts and aspects must be capable of interaction—otherwise we could never have any awareness of the other part. At the same time, there may be parts or aspects of the world so foreign to our everyday thought and experience as to justify separate treatment. There are recent examples: *e.g.*, the phenomena of electromagnetic radiation, outside of the visible spectrum, represent an extremely important aspect of the universe, yet one entirely unsuspected until modern times; in classic Greece, radio waves and X-rays might as well have existed in a different universe.

The evidence for psychic phenomena, in the sense of extra-sensory perception, seems extremely weak. Nevertheless, some investigators are convinced of their reality, and of their dramatic divergence from the ordinary phenomena of physics; for example, Professor Joseph Rhine believes that certain effects are unaffected by distance or time.[143] Likewise, the seance-spiritualists have not convincingly demonstrated their "ectoplasm," yet it is at least conceivable that some quasi-material "soul" somehow inhabits and directs the body.

We do know that very sensitive linkages exist in nature, pivot-points where extremely subtle influences can exert profound effects: for example, some years back a few pounds of copper threads were put in orbit around the earth for certain tests, and some scientists thought there was danger of the earth's entire climate being disturbed! Professor J. C. Eccles, a prominent neurophysiologist, has written that the brain is indeed the sort of machine a ghost could operate; *i.e.*, the mind might be a very insubstantial kind of director, needing only to nudge the brain very slightly at crucial spots to make it carry on their mutual business in the desired way. While this kind of dualism seems most far-fetched to me, so far neither necessary nor fruitful, one cannot make a final judgment. Neutrinos certainly have almost a ghostly quality, and so do tachyons, if they exist; it may conceivably turn out, after all, that the spiritualists have erred chiefly in language and attitude.

Without filling in the details or soft spots, maybe we can picture something like this. The mind is different from the brain—material, but extremely subtle, even harder to detect by ordinary methods than the neutrino. This mind, essentially, is the person. It is symbiotic with the brain, in a sense; or perhaps we should say that only the mind is "alive," the brain being merely an appendage of the mind, as the leg is an appendage of the person. Both—brain and mind—are essential, and both develop together, the reproductive cells carrying both the seed of a brain and the seed of a mind. With present techniques, the mind cannot exist without the brain, but future developments may make it possible for the mind to divorce itself from its gross partner and be self-supporting. Thus we may imagine our transfigured selves as beings of "pure mind," gliding swift and ethereal through the reaches of the cosmos.

Hogwash, in all probability. I emphasize again that the evidence for any such notions is *extremely* slim, with much more likely explanations at hand for all known phenomena. And yet, the realities of the distant future will be *at least* as strange as this.

5

Transsex and Supersex

The sexual superwoman may be riddled with cleverly designed orifices of various kinds, something like a wriggly Swiss cheese, but shapelier and more fragrant; and her supermate may sprout assorted protuberances, so that they intertwine and roll all over each other in a million permutations of The Act, tireless as hydraulic pumps. (We may *have* hydraulic pumps, if we are cyborgs.) A perpetual grapple, no holes barred, could produce a continuous state of multiple orgasm. (Of this, more later.)

A little too vulgar? All right: those who choose spiritual expression of supersex may never touch each other at all, except with tender tendrils of the mind. Each could represent the distilled essence of feminine or masculine personality, and quiver with exquisite joy at an exchange of precisely the right word or glance, and after every such thrilling encounter retire for decades to analyze and relish it in prose, poetry, song, drama and fingerpaints before readying for the next.

Is this too far out also? No—the sober probability is that the above examples are too conservative: supersex could, and likely will, be much stranger. Before exploring the more zestful options, however, let us look briefly at the null possibility.

Is sex here to stay? Some moderately good arguments can be advanced against it. Certainly the need for coitus in reproduction is already unnecessary, since we know about artificial insemination. Soon a race exclusively of women will be viable, through techniques of artificial parthenogenesis, mothers chemically stimulated to bear daughters, no male ever violating their vaginas. Eventually the "cloning" methods could be perfected, with children grown *in vitro* or in "test tubes," starting merely with a scrap of tissue, even skin, from any person. All these facts and probabilities are well documented in the current biological literature.[145] Furthermore, there is the possibility that immortals will not be interested in offspring, that they will neither need nor want them.

As for the psychological need for sex, one might claim that this is just an accident of body chemistry, which responsible engineering can eliminate. After all, innumerable species get by without sex, or with only a pale shadow of it. (Think of the poor fish, whose big moment comes when he swims over the eggs, already laid, and deposits his milt. This can't be much fun, and even less so for the female.) Closer to home, we remember that children are zestful without much awareness of sex or much presence of sex hormones. (Yes, my wife is an elementary teacher, and I realize that some fourth graders masturbate.) Some young adults, such as nuns, seem to miss sexual activity very little even though their glands are normal. And many elderly people are jolly enough, with apparently never a salacious thought. None of these examples is perfect, but they are all suggestive.

Finally, we may encounter the lofty assertion that we are bound to outgrow sex, which is after all rather nasty and suited only to a bestial nature. The ultra-fastidious may tell us that the future holds no place for lusty, gusty, bawdy, raunchy, leering, snorting, panting people, and instead our desexed superman will find much higher and purer delights in adventures of the intellect, beside which the squalid slaverings of sex will be disagreeable at best.

And yet, all this is unconvincing for many reasons, one of which constructs an analogy between the appetite for sex and the appetite for food. Imagine a troglodyte philosopher, slobbering in his dim cave over a greasy bone, or thoughtfully picking the lice out of his beard, cracking and eating them without enthusiasm. Trying to predict the eating habits of men of the future, he might reason that those powerful and enlightened ones would have little interest in food, which would no longer be in short supply and which could scarcely compete, either in interest or importance, with the pressing business of building and exploring. Eating, then, might be expected to become a very minor incidental of life, like bathing.

Ah yes, but you and I know, with our fifty thousand years of hindsight, that eating is not so trivial, nor bathing either. For one thing, the immense variety and delicious taste of modern foods were unforseen in troglodytic times, and the temptation to gluttony unappreciated. Primitive peoples today—such as the aborigines of the Kalahari Desert—are almost uniformly skinny, even when there is no scarcity, simply because the food is bad. A piece of tough or halfrotten meat, raw or badly cooked, a few staple roots boiled or pounded to a watery paste—these are eaten only by the hungry. A strawberry shortcake, on the other hand, is eaten because it is there. (Despite the proverb, hunger is not always the best sauce.) And of course the greatest invention of modern times is that which allows us to eat *and* work—the businessman's lunch.

This, then, may be the future of sex—a kind of naked lunch. Other things may be more important, and people may not often *concentrate* on sex, nor devote much time to it *exclusively*, yet it could remain a very pleasant byplay. (We remember that "pleasant" in the lexicon of superman translates in the languages of homo sap as "ecstatic," "wow," or "out of sight.") This byplay will develop undertones and overtones, ramifications and extensions, intensifications and innovations such as we can scarcely guess, and in the far reaches of time and space we are likely to try just about everything. Straining our myopic eyes, let us squint a little into some possible futures, beginning with what is least remote in time and tradition.

When I was a freshman at the University of Michigan in 1937, I went to a Communist meeting, enticed by rumors of "free love". As it turned out, there was no love to be had, or even simple sex, and the girls were dogs anyway. I learned a lesson then: never trust a Communist.

The Communists have more or less faded from the American scene, but the to-do about "free love" is livelier than ever, although we should have learned some lessons by now. Is our system wrong in its regulation of love and marriage? Is the system right, but in need of stricter enforcement? Or is it simply the nature of the beast continually to rebel against just and necessary restraints?

The trend seems clearly toward a more pluralistic and permissive society, toward experimentation and individual freedom. Perhaps a good way to provide an orderly transition would be to *make the marriage contract explicit.*

Certainly marriage is not a contract in the technical legal sense, but it has important contractual elements; and the hilarious horror is that most people marry in ignorance of many of their legal rights and obligations. To make sure they know something of what they are getting into, each state might codify all the laws pertaining to marriage and divorce, in the form of a contract which the applicants for a marriage license must read and sign.

The immediate benefit would be another nudge toward prudence and preparation in marrying. A slightly more delayed benefit would be the impetus toward legal review and improvement of the marriage code, with the more glaring inconsistencies and inequities removed. And somewhere along the line, some state would accept the implicit invitation to write *options* into the contract, however few and conservative at first. Eventually, subject to such limitations as experience may prove wise, there would probably develop a wide range of choices, amounting to individually negotiated contracts representing a broad range of marriage styles.

One can imagine this custom, contracting sex relations, being carried to extremes—even to the extent, say, of signing a paper before knocking off a casual piece in the back seat of a Chevicopter. Yet one might make a case even for this—because otherwise, for example, one party might claim the other took advantage of her (him), or owed her (him) money. In the beginning, however, contracts will doubtless be limited to more or less formal and extended liaisons.

Varieties of Marriage

Every style of marriage and family life that has even been successful or shown promise is likely to be tried in the future; one of the first was polygymy—one husband, more than one wife. It may have dominated much of human existence: the strongest men took the women, and subdued them, and used them, and reproduced their kind. And what adolescent does not dream of romping barefoot over acres and acres of bare boobies and behinds? Of course, there has always been a price for this ego satisfaction and variety, in wear and tear both nervous and physical. Margaret Mead reports the irritable complaint of the Iatmul husband, with each wife trying to tempt him to her hut: "Do you wives think that I am made of ironwood, that I am able to copulate with you as much as you want?"[117]

It is claimed polygyny worked farily well among the Mormons and the ancient Hebrews. First wives were glad to have the household help and companionship of junior wives, and the junior wives often preferred this status with a first-rate man over monogamy with a second-rate husband. In some cases, there may also have been subtle sexual advantages for the woman: a wife with little libido had fewer demands upon her, while a lusty but nervous woman could relax and enjoy it in the knowledge that she did not bear sole responsibility for pleasing her man.

But polygyny carries an almost overpowering suggestion of *property* rights in women, and seems likely to survive only in rare cases. One such circumstance might involve a frozen and revived wife, rejoining a husband who had meanwhile remarried. Other cases might involve an extremely charismatic man, able and willing to take on several wives; or sisters who preferred marrying the same man rather than separate.

Of course simple arithmetic assures that polygyny cannot work on a long term basis, unless the extra men find some other outlet. But the arithmetic is subject to change. The birth ratio of males to females may shift in the next century—but in which direction is hard to say. According to Dr. Augustus B. Kinzel, president of the Salk Institute for Biological Studies, by 1980 (so soon!) we shall be able to choose the sex of children in advance (as well as slow down aging). Some people expect this will result in a heavy shift toward a male population, at least for a generation. In that case, it might be necessary for a while to resort to polyandry—one wife, more than one husband. This has rarely been tried in history, but it has not been unknown. M. D. Singh writes about the Sudras of India in 1907:

> When a Jat is well-to-do he generally procures a wife for each of his sons, but if he is not rich enough to bear the expenses of many marriages, he gets a wife for his eldest son only, and she is expected to, and as a rule does, accept her brothers-in-law as co-husbands ... the wife not infrequently bestows her favors on all of them equally, by turn, one evening being reserved for each . . .[19]

In Tibet and Nepal, according to Levi-Strauss, ". . . polyandry seems to be explained by occupational factors . . . for men living a semi-nomadic existence as guides and bearers, polyandry provides a good chance that there will be, at all times, at least one husband at hand to take care of the homestead."[101] The future may also include a nomad, viz., the astronaut: a woman might be the wife of several sailors, each of whom spends most of his time between planets, or between stars. This might result in polyandry for the stay-at-home wives, and polygyny for the astronaut with a wife in every port, if we colonize other planets and star systems, as we almost surely shall. (There might also, of course, be female astronauts, with everything reversed; and in some cases there could be space-faring couples or families.) This interlocking polygamy would represent a strange life indeed, from where we sit; yet for adventuresome immortals it might be one way to find both security and diversity, each encounter carrying both the warmth of familiarity and the spice of change, not to mention all the wonderful opportunity for gossip.

At this point one might ask why we are so concerned with marriage—how do we know there will *be* such a thing as marriage among fully liberated, financially independent people? Why not casual relationships? The answer, of course, is that most of us need the security and comfort of an intimate, loyal companion; yet we are foolish and irresponsible enough to need the bracing of a formal contract. This will doubtless change when superman becomes sufficiently super, but this may take a while.

It is tempting to view group marriage as the wave of the future, with its apparent advantages of sexual variety and clan strength—a milieu of warmth and nurture for the young, of stimulation and support for the adult, where no one ever lacks the services of a husband or wife, a mommy or daddy. Science fiction writers have been fond of this theme, but the rather scanty evidence seems to point to failure; the complexity seems to increase nervous stress, rather than relieve it. Perhaps superman could handle it, but he isn't likely to need it, even for variety in a very long life.

As remarked in another chapter, increasingly sophisticated cosmetic changes are likely to become possible, and gradually less costly relative to income. A contemporary wife or husband can take advantage of dyes and wigs, false teeth and colored contact lenses, even face lifts and silicone implants, to counteract flagging interest; but the choices of the future are expected to be far wider, including quick and easy changes in skin, hair, and eyes, more expensive and less facile changes in physiognomy and body contours. Furthermore, changes in body chemistry and glandular balance could modify the personality in ways interesting to the individual as well as the partner; they would not have to pretend to be different, but *would* be different.

There are dangers for you and me in admitting interest in such possibilities. First, our wives or girl friends, or vice versa, may accuse us of being dissatisfied with what we have; second, it may seem an admission that we lack the imagination and sensitivity to appreciate existing opportunities. The correct answer is simple: what we have is good, even marvelous, but what we can have will be better still. Remember the strawberry shortcake.

Suppose your wife was a statuesque brunet, voluptuous and languorous, lusty but primarily receptive. After a short business trip, you return to find she has invested in a major styling change. She is slimmer, shorter, quicker-moving; she has no pubic bush but is covered with downy-fine blond hair; her breasts are smaller and firmer, her nipples harder; her breath and bodily secretions have subtly altered, so that she smells different; her tongue is slightly roughened, although not so much as a cat's.

The change in her is exciting for both of you. In caressing and being caressed, the sensations are quite different, whoever is stroking what part of whom with what. The balance of aggression is altered, the old patterns discarded. There may even be a hint of titillation through guilt, the Puritan in your subconscious (if any remain) feeling pleasantly wicked and disloyal in enjoying this new woman. Enjoy, enjoy!

Blood and Water

Whether or not formalized by contract and law, and whether it settles mostly into the small conjugal unit of contemporary America or the extended unit (clan) of other times and places, the *family* can be expected to persist. We millenials must remember that institutions are less permanent than people, and less comfort in the long run. If any external stability is to be found in the world, it will probably have to be in the ties of kinship and friendship, remembered and ever renewed.

The family will both help produce and help mitigate that relative anarchy which may result when the all-purpose machine makes the individual economically independent. (The family is the antithesis and enemy of the totalitarian state; Nazi Germany and Marxist Russia and China, as well as ancient Sparta, all started out by degrading the family.) With values concentrated in the individual and the family, no despotism or oligarchy can easily persuade people to die for it, and all top-heavy structures of government, if not of business, are likely to collapse. The family should put a lower bound on fragmentation, and perhaps provide the bridge for whatever degree of larger collaboration may from time to time be deemed good.

But the family, extended or restricted, will not necessarily be defined by the same blood ties as now. To begin with, the sentimental value of shared genes is somewhat dubious and unreliable. Although children have, on the average, half their hereditary traits through each parent, this varies according to the laws of chance; furthermore some of the traits may be only *carried* (in latent form, from previous generations) by the parent, and therefore not held in common—this means that sometimes a parent and child may have the "same blood" only to the extent, say, that cousins commonly do.

By the shared-gene criterion—which seems to be the only biologically meaningful one—the highest degree of kinship is that of identical twins, who have exactly the same heredity, all genes in common. The next highest degree is that between parent and child, or between siblings who are not identical twins, in each case half the genes, on the average, being held in common. But love is not rationed out on the basis of gene count: we usually love our wives better than our cousins, and for that matter, we sometimes love our dogs better than our grandchildren. In any case, the children will not necessarily be reared by the biological parents.

"Fosterage"—children raised by someone who could offer them more, or needed them more, than the parents has not been uncommon in the past—this custom has been recorded, for example, in parts of Africa, in Polynesia, and in European feudal society.[153] Apart from orphanages, it is a rarity with us, but customs change. In 1967, a college professor in East Lansing, Michigan, advertised in all seriousness to trade his teen-aged son for another teen-ager, hoping a change in environment would benefit everyone.[7]

Certain technical developments will surely favor this

type of fosterage in the future, as artificial insemination already has done to some extent. We are likely, for example, to see double artificial insemination—both sperm and egg taken from banks, joined, and implanted in a host-mother.

Beyond this, we foresee the means for mixing genetic material from any two people, or more than two, or "cloning" from a single cell, so that a child could have two women as parents, or two men, or one woman, or one man, or several people, or even none at all! The last case would correspond to building a baby from scratch—that is, constructing the germ cell, then growing the baby. (Concerning the multi-parent possibility, it has already been reported that a mouse has been grown with four parents—genetic material mixed together, in the fertilized egg, from four different mice.) If most parents choose to optimize their children, by creating or borrowing the desired genes and not just by selecting the best from their own pool, then the "blood" relationship will be small or nil, and the reality, whatever it is called, will be foster parentage.

The pressing need for foster parentage will diminish, we hope. The historic scandal and sorrow of children produced and raised by unskilled labor may eventually be corrected by law or custom imposing standards of competence. But for some decades or centuries varieties of temperament may allocate some people the task of child-rearing, and others the training of youthful adults, and so on. Family ties might be created in these connections, ties cemented by love and tradition, with or without the "blood" bond. Perhaps inclination and happenstance will combine to give some of us the responsibility of rearing our own great-great-great grandchildren. What shivery stories we could tell them of the benighted twentieth century! And what feelings of security, stability and responsibility the presence of remote ancestors might tend to produce in the children!

On the other hand, there is the opposite possibility: future families averaging a higher degree of kinship. There is no guarantee the incest taboo will be fully retained, even though it has generally prevailed. The Ptolemies of

Egypt married brothers to sisters for centuries without apparent ill effect. And for a partial parallel we can turn again to Levi-Strauss:

> . . . the Siberian Chukchee were not in the least abhorrent to the marriage of a mature girl of let us say about twenty, with a baby-husband two or three years old. Then the young woman, herself a mother by an authorized lover, would nurse together her own child and her little husband. Like the North American Mohave, who had the opposite custom of a man marrying a baby girl and caring for her until she became old enough to fulfill her conjugal duties, such marriages were thought of as very strong ones, since the natural feelings between husband and wife would be reinforced by the recollection of the parental care bestowed by one of the spouses on the other. These are by no means exceptional cases . . .[101]

In connection with the possibility of sanctioned incest, we note that, among immortals, no adult would be any older than any other in physical appearance, unless he chose to be. With everyone equally spry and modern, this might blur the distinction between the generations.

While mother-humping and daddy-diddling are nowadays regarded as very nasty, we should remember how scornfully Caesar spoke of the English barbarian: "He thinks the customs of his tribe and island are the laws of nature."

A Freeze on Fidelity

The transitions to new freedoms and strange options will entail special problems for those jumping a long time-gap (those frozen in the near future and thawed after many decades or centuries). In particular, when married people are planning cryonic suspension, should they make marital commitments for the future?

At a television broadcast a couple of years ago, a woman in the audience asked me whether she and her husband would be thawed together; when I answered that this could probably be arranged, she said, "In that case, count me out." At a club meeting on another occasion, a

94

vivacious middle-aged woman said, "I don't want him (her husband) when I'm thawed; I want five hundred years of free love." On the other hand, many people seem emphatically to believe that, without assurance of the family remaining together, extended life would be meaningless; and a number of husbands and wives have promised each other not to remarry if one should die and be frozen unexpectedly early.

If the parties are fond of life and of each other, such pledges may seem reasonable: the family that agrees together will freeze together. But if one of the partners should die young, ought the survivor be expected to accept many years of loneliness? Ought the children to be brought up with only one parent? And will the dying partner have confidence that such a difficult pledge will be kept?

In Germany, after the Thirty Years War, the shortage of men was such that for a generation polygamy was common. Undoubtedly the senior wives would often have preferred sole status, but they recognized the force of unusual circumstances and accepted a realistic portion. Perhaps we can find a parallel here. The dying partner wants assurance of not being abandoned, and does not want the family funds dissipated among strangers; at the same time, perhaps the chains on a young widow or widower should not be too heavy. Some people might settle on an agreement for loyalty, but not necessarily *exclusive* loyalty.

The Trouble with Men and Women

Looking a little further ahead, some of us may question the very premise of two sexes. That well-known Gallic sentiment—*vive la difference!*—sounds cozy enough, but there is an eloquent if not persuasive school holding, with Philip Wylie, that most of the evil in the world stems from the way men treat women and the resulting psychic damage to both. During most of mankind's existence, most women have been subjugated and mistreated, and of course abuse always tends to warp both the victim and the perpetrator. Even in modern America, girls are often discouraged from displaying initiative and daring, while little boys

95

yearning for affection may be treated roughly by fathers fearful they will not be "he-men".

In the forthright and engaging science-fiction tradition, Theodore Sturgeon accepts the thesis and carries the argument to one of its ultimate conclusions: in his utopia, he proposes to eliminate sexual differences altogether.[164] It might seem impossible to write a whole novel (*Venus Plux X*) about a race of hermaphrodites without provoking yawns or leers, but he carries it off.

We learn that the "Ledom," who apparently have replaced homo sapiens as the dominant species of our planet . . . clearly possessed both sexes, in active form. First of all, the intromittent organ was rooted far back in what might be called, in homo sap., the vaginal fossa. The base of the organ had, on each side of it, an *os uteri*, opening to the two cervixes, for the Ledom had two uteri and always gave birth to fraternal twins. On erection the phallos descended and emerged; when flaccid it was completely enclosed, and it, in turn contained the urethra. Coupling was mutual—indeed, it would be virtually impossible any other way.

The *raison d'etre* is not just a case of "double your pleasure, double your fun," although there may be an element of this. A Ledom and a human converse:

"The greatest occasion of sexual expression is a mutual orgasm, wouldn't you say?" "Yes," said Charlie as clinically as he could. "And procreation is a high expression of love?" "Oh yes." "Then if a Ledom and his mate mutually conceive, and each bears twins, does not that appear to be a fairly transcendental experience?" "F-fairly," said Charlie in a faint voice, overwhelmed.

Before accepting such a radical solution as hermaphroditism, however, even if it were feasible, we should look at the premise—the notion that men and women are inherently unequal, *and must remain so*.

Are Women Equal?

Schopenhauer—or perhaps it was Nietzsche—one of those fellows said that the difference between men and women is so profound, they should be considered separate species. And Nietzsche—or maybe Schopenhauer—said, "When you go to woman, forget not thy whip." These amiable attitudes fit in quite well with the idea mentioned above, attributed to Wylie and others, that the abuse of women by men underlies much of the evil in the world. But there seems to be emerging a normative pattern keyed to individual needs and choices, with a de-emphasis on assigned roles. In other words, the future may have large percentages of dainty men and aggressive women, but that isn't as bad as it sounds.

Whether there is such a thing as a "masculine" or "feminine" personality, and the relative importance of nature and nurture are still in dispute. For example, sex hormones affect the brain, and testosterone (male sex hormone) given to infant apes and monkeys apparently affects their "instinctive" behavior, which normally shows greater aggressiveness (both sexual and general) for the male, and more interest in infants and in grooming for the female.[65]

But this is only suggestive as regards humans, and there is also opposite evidence. Some studies indicate cultural or social factors are much more important than heredity in the development of personality differences between boys and girls, and in the roles they accept. The most striking examples concern cases of congenital adrenal hyperplasia. (Hormone disturbance before birth may result in a child—who would normally be a girl—having an enlarged clitoris, resembling a penis, and fused labial folds, resembling a scrotum.) Apparently the child will grow, with a reasonable degree of mental health, conforming to whatever sex is assigned at birth, even though there may be ambiguous or even contrary genital appearance.[124] Thus, at least one team of workers has hypothesized that gender role is *entirely* the result of learning, and is independent of chromosomal, gonadal, or hormonal sex; it depends only on whether the blanket and booties are blue or pink![125]

There are unequivocal differences between the sexes in average size, strength, quickness, disease resistance, sensitivity to heat, cold, and pain; but the importance of these differences seems greatly exaggerated in modern conditions. Certainly the races of man differ more in these respects than do men and women of the same race; and even in a given race, many individuals differ from the average of their own sex more than the sexes differ from each other. We are fond of saying no one should be penalized politically because of his background; likewise, people should not be pigeonholed on the basis of sex. A delicate man should not be forced into a rough occupation, nor a sturdy woman denied its opportunity. (The ever-forward-looking Russian Empire has beaten us again in clear enunciation of the principle, and permits many of its women to be streetsweepers and hod-carriers.) But all this will probably become irrelevant when we are supermen and bodily parameters are matters of design and choice; on the average, then, women may be as big and strong as men.

As to relative sexual desire and performance, this is still a matter of some disagreement. Dunlop says that young female virgins, in contrast to young men, are not easily aroused, and that in many women the desire is very slight until developed by repeated stimulations and experiences, and may thereafter be powerful and easily aroused. Indeed, many woman still claim they are not much stimulated by talk or pictures, or anything short of the act itself, which they enter at first in a spirit of affection and accommodation only. The reason, some say, is that the woman's main organ of sexual sensation, the clitoris, is much less developed than the male penis; also, there is some evidence that male hormones may be linked to sexual desire in both men and women.[124]

On the other hand, many observers agree with Dr. George R. Bach:

> Freed from the crippling effect of anxiety (about pregnancy), woman is not just man's sexual equal; it turns out she is his sexual superior. Her physical capacity is greater, her responses deeper, her emotions richer. Man's claim of being the stronger sex turns out to be one of history's great frauds.[153]

Whatever may be true of the average woman, it seems clear that small anatomical and physiological changes can produce strikingly modified behavior, as indicated in a report by J. Money concerning women with enlarged clitorises and unusual hormone balance:

> Erotic arousal (results) from the stimulation of visual and narrative perceptual material (and is) accompanied by erection of the clitoris . . . and masturbation or the willingness for sexual intercourse with even a transitory partner. (However,) the imagery of the erotic thoughts and desires is all suitably feminine . . . ; the unfeminine aspect of the experience applies only to the threshold and the frequency of arousal, and to the amount of sexual *initiative* that it might engender.[124]

Since in the future we expect complete understanding and control of body chemistry, women will be as randy as they choose to be, besides being the equal of men in size and strength (if they wish). Eventually, also, men will be given the means to keep up with the women—but what can men do right now, and in the near future, to match the liberated women?

It is well known that the average American has only one testicle. However, a promising new development at the University of Michigan, not yet published, is a technique akin to hypnosis that can allow a man to achieve "clitoral orgasm"—that is, to experience intense, multiple, and long-lasting spasms heretofore believed restricted to women. Thus we see again that, in some ways, supermen may be more feminine than men, just as superwomen are likely to be, in many ways, more masculine than human females.

Attempts to make women "equal" have seemed hopeless (as well as indecent) to some in view of apparently changeless biological function—carrying children in the womb, child-bearing, and suckling. These represent physical handicaps which have given women nearly slave status in most cultures; but they also account for her elevation to a position of acknowledged nobility and special claims. A father is just a man, but a mother is a martyred saint. This situation, however, seems near an end.

Actually, it is a little hard to see why suckling or carrying a child should produce a special bond, any more than in other forms of parasitism. Does one feel special tenderness toward his tapeworm? It is true that some pediatricians have claimed advantages for breast feeding, but I imagine few mothers of bottle babies will admit to a lesser intensity of motherly feeling. Likewise, even though fathers desert their families somewhat more frequently than mothers, I doubt very much that the average father is any weaker in ability to love than the mother. (The desertion rate is affected by many other factors, including greater job mobility for men.)

Certainly breast feeding is on the way out, despite occasional flurries of fashion. It must go because in too many ways it degrades the woman. It reduces her to a biological machine, an elemental function rather than a fully human person. It restricts her, physically and psychologically; it sets narrow limits on things she can do and times she can do them. It interferes with her career. It may alter her sex life. In short, it is an intolerable imposition, which was once a virtue only through necessity. It is attractive now, one suspects, mainly to those women who want to be career mothers, who seek status in the easy way available even to the laziest and least capable, or else to those who are confused and misled. (Of course, the lazy and incapable have to live too, and we must also take account of exceptional temperaments. No doubt for a while there will be a place for the career mother, if she can latch onto a career father.)

Well within the next century, the term "bottle baby" could apply not just to nursing, but to gestation. Ectogenesis, or extra-uterine gestation or "test-tube babies," will become feasible according to expert prediction, and as soon as the practice is economical, it may very possibly be quickly and almost universally adopted. There has already been partial success in joining sperm and egg and growing the foetus in an artificial womb; when the technique is perfected, women will be fully emancipated from the bondage of their bodies.

In Aldous Huxley's *Brave New World*, babies were "decanted" rather than born, and "mother" was a dirty word.

Huxley's world was an anti-utopia, but for confused and not entirely valid reasons. Many women don't believe it, but I am convinced ectogenesis will be a nearly unqualified benefit, and that almost all women will welcome the chance to be "fathers" instead of mothers. At first, they will claim their main reason for approving of it are that the foetus will receive greater protection and more reliable care under controlled conditions, and possibly that husbands will have less inconvenience, but they won't miss the swollen bellies and the backaches either. If some women insist on carrying the unborn "under their hearts" (and over their bowels), perhaps science will still serve them, and provide them with marsupial pouches so they can continue to carry the young after birth, like the kangaroos, giving them even more transcendental motherhood.

Men Without Women and Vice Versa

The discussion to this point has centered on bisexuality, but there are other possibilities. A 1967 newspaper story stated, "Two male homosexuals have been secretly 'married' by a Roman Catholic priest in Rotterdam ... The pair had ordered a mass to confirm their lifelong friendship. During the mass, which was held in private and attended by the families of both men, the men exchanged rings."[47] Recently, there have been quite a few reports of homosexual weddings. Strange and distasteful as it is now to most of us, homosexuality may have a future; it may even dominate whole cultures or subcultures.

There are at least two possible benefits in having a single-sex society. One is the elimination of discrimination (in both directions) and mental strait-jackets, with the resulting neuroses. The other is population control.

Isaac Asimov, a biochemist and writer, has suggested (how seriously is something else) that homosexuality might control the population surge. It isn't clear whether he means that the practice should merely be tolerated, or encouraged for those so inclined anyway, or whether it should be universal with test-tube babies *a la* Aldous Huxley, or what. However, other writers have created fictional all-female or all-male societies, and claimed them advantageous.

Technically, as already indicated, the possibility of such societies may not be far in the future. Parthenogenesis, or virgin birth producing females only, is already feasible with many animals, including turkeys; the cock turkey is superfluous. But similar results have not yet been achieved with male seed, nor are there yet techniques for mixing genetic material from two females (or two males) to produce desired genetic variation; but there appears no reason in principle why this could not be done. Of course, people and societies dependent on sophisticated procedures for continued existence would be vulnerable to disasters, but to some extent this is already true, *e.g.* without insulin, the diabetic would die, and without commerce, New York city would die.

In the currently dominant tradition, we not only disapprove of homosexuality but despise it; we fear and hate it. Writer Theodore Sturgeon views us as "... a people of unbreakable and hidebound formality, a people with few but massive taboos, a shockable, narrow, prissy people obeying the rules—even the rules of their calculated depravities—and protecting their treasured, specialized pruderies. In such a group there are words one may not use for fear of their fanged laughter, colors one may not wear, gestures and intonations one must forego, on pain of being torn to pieces."[165]

The extreme revulsion most of us feel toward homosexuality is revealing in itself; we seldom hate anything truly alien, but rather we despise most that sin whose seed we suspect lies also in ourselves. And there are many reasons for believing we all have the homosexual potentiality—reasons having mostly to do with the strange relation between romantic and physical love.

As one hint, let the male reader ask himself this nasty question: What would he do if he fell in love, unknowing, with a female impersonator? Shake you up a little? (Something like this happened in a film comedy with Joe E. Brown as the groom and Jack Lemmon as the "bride;" when Lemmon was unmasked after the wedding, Brown said, "Well, nobody's perfect.")

As another, consider the problem of a humanly intelligent horse. Except for size, there is little outward distinction between male and female horses; secondary sex characters are not pronounced, and except for the actual genitals, it may require close inspection for an ordinary person to tell the difference. If horses were people, and their sex arousal were not related to smell or female cycles, would homosexuality be more of a problem than with us (because more easily fallen into) or less (because not socially condemned)? On the other hand, what about chickens? Can anybody imagine a homosexual rooster?

In any case, homosexual love appears to be at least as "spiritual" as the heterosexual. Will Durant writes:

> The attachment of a man to a boy, or of a boy to a boy, shows in Greece all the symptoms of romantic love—passion, piety, ecstasy, jealousy, serenading, brooding, moaning and sleeplessness. When Plato, in the *Phaedrus*, talks of human love, he means homosexual love; and the disputants in his Symposium agree on one point—that love between man and man is nobler and more spiritual than love between man and woman. A similar inversion appears among the women, occasionally among the finest, as in Sappho, frequently among the courtesans; the auletrides love one another more passionately than they love their patrons, and the *pornaia* are hothouses of Lesbian romance.[40]

It is extremely suggestive that homosexuality seems to have flourished most among men in those societies which kept women ignorant. Apparently some men, at least, chose male companions, not because they preferred their bodies, but because they preferred their minds! From the standpoint of our culture, if a man cannot find an intellectually satisfying woman, he should make do with an inferior woman (assuming he cannot educate her), rather than turn to homosexuality. But is this not a kind of bestiality? Is not concubinage a perversion? Is it not inhuman to use a person on a glandular level only? Can there be a marriage worthy of the name without a substantial degree of spiritual intimacy and understanding?

Immovable as our emotional blocks may be, logic can

103

tell us what might happen in the relatively near future if there were no cultural prohibition against homosexuality. Since the hunt for a well-matched mate is always difficult, and since differences of temperament are likely to be more important than physical ones, it seems entirely possible that homosexual pairings might sharply increase.

In other words, it appears that romantic love depends primarily on personality traits, shared ideals, and psychological needs generally, and that our bodies (or our lower-brain centers) are not all that choosy about modes of physical relief and comfort. Coupling this conclusion with the trend toward increasing individual freedom, we may predict with moderate confidence that eventually these matters will no longer be regulated by taboos, written or unwritten.

Changes of Sex

Apparently some categories of homosexual want to play the opposite sex, and now let us look at their problem a little differently. Assuming he or she cannot be "cured", should the person *play* the opposite sex or *be* the opposite sex? We look to the day when those with personalities unsuited to their inherited sex (assuming such basic personality differences exist) can be assisted to make a biological change—to some extent, in fact, this is already happening.

We know there are at least three separate criteria of sex: (1) the genetic character, specifically the presence or absence of the XY pair of chromosomes, which normally determines the future development of bodily sex; (2) the somatic character, or the anatomical and glandular structure of the individual after birth, which due to prenatal accidents is not always in accord with the genetic character; (3) the personality, which may cover a wide and complex range in either sex.

Not uncommonly, the external sex organs of babies are difficult to identify, and surgery and hormone therapy are sometimes necessary to make the individual definitely one sex or the other. Furthermore, the effect of abnormal early hormone activity may have been such that the better choice is *not* the sex indicated by the chromosomes; e.g., a boy's sex organs may have failed to develop, and may no longer be capable of adequate development, hence he can more successfully be made into a girl than a boy. Finally, many respected and responsible physicians and psychiatrists (although by no means a consensus) agree that the psychological factors, whatever their origin, may be the most important of all, and surgeons sometimes agree to alter men into women or women into men simply because they are convinced they would be happier that way. A man can be given breasts and a vagina, and a woman can be given a beard and a (non-erectile) penis.

Today, the wisdom of such operations is doubtful for many reasons; nevertheless, one can make a good case for revolting against the tyranny of the chromosomes. Frederik Pohl has carried these ideas into a fiction story, "Day Million" (the millionth day of the Gregorian calendar).[140] He tells us that the heroine, Dora,

> ... was a boy ... (but) if you were to see this girl you would not guess that she was in any sense a boy. Breasts, two; reproductive organs, female. Hips, callipygean; face hairless, supra-orbital lobes nonexistent ... It didn't matter to her audiences that genetically she was a male. It wouldn't matter to you, if you were among them, because you wouldn't know it—not unless you took a biopsy cutting of her flesh and put it under an electron microscope to find the XY chromosome ... These people were able to determine a great deal about the aptitudes and easements of babies quite a long time before they were born ... and then they naturally helped these aptitudes along. Wouldn't we? If we find a child with an aptitude for music we give him a scholarship to Juillard. If they found a child whose aptitudes were for being a woman, they made him one.

Pohl's argument has soft spots; not only are there other alternatives, but the very existence of strong innate tendencies to a particular gender in personality is in doubt. (And in the more distant future, the question probably will not arise at all, because the baby's whole blueprint will be designed in advance, with no inconsistencies.) And for the present, with medical techniques limited and taboos powerful, surgical sex change seems a dreary choice;

one might be better off as an ordinary homosexual. Or the troubled individual might simply be continent for a few decades, relying on the millenial outlook to give him patience.

Autosex and Worse

Even if the "gay" life loses its stigma, what about the person who simply does not want a partner, man *or* woman, even a transitory one? What outlet is he or she to find? This may seem a monumentally unimportant problem, yet the possible fragmentation of life in the near future may produce many loners. One possibility lies in creative masturbation.

While sexual liberals have nothing against masturbation, morally or medically, they regard it as inferior to enjoyment with a loving partner. Yet one of the celebrated findings of Masters and Johnson is that self-induced orgasms are the most intense ones.[114] Add to this a narcissistic personality, or one that doesn't want to be bothered with pleasing a partner, and what do we have? Or rather, what do *they* have?

At a minimum, one can expect more elaborate gadgets for women and the development of devices for men. Japanese women are said sometimes to put steel balls between their legs, so that as they sway rhythmically in rocking chairs they enjoy hours of voluptuous sensation, culminating every fifteen minutes or so in orgasm. American know-how has produced the electrical dildo, phallus-shaped vibrators that are said to bring climax in seconds. Minimum improvements to be expected soon include controlled frequency and amplitude of vibration, thrust in addition to lateral vibration, temperature control, variable size and surface texture, and a wide choice of lubricants. Beyond this, for those who want it, there may eventually be coitus machines or handyrandies, robots that will not only provide any amount of service demanded but can be designed in any shape and programmed to supplement their caresses with compliments. And when she is done, the lady doesn't have to cook supper for the stud—just stand him in the closet until she wants him again. That's modern convenience for you. Similar devices can be made for the male.

But suppose robots remain out of reach for a long time, and the cruder forms of masturbation pall—what then? Some will probably take their cue from the shepherd, Leda the swan-lover, and others in history and literature who have coupled with "the beasts of the field". There are some clear advantages: a real, live, warm, loving partner, and yet one that can be kept in his (her) place and used more or less at convenience. There have always been people who treat their pets better than other people treat their lovers. Furthermore, if techniques develop to train and tame animals far beyond present capability, new kinds of excitement present themselves. According to the author of *The Sensuous Woman*, some women fantasize being ravished by a tiger; perhaps the safe actuality will become available.

The use, or abuse, of animals in this way will strike most people as very kinky indeed, and it may be; there seems to be something inherently nasty in perverting the minds of helpless creatures. Yet it is too soon to be sure, and even if it is decisively proven vicious and destructive, we can be fairly confident that some will try it. This is, after all, among the possibilities.

The Future of Chastity

For a semblance of balance and a brief change of pace, let us examine the claims of the chaste.

The arguments *against* rigid, traditional Judaeo-Christian standards are wearisomely familiar to moderns: it is harmful to repress natural biological urges; bombarding children—especially girls—with chastity sermons may permanently maim their capacity to enjoy physical love, even after marriage; guilt feelings may so terrify a girl that if she does slip, she may do something desperate and be afraid to go to her parents for help, or be left with feelings of self-contempt that will permanently warp her personality. And especially for the future, the prospect of long life makes it absolutely intolerable that any one social error should doom anyone to perpetual punishment.

The last argument is unassailable: however high we set our standards, there must always be avenues of recovery and correction. Human pity cannot conceive of such a thing as an "unforgiveable" sin, in the fullness of time. Yet the traditionalists are certainly correct in pointing out that, at present, most girls are emotionally and socially vulnerable, and can feel great distress after "slipping." (They see to it that she does.) On firmer ground, they note that our young people are slow to mature emotionally, and it isn't easy to unscramble the eggs.

Their philosophical case has some merit, if not much. Is it true that "free love" debases sex, that what is casual cannot be valued, that the splendor and glamor and romance of love are lost if one gives love too easily? Can we compare love with diamonds, whose value depends on scarcity as well as intrinsic beauty? If so, are we justified in deliberately creating scarcity? Is the sum total of happiness increased by rationing pleasure? Some people are likely to continue to buy these ideas, and science can also serve the ideal of complete and perfect monogamy.

Potential mates could be computer-matched, by means not yet available, with personality traits optimally selected out of all the population in the appropriate age-bracket. Any physical disparities could be corrected beforehand. If circumstances warranted, sexual maturity could be delayed or sexual urges suppressed by effective but harmless medical techniques until time for marriage. Thus, one would not have to sacrifice the element of purity and uniqueness.

In the slightly more distant future, when we are more nearly supermen, we can expect more sophisticated solutions, such as highly reliable protocols for the molding of character. When the anatomical and physiological bases of mind and temperament are thoroughly understood, then no one need be the victim of unlucky heredity or environment; therapeutic techniques of education, medicine, and surgery can be expected to produce any type of person desired, complete with a moral code endorsed by the church and the FDA. I prefer things a little looser, but perhaps all us reprobates will be converted.

As a species, humans are already very sexy, and it might seem presumptuous to want more. Among bees, for example, only one drone of many catches the queen, and even he enjoys her only once. Among some spiders, the male's mating and execution coincide. Salmon spawn once, and die. Among many antelope, according to Ardrey, only a few males have any intercourse at all, and the females infrequently.[4] The activity of most mammals is limited to a rutting season. Some humans can psych themselves with the old line, "I wept because I had no shoes, until I met a man who had no feet;" but it is cold comfort we get from the misery of others.

On the other hand, there is a male mosquito whose member is about as large as himself, and who can copulate for more than an hour—corresponding perhaps to a *week* straight for a man. In a certain species of octopus, the male has his intromittent organ on the end of one of his arms—the third right. Ardrey says a pair of lions was observed copulating one-hundred seventy times in a period of two and one-half days, about every twenty minutes around the clock.[4] (You'd roar too.) These observations provide a few of the present clues for supersex, with many more coming from extrapolations of our own experience.

Man will hardly emulate the mosquito, but most men would probably like a somewhat larger organ—ideally, perhaps, a telescoping, fully adjustable variety; and nearly every man, beyond the flush of youth, would like more stamina, or the ability to reach orgasm without ejaculation. Many women would like better control of vaginal muscles and secretions, and a relaxed nervous system permitting full exploitation of their physical potential. As for the hint provided by the octopus—or for that matter in women, who have erectile tissue in at least three places—it is simply that erotic sensation and its organs can have many locations in the body.

The *chief* sex organ, to be sure, is singular and unique —the brain. Erotic variety and intensity could be immensely increased with no outward changes at all, simply by modifying the nervous system. As noted above, men could be given the sex capacity of women by making orgasm an occasion of muscular spasm and nervous release, but not the discharge of sperm (unless desired). More radical possibilities also suggest themselves, *e.g.*, the neural circuits might be rigged so that orgasm (again, only when desired) could be achieved by a kiss—science serving a more "spiritual" love! Going still further, one might imagine the "ogle orgasm"—climax (without ejaculation, and only when desired) simply by *looking* at a pretty girl, or a pretty something. Going all the way, it is known that "pleasure centers" in the brain can be electrically excited with enormous frequency by *current* technology[132], and we can conclude that sooner or later—whenever our maturity of responsibility allows—we shall be able to achieve orgasm simply by an act of will, anytime and anywhere.

Most of us, perhaps all, have not fully explored our *current* potential, futuristic technology aside. For example, custom frowns on the recognition of non-sex-specific eroticism. The author of *The Sensuous Woman* recommended detailed techniques for appreciating an ice cream cone, savoring it slowly and licking and sucking it in complicated patterns. What she was leading up to, to be sure, was the substitution of a penis for the ice cream cone as the recipient of the loving licks, but there is a prior and perhaps more important point—that voluptuous, erotic feelings can attach to many non-sex-specific things and actions. A warm breeze can caress one's body more deliciously, in some ways, than a person; and so on and on.

It is also true that relatively crude and early technology will offer interesting opportunities, without tampering with the body. The waterbed is a fairly recent example. And when we have colonies in caverns of the moon, the one-sixth gravity will permit extraordinary bedroom athletics, less fatigue, and less awkward weight; it may be a little like making love in a bathtub, but without danger of drowning.

Yet the current potential, however large, is limited, and surely some will go beyond it. Biologists may design entirely new sexes and new sex organs, aimed at accomplishing reproduction by mixing genetic material from several people: a mating occasion might look like a Conga line, or perhaps a football huddle, or possibly a human pyramid. But even if we restrict ourselves basically to bisexuality, there are amazing possibilities, as suggested at the beginning of this chapter.

Let us return to the Swiss cheese and the naked lunch, even though we are likely to be far off the mark. Our female superperson has not just one specific sexual orifice, but several, each with its characteristic dimensions, texture, musculature, secretions, and nerve supply, adapted to appease and tone up specific aspects of the psyche; she also has organs and aspects corresponding to secondary sex characters—breasts, buttocks, throat and thigh curves, eyes, lips, etc., etc. The male also has specialized organs and qualities, including varied or variable penises, tongues, hair patterns, skin textures, voices, exhalations and secretions. Their designs are intended to fit exquisitely together and to realize every erotic possibility we know or can imagine—indeed, every possibility *they* could imagine, which would be vastly more.

Their enjoyment is frankly physical, but not *only* that; they also far exceed us in delicacy, subtlety, and sensitivity. They probably have something tantamount to mental telepathy, although it may only be a rapport based on intimate experience and a kind of "muscle reading", on sensitive inference rather than direct communication. Imagine how it would be then between lovers, every nuance of thought and feeling being shared and reflected, reverberating between two beings with dazzling interplay of refraction and resonance. To know another as she knows herself, and to know yourself as she knows you, and to feel—not just guess, but feel—her inmost response to you! Is this not one of the things worth waiting for?

Transsex

Our superpeople could enjoy the physical act of love as much as they pleased, which might be most of the time. But this isn't all they would be doing remember: there are many channels of communication (telepathy? radio?

something else?), and many facets or compartments to their minds, so at the very same time they are reveling in each other with full attention and appreciation, they are also attending to business—looking after their interests in the world of economics, politics, science, art, or whatever. By some measures, these other interests will probably be bigger and more important than the sexual ones.

The universe, both of nature and of man, is larger than any single emotional pattern. We shall grow sexually, to be sure, but we shall surely grow even more in other directions; our energies and satisfactions will take many channels, as they do now. Marshall McLuhan and George B. Leonard have said something similar, in suggesting that all of life will become more "erotic," sex in the narrow sense becoming less important:

> Sex as we think of it may soon be dead. Sexual concepts, ideals and practices are already being altered almost beyond recognition. Marriage and the family are shifting into new dimensions. What it will mean to be boy or girl, man or woman, husband or wife, male or female may come as one of the great surprises the future holds for us ... In future generations, it seems most likely that sex will merge with the rest of life, that it will settle down and take its place within a whole new spectrum of experiences ...[116]

My prediction is somewhat different: I have specified some of the changes and innovations we may see, and indicated that the "settling down" of sex will not take place, if at all, until after a long, hot fermentation of experiment, far beyond the current bounds. But eventually it will indeed become a smaller aspect of life than it now seems— not because sex will shrink, but because life will expand.

6

Growing Pains

It is all very well to surmise what we supermen will *be* like; but an equally important question, so far largely skirted, is what it will *feel* like.

Miserable, maybe. In one of Robert Heinlein's early stories, "By His Bootstraps," the protagonist briefly encounters superhuman creatures via a time-travel machine, and his mind nearly crumbles:

> It had not been fear of physical menace that had shaken his reason, nor the appearance of the creature—he could recall nothing of *how* it looked. It had been a feeling of sadness infinitely compounded ... a sense of tragedy, of grief insupportable and unescapable, of infinite weariness. He had been flicked with emotions many times too strong for his spiritual fiber and which he was no more fitted to experience than an oyster is to play the violin.[75]

There is ample precedent for this kind of conjecture. "Ignorance is bliss." "Whosoever increaseth knowledge increaseth sorrow." Perhaps our powers of perception, comprehension and sympathy will outstrip our ability to mainipulate the world and ourselves, leaving us in the horrifying position of feeling and foreseeing every hurt, while helplessly watching universal tragedy unfold. It is even possible that *this* explains the apparent absence of superior alien visitors: cosmic truth, revealing itself at a slightly superhuman level, may be too terrible to be borne.

Optimists have not been lacking either, but their views have often been simplistic. Countless gospel-bearers have insisted that some ritual, or talisman, or slogan would make us moral and emotional—if not intellectual—supermen, with what small results we well know. And this penchant survives in the modern era: Arthur Koestler speaks of a "harmonizing pill" that will somehow reconcile our warring impulses and civilize us through chemistry.[95]

Since it is very unlikely to be that easy, many pundits refuse to consider basic change at all. René Dubos has written. ". . . I believe that any attempt to alter the fundamental being of man is a biological absurdity as well as an ethical monstrosity." Also, ". . . the biological and mental nature of man . . . is essentially unchangeable."[39]

But the "absurdity" remains to be seen, and the "monstrosity" is something we should be able to accept, albeit it will require some very nimble psychology. Expressed a little differently, it should be within our power to choose to grow up.

To a child, the normal adult has some monstrous qualities, including his inscrutable values and motivations. The boy is incapable, for example, of believing that one day girls will be alluring to him, or that lollipops may not be; and he cannot always understand the perspective that produces the apparent cruelties of punishment and discipline. Many children would opt for Peter Pan, and most adults today would choose humanity. To undermine this prejudice, we must try to show that the suggested changes will indeed constitute growth, development, and improvement. The most crucial changes—the most threatening and promising ones—are those relating to intellect and personality. By investigating these, perhaps we can gain some inkling, some faint intimation, of what it will feel like to be a superman among supermen.

We can begin with something relatively simple, explicit, and palatable: the improvements in intellect associated with supertongue.

> *But what we can't say we can't say,*
> *and we can't whistle it either.*
> F.P. Ramsey

Since man is sometimes characterized as "the animal that talks", perhaps superman is "the animal that talks more", or "the animal that talks better".

Many scholars have been profoundly impressed by the idea that language does not merely *express* thought, but shapes it. Emerson said, "Bad rhetoric means bad men." Ludwig Wittgenstein said, "The limits of my language are the limits of my world." In Orwell's world of 1984, "Newspeak" made it nearly impossible to express or even entertain thoughts outside the party line. Korzybski, Hayakawa and other students of semantics have laid great stress on the traps and pitfalls in everyday speech and symbolism.[71] And the great exponent of the hypothesis of linguistic relativity, or linguistic *Weltanschauung*, Benjamin Lee Whorf, wrote: "The world has to be organized by our minds—and this means largely by the linguistic systems in our minds ... we cannot talk at all except by subscribing to the organization and classification of data which the agreement (of the linguistic community) decrees."[181]

This means, for example, that if your language is rich in special names for colors, you will have enhanced ability to recognize and identify particular hues from memory; and laboratory evidence has been compiled for this.[18] It has also been shown that if objects or stimuli are given the same name by the experimenter, the subjects are more likely to respond to them in the same way.[23] Yet many attempts to prove more sweeping claims have failed, and most linguists seem to remain skeptical of such assertions as, ". . . the structure of a particular language may channel thinking and thus cause the users of that language . . . to arrive at different conclusions or different solutions to problems from what speakers of the other language would do."[23]

But this skepticism seems to be based on attempts to compare natural languages, with all the attendant difficulties in trying to sort out the linguistic effects from those of culture, heredity, etc. We do have good evidence, objective and subjective, that the languages of mathematics and technology permit and promote different and more effective styles of thinking. In the words of Sylvain Bromberger:

"... some of these (scientific) questions may not be expressible in English at all, especially so if by 'English' we mean contemporary, 'ordinary' English. 'Why is the emf induced in a coiled conductor a function of the rate of change of magnetic flux through it and of the resistance of the coil?' could probably not have been asked in seventeenth century English, and a similar situation may hold for questions that have not yet risen."[16]

An even better example occurred in one of my classes a couple of years ago. Male students would go to almost any lengths to avoid the draft. Why? So as not to be killed in Viet Nam. But what was the probability of being killed there? Oh, fifty-fifty, was the usual answer. How do you know? Shrug. Don't you know that about 40,000 have been killed, out of about 4,000,000 who have served? Shrug. The *probability* of an event is defined as its relative frequency of occurrence, in a suitable sequence of experiments—it is the number of times it *does* occur, divided by the number of times it *might* occur. Calculate the probability of being killed in Viet Nam, if the war goes on about the same. Well, what do you know—the probability of being killed is only 0.01 or 1%.

Hell no, they still won't go, but at least their eyes have been opened a little bit, and if faced with really grim alternatives—jail or exile—the choice might now be different. One little technical word, and the concept it embraces, can change a whole life.

Again, the languages of science tend to reflect the "operational definition," which separates information from mere labels. It was not so long ago, remember, that Moliere had to chide physicians for saying, in all seriousness, "Why does opium put people to sleep? Because it has dormitive virtue." ("Because it puts people to sleep.") We have much less tendency nowadays to talk about "virtues" and "essences" and "humors," and this represents real progress.

Likewise, who can deny that quantitative thinking became much easier with the transition from Roman to Arabic numerals? (Imagine a Roman engineer trying to multiply LXIV by MCIX.) And who can doubt that the incredibly clumsy Mandarin writing exhausted the talents of generations of Chinese scholars? As Parkinson says, ". . . the process of becoming literate in China is one for which life hardly seems long enough."[136] Although the Chinese invented movable type, the 40,000 characters of the written language prevented its use.

True, one might speculate that the very difficulties mentioned above tended to produce bright people; the Romans were, after all, effective engineers, and the Chinese did devise ways to put their language to work. But it is much more natural to recognize liabilities for what they are, and to agree, for example, with Professor Nakamura's statement:

> The (Japanese) language lacks the relative pronoun, "which", standing for the antecedent, that helps develop clarity of thought. The absence of such a relational word makes it inconvenient to advance closely knit thinking in Japanese. It is difficult to tell what modifies what, when several adjectives or adverbs are juxtaposed. Because of these defects, Japanese presents difficulties for exact scientific expression and naturally handicaps the development of logical, scientific thinking among the Japanese people, which has actually brought about grave inconveniences in their practical lives.[128]

Although Dr. Nakamura speaks here only of "difficulty" and "inconvenience," much more than that is at stake. It is indeed difficult to compare the effects on culture of the natural languages (a) because it is nearly impossible to separate the non-linguistic factors; (b) because a natural language, such as Chinese, that is deficient in one area may be superior in another; and (c) because all existing natural languages, including those of "primitive" peoples, are very old and complex. But by comparing natural languages on the one hand with the protolanguages of the distant past, and on the other hand with the languages of science and with imagined languages of the future, we can convince ourselves that language holds a key to qualitative improvement in thought.

For example, modern Chinese is said to be rich in words for the concrete and particular, but very poor in words for the abstract and general; it also lacks simple forms for the plural of nouns or the tense or mood of verbs.[128] Thus they have no word meaning "old"—one must specify *how* old, *e.g.*, "seventy or more," "eighty or ninety," etc. Likewise, one cannot speak of a "fast horse," but must say something like "a horse good for a thousand *li*." The same word may signify "a man," "the man," "some men," "mankind," etc.

Of course the Chinese have long since found ways to minimize the deficiencies of their language, while exploiting its advantages. But what about proto-Chinese? There must have been a time in prehistory when Sinathropus (or some such) was just learning to speak, and there existed words *neither* for "old" nor for particular numbers, neither for "fast" nor for units of distance, neither plural forms of nouns nor substitute expressions. Surely then, speech and thought must have been dim, vague, and ambiguous enough to merit the epithet "subhuman".

Looking to the future, some opportunities are obvious but striking, as in the reduction of ambiguity. Questions in English, beginning with "Why," are of so many subtly different types, demanding so many different *kinds* of answers—often not the kind anticipated—that professional philosophers and linguists must write yards of jargon to extricate and explicate the meaning.[16] Supertongue should have all of these nicely categorized, with immense saving not only of time but of misunderstanding and frustration.

Terseness is itself a virtue insufficiently appreciated. Who has not had the experience of reading a long sentence, involving difficult concepts, or complex relations, and found that at the end of the sentence he had forgotten the beginning? If you cannot express an idea briefly, then a combination of ideas may become so awkward that its expression is not just difficult, but impossible. Yet in English, for example, we use unnecessarily long words because *most of the one-syllable words have not been allocated*.

Consider, say, the one-syllable words that could be formed by combining three sounds—the first vowel, the first unvoiced consonant, and the first voiced consonant, viz., ä (ah), b, f. Even if we delete the most awkward combinations (fbä, bfä), there are still four words (äbf, äfb, bäf, fäb) only one of which (fäb = "fob") is in use. If we consider the sounds ä, b, f and r, the feasible words are ärbf, ärfb, bärf, bräf, fräb, and färb, *not one of which is in use*, except for the colloquial use of "barf". In fact, linguists believe that with moderate ease we can speak and hear at least 100 simple sounds[140]; whence it follows, with reasonable assumptions, that the entire unabridged English vocabulary could be reduced to words of one syllable— still leaving plenty of room for redundancy, synonyms, poetic variation, and the monosyllabic rendition of a large store of common phrases!

Our languages are exceedingly weak also in the description of contoured surfaces, including faces; we can easily recognize differences of physiognomy and expression that we are nearly helpless to communicate verbally. Consider how laborious it is for a witness to help a police artist reconstruct a face; or, better yet, consider the well-documented story of Clever Hans.[189]

Hans was a horse—a horse that apparently could do arithmetic, understanding the questions spoken in German (this was in Berlin in 1904), and responding with the correct number by tapping his hoof. Visitors, including eminent scholars, came from far and wide to view the marvel; and many were convinced of the genuineness of Hans' intelligence, because he succeeded with strangers as well as with his master, even in his master's absence. Eventually, however, a shrewd observer named Pfungst noticed that Hans did poorly in failing light, and with that clue the puzzle was quickly solved. Hans had no talent whatever in arithmetic and no understanding of German; what he did possess, however, was an amazing ability to read human

119

emotions from facial expressions and bodily attitudes. He simply (!) watched the spectators carefully, and could tell by their appearance when it was time to stop tapping. We can expect languages of the future to have thousands of new words and coded combinations, both to allow the communication of subtleties of facial expression and to help perceive them.

Again, we need to develop the verbalization of kinaesthesia—articulate the sensations relating to balance and coordinated movements. At present, in order to teach someone how to ride a bicycle, for example, it is necessary to demonstrate and then let him practice. Conceivably, with adequately developed language, one could simply give description and directions, and the feelings and muscle responses would be so clearly conveyed that the student could ride at once, or at least with greatly reduced practice. (Fortunately, new techniques of memory training are likely to be at hand even before we have biologically improved brains.)

Oddly enough, some bright people have failed to recognize the opportunities in more sophisticated language. The philosopher Michael Polanyi, for example, actually appeares to accept the present limitations of language as natural and permanent, and uses them to "prove" (!) that some kinds of knowledge cannot be made explicit, that certain things can be known only tacitly: bicycle-riding is one of his examples.[141] Now, it is not self-evident that the feel of a bike can be fully conveyed in words, but at least the approximation is presumptive. If one can remember or imagine a set of feelings, then one can associate these with a spoken cue. The problem then reduces to building an adequate store of feelings or responses on the one hand, and symbols on the other.

Thus, superman will gradually build—and be built by—the richness and subtlety of supertongue, and there will develop qualitative changes in our mental world, if these suggestions prove sound. We should be able to express details, shadings, and nuances that now perforce we must either gloss over, or else honor at the cost of excessive labor and time. Our perceptions of the world, and of each other, should in turn become sharper, broader, and deeper.

Thoughts which formerly could be expressed, or even entertained, only slowly and laboriously if at all, could then become for everyone the casual exercise of a moment. What godlike power, just in the enrichment of verbal language!

Eventually, the demands of "channel width" for high-density communication, or the simple joy of exploitation, may lead us to explore visual, tactile, and olfactory dimensions of language, despite the seeming handicaps. We may learn how to create appropriate signals with muscles or glands, or even directly by cerebration, as well as how to amplify these signals and beam them over space, and how to use suitable transducers for direct input to the nervous system of the listener. But such exotic techniques will not soon be needed. Sound alone provides vast room for the expansion of language.

The consequences are in some respects unnerving. It gives one pause, for example, to note—as I have elsewhere—that within a few centuries Shakespeare is likely to be a dead letter, his wonderful works of no more interest than the grunting of swine in a wallow. At best, they may retain a certain quaint charm for scholars of antiquity, somewhat as Egyptian hieroglyphics do for us; but ancient Egyptian writing is simply too stiff, narrow, cumbersome and tedious to merit much interest among moderns, even though it was created by people just as intelligent as we. It was a feat in its time and served a purpose, but now it is over and done with. If we would not remain children, then at the appropriate time we must put aside childish things.

The Human Condition and Beyond

An adult differs from a child in more than size and strength, and we can expect our thoughts to develop in more ways than speed and accuracy, as well as anticipate a different balance in our feelings and an altered focus in our motivations. Our guesses will be informed by a review of certain aspects of human psychology.

First we must clear away certain fallacies widely held among "educated" laymen, (for example, many physicians), such as the notion that the most powerful of our drives are those related to survival, food, and sex. For people to risk their lives, and to abstain from food and sex in varying degree in response to social pressure, individual idiosyncrasy, or mere habit, is more the rule than the exception. (Think of soldiers, smokers, dieters, chaste teen-agers, etc.). While our elementary animal needs are in a sense "basic", still the tail has come to wag the dog, and the higher drives are nearly autonomous. Gordon Allport has not much overstated the case in saying, "The motives of a mature person are so far removed from the original physiological drives that nothing can be gained by attributing the social behavior of an adult to primary physiological drives."[1]

Another mistake is the notion that we are governed, or ought to be, by some principle of "homeostasis" analogous to the tendency of an individual cell to maintain a constant internal environment in the face of changing external conditions. Only some aspects of our behavior, and those not the highest, are of this defensive type, aimed at redressing balance and seeking some peaceful haven. (This is the trouble with virtually all utopias.) A somewhat similar error is the idea that one of our basic motivations is to seek "adjustment" to the world. Probably most of our highest drives are related to the non-homeostatic, aggressive drives of curiosity, play, manipulation, and exploration. At any rate, happiness cannot be equated in any simplistic way with comfort or pleasure, else the opium eater and lobotomy patient would have to be considered among the most successful people.

Then there are several interrelated fallacies, seldom explicitly stated by prevalent, concerning "natural" man, already touched upon. One is the assumption that our most basic motivations and values are mutually consistent, so that a "correct" attitude and course of action is always possible in principle: this is far from clear, and to avoid permanent residence on the horns of a multiple dilemma it may become necessary to excise certain motivations from our psyches—a painful process. Another is the idea that man is normally well integrated, despite the many-layered accretion of disparate elements in his brain and mind gathered during the development of the species and the individual. Still another is the assumption that the more basic drives, at least, are overwhelmingly adaptive, for example, that fear is almost entirely a useful response that prepares the organism for "flight or fight"; but M. B. Arnold has shown rather convincingly that fear is more often enervating than invigorating, and while it may be useful for caution it is maladaptive for flight.[5] Finally—to cut the list arbitrarily short—there is the idea among many laymen that needs and appetites are always well correlated; but P. T. Young points out that this is not so, e.g. that when a rat's diet is deficient in magnesium, it may actually develop an *aversion* to the needed element.[185] In short, it seems nearly certain that man is not consonant either with himself or with even an idealized environment.

Those who speak of the "human condition"—especially novelists and philosophers—often embrace all of these fallacies and many others. In their moments of relative optimism they may rationalize pain and failure as necessary counterpoints to joy and triumph; or they may see tragedy as the penalty for forsaking the "natural man" within us, the generic angel sullied and crusted over by individual and cultural mistakes. These are not very productive ideas—little more than breast-beating. In their more pessimistic musings, such writers are likely to see the failure of man as an existential necessity, hungers unsatisfied and tensions unalleviated as the way of the world—but again they only bewail man's fate or acclaim his noble martyrdom, and neglect the close analysis of the problems that might reveal paths to solutions.

As one small example, it is suggestive to imagine the plight of a young man in the Old Stone Age, seeking to "find himself." Why can he not adjust to his time and place, as might be expected of a "normal," healthy animal? Why is he restive and discontented, even though his life may be comfortable enough in a good year, with clams for the digging, fruits for the picking, a complaisant woman and a balmy breeze? Perhaps he is really a jazz musician, and he can't find a clarinet. Possibly he needs to do fine wood carving, and the flint hand-axe isn't adequate. Or maybe—just like some moderns—he needs to scratch his fanaticism itch; he needs a "cause," and no satisfactory banner is in sight. ... Well, there was little he could do but kick the dog, squint wistfully at the horizon, and grumble about the "human condition." But our position, at the watershed of history, is different; we have the knowledge, the tools—and the time. To plan our strategy, we need among other things the clearest possible understanding of motivation and emotion, some of which seems at hand.

Motivation: Hierarchies and Feedbacks

There are several related words which differ in many ways—between themselves, from psychologist to psychologist, with respect to inheritance vs. learning, etc.; these words include *motivation, drive,* and *instinct*. We shall not trouble ourselves overmuch with the distinctions, but use them (as Humpty-Dumpty did) at our convenience.

As good reductionists, we recognize that at the basic physiological level our nervous systems (hence our personalities) are *programmed*, and that a motivation (drive, instinct, reflex, habit, etc.) is an element of the programming. At some stage, presumably, the programming and its principles will be fully understood and it will be within our power to modify it physically, by brute force if necessary, thus becoming whatever we choose to be within whatever limits may exist. At the very least, each of us should become equal to the best of us in all respects.

But this is rather vague and distant. For the near term, we must work at a different level and more indirectly; and of course we acknowledge that the programming of an animal is far different from that of a computer, primarily because, even in self-modifying computers, there is a clear separation between the "nervous system" (the program) and the balance of the beast. In a biological organism this distinction is not nearly so sharp and the feedbacks much more complex, including the likelihood of internal anomalies or inconsistencies, such as the simultaneous need to dominate and to submit.

In Abraham H. Maslow's frequently-cited theory of motivation, various drives or goals are roughly ranked in order of "prepotency" or urgency, and the "lower" drives must be satisfied before one can turn to the "higher," in general.[113] For example, hunger usually takes precedence over the sex drive; and most of us require our social approval urge to be satisfied before we can turn fully toward self-actualization or fulfillment of creative potential. (Sometimes, of course, the same activities may serve both ends.)

Maslow's theory, although crude and incomplete, is not merely descriptive but useful and fruitful. It organizes motives into hierarchies (which admittedly are not always clear-cut), and it also distinguishes between "deficiency motivation" (such as hunger) and "growth motivation," of which the highest is self-actualization: a man *must* do what he *can* do. (As Henry W. Nissen put it, "Capacity is its own motivation.") Among other things, these ideas, when judiciously interpreted, give us a new perspective on the autonomy of the higher motivations and the possible dispensability of some of the lower ones.

As a trivial example of the partial dispensability of one of the lower drives, consider hunger. Modern man—let alone superman—does not need gnawing, ravenous hunger to produce needed action; if we happen to be busy, we should be able to ignore hunger for several days without severe discomfort. There is no danger of starvation; we know our bodies need food, and it will be available at our convenience. Instead of a raucous "alarm clock" clanging *feed me, feed me,* there should be a decorous, gentle "chime" growing more insistent only very gradually. Ideally, of course, the "alarm" should be adjustable by an act of will, so that when we decide to enjoy the act of satiating a vigorous appetite, the appetite will be there. To attain these improvements should be a relatively easy task of physiological engineering, if indeed not merely of conditioning.

At the second-highest level in Maslow's system is the need for *esteem,* that of others and of oneself. A great many people are more or less stuck at this level, their major activities organized by this need, which never seems quite satisfied. There seem to be two main reasons for this: first, the need was insufficiently satisfied early in life, and the deprivation, according to Maslow, permanently weakened the individual in that respect—made him *less* able to bear that kind of deprivation than a normal person; second, the deprivation instigated activities that became fixed as habit patterns, so that esteem-bringing activities (making money, earning acclaim and admiration, etc.) became essentially autonomous, the core of the individual's personality, dominating all other needs and activities, at the expense of his further development.

It is fairly clear that, as supermen, we can largely dispense with the esteem drive also. (We bypass for the moment the question of how to reorganize personalities already stuck at that level.) By way of analogy, normal people in civilized countries and quiet times (there have been such) are very little driven by their "safety needs" (the second tier in Maslow's hierarchy) because family and society have always provided ample protection, and the adult need merly allocate an occasional cursory review to his arrangements for physical safety. Likewise, superman should have ample confidence in the esteem-worthy character of his personality and actions, and thus be able largely to ignore the question, except for occasional routine review on a conscious level.

If superman is going to eliminate or minimize all motivations except self-actualization, this seems to tell us something about the nature of "happiness"; it does not depend primarily on comfort, certainly not on safety, and not even on love or self-esteem, although all of these are needed in their time and place; it depends ultimately on a certain tension, and a certain rhythm, in the stretching and exercising of one's capacities—not homeostasis, not any static bliss, but a dynamic and intricate pulse and surge of challenge and growth. Happiness is better than comfort, joy, or even ecstasy; and its main features seem to relate to the binding of time and of the personality—it seems to tend, in a preconscious way, to depend on rhythms of satisfaction extended over time and over several facets of the self.

While these notions barely broach the subject, and while vast areas of great interest must be omitted entirely (such as the nature of the unconscious and the possibility of making it rational and accessible), still we may get a glimmer of the transhuman psyche by looking at some further aspects of motivation, usually either from a Maslowian or a Darwinian point of view, and with no special concern for redundance. But before looking at some specific motivations, we should clarify again the possibility and desirability of a higher level of uniformity, and a much larger pleasure/pain ratio, in our transhuman world.

Designing Personality and Prescribing Happiness

When we learn what factors of personality are most conducive to external effectiveness and to internal satisfactions, everyone should have the option of optimizing the circuits in his nervous system, whether through surgery, pharmacy, and electronics or through simple learning. Then almost everyone might be highly efficient and nearly always content, maybe even euphoric; yet contemporaries are apt to view such prospects as distasteful or worse. We must try to show that the fear and repugnance many feel are founded mostly on misunderstanding.

Part of the fear pertains to a well-meaning but clumsy and doctrinaire paternalism in the manner of *Brave New World*, which some humanists foresee, a world in which you will not only be forced to conform, but will jolly well be forced to *like* it. The fear of being *made* to like what you don't like strikes at the ego, the self; a threat of forced personality change is, in a sense, a death threat.

The possibilities of abuse and tragedy are real enough. But such errors represent aberrations and not necessary consequences of human engineering. As for the feeling that *any* major personality change is a mortal danger, that is just an excess of wariness and want of thought; the feelings that make our hackles rise are not always reliable guides to behavior. Major progress must involve major changes in intellect and personality, and there need be no trauma unless the change is too rapid or disorderly. If we have time to digest and integrate the new information and relationships so that all aspects of the self can be kept or brought in phase, then these personality changes will represent not mayhem but simply growth, and in many cases healing.

Even less valid is the notion that some of the spice will be taken from life if we cold-bloodedly study the psyche, learn its mechanisms, and then tailor the individual to exploit this knowledge. It takes all kinds to make a "human" world, we are told; some even go so far as to say it is our very defects that are endearing!

Perhaps it is the contrasts in the world which provide some of its interest. But who would conclude thereby that we ought carefully preserve a quota of victims, a class of clowns? Must there be dwarfs, and blind men, and hunchbacks, just so the rest of us can savor our good fortune a little more? Must we force or entice some to remain simpletons, so the rest of us can the better relish our superiority? The absurdity of such proposals is obvious; it would be even worse than to retain a class of poor people, just to titillate the rich.

Even if it *were* true that the world would lose some savor thereby, it would still be morally and practically necessary to allow everyone the information and facilities to optimize himself, to enjoy the best available. But in fact it is not true, for at least two reasons. First, it would require a warped mind to enjoy the unnecessary misfortune of others. Second, superman's capacity for perception is unlikely to require the crude, physical, temporal presence of contrasts of misery; if he realizes fully that misfortune *has* existed, and *could* exist, that should suffice for any requirements of contrast.

In similar vein, some philosophers have gone so far as to assert that pain is necessary for pleasure, occasional misery is essential for the possibility of joy, good cannot exist without evil, and indeed life can have no meaning without death. This falls just short of being self-evident drivel; it has just barely enough plausibility so that it sometimes fools people.

The answer, first, is that it just isn't true; it is an assertion with a certain ring to it, but virtually no substance. There is no solid evidence behind it, and there are plenty of counter-examples. There are many people who are generally wretched, and others who are generally contented. Many people show a life-long surplus of joy, and others a deficit.

If the claim is made that at least a substantial *danger* of pain must be present, that at least a looming *threat* of tragedy must underlie the enjoyment of life, again the case is, at most, unproved. To some extent, the argument can be reversed: the near presence of unfortunate people and the dark shadow of peril can warp the personality, producing feelings of guilt and anxiety that make happiness impossible.

In any case, as already indicated, superman should fully appreciate the dangers and tragedies in the world of space and time, and be able to utilize any desired sense of contrast. Furthermore, we do not expect this functioning to depend on the crude animal drives which governed our predecessors and ourselves until now; for superman, gradations of pleasure ought to provide motivation just as efficient as did the contrasts of pleasure and pain for man and pre-man. Keenly alive to the implications of small differences, he can be happy at all times and comfortable most of the time, yet far quicker and more energetic than we in responding to—and creating—demands for action. This qualitative improvement is something we can scarcely understand until we experience it.

Habits Good and Bad; Phasing Out Fear

With no effort to be systematic, let alone exhaustive, we can now look at a few specific drives and ask whether to cultivate or weed them out.

While we are being very cavalier in the use of terms, there seem to be very few, if any, true "instincts" in man above the cellular level—only genetic tendencies or capacities which are stronger or weaker, more or less specific. (It used to be said that infants have two universal instinctive fears, namely of falling and of loud noises, but this seems to have been disproved.[5]) One is tempted to speak of a universal tendency to avoid the painful or unpleasant and seek pleasure, but the spectacle of a sadist and masochist interacting is enough to cure us of that; adequate definitions of "pleasure" and "pain" are not yet at hand.

Having bowed to some of the many difficulties, we can now proceed to ignore most of them and make some judicious speculations. Our first and easiest include the continuation, without radical change, of the drives of *self-preservation, curiosity,* and general *aggressiveness.* It is not claimed that there are "basic" in any physiological sense, and it is even possible that aggressiveness and self-preservation may have neurotic elements from some valid point of view; but it is reasonably clear that these traits will persist simply because their lack would probably prove fatal in the end. It is true that clams have done well enough, as a species, without notable curiosity or aggressiveness, and even some varieties of man—Egypt's fellahin, for example—have sometimes found protected niches; but on the level of technological man, and for the long term, a lack of curiosity and aggressiveness will surely be suicidal. (Their presence may also, of course, but less definitely.) To him who merely sits and waits, assuredly will come at last his nemesis; constant reconnoitering and probing is the only defense that has a chance. The only way to avoid disaster is to go looking for it.

Drives likely to be extirpated include *zealotry* (idealism, fanaticism, militant enthusiasm, etc.) and the "territorial imperative," if the latter really has a specific genetic basis. These are not only unnecessary, at a superhuman intellectual level, but obviously troublesome; we shall expand on this in the next chapter. *Shame* will probably be weeded out, no longer being needed as a counterweight to pride; instead, there could be simple acknowledgements of factual shortcomings, and calm regret when we blunder, followed by efficient corrective actions. On the other hand, we may well retain *pride* and *vanity,* despite their elements of neurosis, because they may continue to be important constituents of our psychic fuel.

More impressive than any of these, however, will be the expected phasing out of *fear*.

Fear has both emotional and motivational aspects. It seizes the viscera and alters the metabolism, often squeezing

130

the heart and blanching the face; and it provides powerful motivation in a wide variety of useful avoidance habits. It is usually assumed to be a biological basic, and of all Franklin Roosevelt's Four Freedoms, freedom from fear might seem the least likely of attainment. Short of utopia— short of total control of the environment and a stable society—must there not always be dangers? And is not fear a necessary response to danger? Would not a fearless being tend to die rather quickly? Is not fear tightly bound up with the survival instinct? So it might seem: neveretheless I think that, as supermen, we shall be nearly fearless.

For this discussion we must disregard most of the complexities and subtleties, such as the relation of fear to the feelings of anger and awe. Then the evolutionary bases of fear and courage seem fairly clear, and these form a dynamic tension somewhat analogous to that of self-preservation vs. self-sacrifice, discussed in Chapter 7. This tension, also, could become radically displaced.

The utility of fear is obvious in avoiding physical peril (a predator, an enemy, a storm). Fear leads to flight or avoidance, and flight or avoidance may lead to safety; hence the timid tend to survive. But the meek have not inherited the earth, because flight or avoidance does not solve all problems: if predators lurk around the only water hole, then those who cannot overcome their fear will die of thirst. Warriors in a war-like tribe may lead risky lives, but they tend to acquire women, land, and slaves, thus consolidating their ferocious traits. (It is said that, a few centuries back, the life expectancy of the sons of English earls was about twenty three, most of them dying violent deaths.) There is probably no single gene for fear, no simple hereditary basis for courage or aggressiveness, but we all have both tendencies in varying degree.

Some of the disadvantages of a fearful disposition are manifest. To begin with, it is unpleasant. If excessive, it can be drastically counterproductive: useful caution may deteriorate into harmful terror or panic. On a more subtle level, in modern circumstances, fear may be diluted or "referred", expressing itself as guilt, anxiety, and indecision. Do these represent the inescapable price we must pay for a biologically essential response? I think not.

At the very least, the average level of fear can be sharply reduced. A child needs fear, because he is too immature to be governed by reason based on experience and understanding; only a healthy respect for parental anger will keep him out of the street. The adult, on the other hand, does not have to be terrified of automobiles to avoid them: he dodges the taxicabs efficiently but calmly, using his brains and rarely calling on his adrenal glands for assistance.

When we are sufficiently alert and aware, we should not need the spur of fear, nor tolerate the confusion it tends to bring. Our glandular responses can probably be brought almost entirely under conscious control, by techniques we are already beginning to learn.[88] Again, this may convey images of aloof, imperturbable automatons, cold and hard, but this is not the right picture. After all, when we grow up today and leave behind our temper tantrums, this does not make us less human, only less childish.

It is commonplace—especially in war—to say that everyone has fear, that courage is not the absence of fear but the ability to overcome it. The first part of this saying is an egalitarian myth, as I am convinced by observations of different people and of myself at different times. There are wide variations in habitual fear levels and fearful response habits, and there is indeed a type of bravery based on lack of fear; there really is a temperament which is cool and steady in the face of danger. Two fighter pilots, for example, may be perfectly equal in willingness to accept and seek risks, but the one with less fear to subdue is likely to be more clear-headed and efficient.

This cool temperament is partly inherited, but it can also be acquired. In my middle age, I am much less fearful than I was as a child or youth. Some of this fear reduction may result, to be sure, from diminished sensitivity—our antennae become stiffer with age—but introspection convinces me that some of it represents genuine learning and growth, the ability to size up dangers, put

132

them in perspective, and handle them in a relatively calm way.

Phasing out fear is only one small aspect of the improvement expected in our personalities as supermen, but it is one most of us can understand and appreciate readily. Not to shiver, not to quake, not to feel the knot in one's stomach, not to be gripped by the shrinking confusion of mind or paralysis of will—not to be afraid any more, how marvelous!

The Action Approach

If wishes were horses, beggars would ride. It is all very well, some may say, to speak glibly of extirpating this instinct or phasing out that emotion or drive, but exactly *how* can this be done?

In part, the question is unfair; if we knew exactly how to do it, it would already be done, and we would be superhuman now. In part, we rely on our sense of history and on the validity of our world-view: presumptively, there is some specific anatomical and physiological basis for every constellation of traits, and the day must come when we can remake ourselves at least to the level of the best that now exists, using either grossly physical (surgical/chemical/electronic) or psychological methods. Beginnings and hints of all these capabilities exist in the current technical literature. In this section we want to review briefly some of the simpler techniques, characterized by Dr. George Weinberg, a New York psychotherapist, as "the action approach."[176]

The basic idea is simple and has been around a long time, viz., that many aspects of personality can be regarded as *habits*, which can be inculcated or eradicated by patterns of behavior that are under conscious control. For a long time attempts to apply this idea had very limited success, but its modern champions are undaunted and apparently making considerable progress.

They are bucking a majority which still takes a gloomy view about the possibility of teaching old dogs new tricks. For example, P. M. Symonds has written, "The evidence ... points not only to the persistence of traits of personality throughout life but also to the great resistance of personality traits to change ... after months and even years of concentrated efforts (by clinical workers) to change personality in clients, basic personality patterns remain unchanged."[167] Gardner Lindzey *et al.* have found compelling evidence for the importance of genetic factors underlying certain personality traits.[103] And the psychoanalytic school, beginning with Freud, holds that events in early life exert influences exceedingly hard to counteract, a view which is certainly consistent with the indifferent success of analytic methods.

What Weinberg calls "the action approach" is related to what others call "behavior therapy," an early proponent of which was William James, who said, "Action seems to follow feeling, but really action and feeling go together, and by regulating the action, which is under the more direct control of the will, we can indirectly regulate the feeling, which is not." (Remember "Whistle a Happy Tune" in *The King and I*?) If we act like the people we want to become, according to James, we shall turn ourselves into those people. But this cannot be done instantly, hence it is crucially important to choose the right strategy in modifying first one, then another of the behavior patterns in question. Weinberg's contribution—which we cannot detail here—lies in the explication of this strategy, and he claims substantial clinical success.

Maslow's views are at least partly consonant with these ideas. He speaks of an "inner core" of the personality, formed in the first few years of life, which must be discovered if one is to find his "identity"; but he also says of the self, "Partly it is also a creation of the person himself ... Every person is, in part, 'his own project,' and makes himself."[111] Again, the tail wags the dog, and at least an important part of the person is simply a bundle of autonomous habits, subject to change.

The better known behavioral therapists, e.g. H. J. Eysenck, have a somewhat different focus in applying learning theory to the elimination of neurotic symptoms, often using a simple "conditioning" approach remindful of Watson's work with animals; for example, a child may be cured of bed-wetting simply by wiring the bed so that a bell rings whenever he begins to urinate.[48]

Needless to say, the analysts vigorously attack the behaviorists, claiming among the other criticisms that a symptom eliminated by conditioning is likely to be replaced by another symptom, perhaps worse, if the "underlying unconscious" cause is not removed; but the behaviorists insist the facts support them, and that in many cases, at least, there is no "unconscious cause," but only the syndrome itself.

Weinberg's position is in some important respects different from that of the classical behaviorists, particularly in his attention to the total patient and his motivations, rather than to isolated syndromes. But he is also attacked by the analysts, and has some wry comments about those who insist that a "seeming" personality change leaves one "really" the same underneath, however great the objective and subjective improvement may be.

We have have not proven that "normal" people can be much improved by the same techniques that are used with "neurotics," but no one is fully normal anyhow, and nearly all of us could probably be substantially improved by the systematic use of existing techniques. If we include "operant conditioning,"[88] by means of which one can apparently attain conscious control even of his heart beat and brain waves, then this partial and current armamentarium alone gives promise of a giant step forward.

Emotional Stability

Despite the foregoing notes of optimism, superman will need all the help he can get in stabilizing his emotions. We think we have troubles now! What must we expect when our expanded intellects interact with a vastly more complex environment?

One possibility is Heinlein's conjecture at the beginning of this chapter—everything scaled larger, including gulfs of grief that humans would dare not plumb, as well as (presumably) peaks of ecstasy that unmodified man could not endure. But we can do without the gulfs, thank you, and there are many ways in which we might cheat the piper, such as simply to tune out or wall off the undesired emotions, possibly for protracted periods, until we can deal with them, perhaps piecemeal, from a more advantageous position Of course this strategy usually fails for the neurotic and psychotic humans who try it, but that is because (a) their unconscious minds are not under control, and (b) they never achieve the more advantageous positions that continual growth should bring.

Another critical problem is that of monitoring one's own conditioning. According to Eysenck, "... dysthymic (despondent) patients and normal introverts are characterized by the quick and strong formation of conditioned responses, while psychopaths and normal extraverts are characterized by the weak and slow formation of conditioned responses. Thus the deviation ... in either direction may prove disastrous."[49] And this is oversimplified; our problem will be to screen endless categories of conditioning reactions and optimize the rate and degree of each. There are some things that we want to learn thoroughly, in a single lesson—mathematical theorems and tables of basic information, how to walk without stumbling in the reduced gravity of the moon, how to recognize poison mushrooms, etc. Then there are other things that we want to learn only through thick (but not impassable) barriers of suspicion—that our value systems are wrong, that a friend is stabbing us in the back, or that it is necessary to betray a commitment, for example.

A related problem is that of adjustment versus responsibility. In contemporary life we all know easygoing people who have apparently made a marvelous adjustment—by blinding themselves to dangers and responsibilities (for example, letting children run wild, untrained and unprotected); and on the other hand, there are those who assume more responsibility than they can handle, and succumb to neurotic anxiety. The latter will be the greater danger for superman, whose longer attention span and heightened awareness of implications may tend to overwhelm him with demands.

Finally, large elements of uncertainty will always be present when we have no fixed ultimate goal, when the horizon continually recedes as we advance, when *being* is subordinate to *becoming* for the indefinite future. As Maslow put it, "Growth has not only rewards and pleasures but also many intrisinic pains. . . . Each step forward is a step into the unfamiliar and is possibly dangerous. It also means giving up something familiar and good and satisfying. It frequently means a parting and a separation, with consequent nostalgia, loneliness and mourning. . . . Growth forward *is in spite* of these losses and therefore requires courage and strength in the individual. . . ."[112]

There is no guarantee that the requisite courage and strength will always be found in time, but I am reasonably confident we can gain sufficient control of our nervous systems, so that the major threats will not be from within.

Empathy Without Altruism

We often assume that superior beings will be characterized by the "civilized" satisfactions and the gentler virtues. Superman mst be *nice*—a kind of Boy Scout idealized and realized. But this notion is probably as unrealistic as its opposite, that of the bloodless logic-machine.

Today we love to be loved, and we need to be needed; the most valued feeling is the feeling of being valued. (That is, most of us are stuck on Maslow's third or fourth level.) But advanced individuals may see maudlin sentiment on the part of their fellows as worse than useless, as a pitfall for the object of affection and a sign of weakness and immaturity by the giver of affection. They may learn to enjoy each other's company and shared activities no less, while still refraining from a generalized and uncritical attachment. Today it is regarded as a virtue to give oneself and to want to give oneself, but this may come to be seen only as a neurotic weakness.

As for the particular trait of generosity, we may be able to throw light on some of its aspects by considering the word itself. "Generosity" is usually construed as giving more than is needful, or more than is expected, or more than is customary. But to understand the anatomy of this generosity, we must ask what is needful, and why; what underlies the expectations and the customs.

What is our purpose in giving more than is needful, or

137

expected, or customary? If it is to inspire gratitude, because we enjoy the gratitude or want to benefit from it, then giving that much was needful after all, and in a private sense the generosity did not exist. If our motives were more neurotic, if we needed to bolster our self-esteem or assuage guilt feelings, then again, in a subjective sense, no generosity was involved. In the last analysis, we do everything to please ourselves, or to please some aspect of ourselves, or to avoid a worse eventuality (even though our actions do not always lead to the desired results); thus we can say, with great generality, that in a proper subjective sense there is no such *thing* as generosity.

This is not to deny that the word has a useful meaning, or that some people are nicer than others. If someone you know has what is commonly called a generous nature, then he doubtless does give beyond the average, by objective criteria, and he doubtless is a more pleasant person to deal with (although sometimes his generosity may have bad results for his family, as well as for himself). But superman may regard the satisfactions of the generous as the delusions of fools, more or less in a class with those who packed off their little ones on the Children's Crusade, feeling full of pious virtue; or with the Stakhanovites who work themselves into early graves for Mother Russia and the Party.

Perhaps, then, superman will regard generosity and niggardliness alike merely as miscalculations, carrying emotional freight only for the immature. (One gives what suits one's purposes, neither more nor less.) Despite this, he may feel the same warm glow a human does when helping and benefiting others; among his other accomplishments, superman will surely not lack the capacity for doublethink, and for falling into child-like attitudes when he chooses.

So in some respects we may indeed come near the cold, aloof, machine-like creature so often depicted in fiction. Surely it will be an advantage to be able to "turn off" or "tune out" one's emotions at will, choosing fully to savor only those that are enjoyable—provided this can be done without impairing judgment and without traumatizing the unconscious mind. Perhaps we may carry to extreme our present habit of "hypocritical" courtesy, showing our acquaintances faces of concern and interest that we may not fully feel, or allow ourselves to feel—not because we are deceitful, but because we recognize *both* their need for sympathy and our need to limit involvement.

But along with his coolness, his ability to make the grimmest decisions without the quiver of a muscle, the transhuman may also be warm and understanding in a way that we see only few hints of today. A "generation gap," for instance, whould be a thing unthinkable. Every parent should understand the most delicate nuance of his child's feelings and the wellsprings of his motivation. In part, we think of the development and training of accentuated perceptions, *a la* Clever Hans, mentioned earlier. "Every little movement has a meaning all its own," and a adult should be able to "read" every twitch and grimace of a child. He should also sense the child's feelings more intensely, for two reasons: the higher "voltage" of his nervous system, in contrast to ours; and his superior ability to extrapolate consequences and perceive the relatedness of situations and developments. All this means he can convoy to the child the breadth and depth of his understanding and sympathy, yet with enormous tact—the total result being a sense of love that we would find inexpressible. Super-mother—whether she "carries" her child or watches him gestate in an artificial uterus—will doubtless look back on human mothers, insensitive and erratic as they are, as little better than the sow that requires only a small disturbance to cannibalize her young.

Man and Superman

Although the foregoing discussion of superman's personality was only a tentative beginning, limitations of space and competence force me to leave it at that. With luck, these speculations may help make transhumanity just a little more meaningful, a trifle less vague and abstract. Possibly more psychologists will be motivated to think in terms of therapy for "normal" people as well as for neurotics; surely this is a major untapped national and personal resource, right now. Perhaps some poets and novelists will be moved to make these ideas more particular and dramatic in the next few years, helping to pave the way for superman and create a more active demand. But might there not be a dangerous interregnum as man is phased out and superman takes over?

The question of race and culture in politics is already volatile, and may become more so. Unless government controls are imposed—which hopefully will not happen— life styles and initiatives will continue multifarious, and for a while many varieties of superman will have to get along with each other, and with man.

One of the more obvious dangers is probably exaggerated: that of nations or societies cloning "superior" types, using newly developed biological techniques to produce thousand-fold "twins" of Einstein, Patton, Eddie Rickenbacker, and others who supposedly might beef up a country's strength. For one thing, these procedures are not likely to be available until the present generation of doctrinaire leaders in the totalitarian countries has been replaced. For another, it should become obvious in time that (1) a hundred Pattons are not a hundred times as valuable as one, and (2) it is nearly impossible to surmise, even a few years ahead, which traits are the most valuable ones for specific strategic objectives; one cannot even be sure whether big men or little men will be better soldiers in the context of the next decade's technology. But most of all, we rest our hopes on the emergence of individual, selfish motives and the millenial outlook, which will view with cold disfavor any holy wars or ideological crusades.

There will still be problems, but to some extent they may create their own solutions. If a new variety is really a superman in all respects, he will realize, far better than we, the error in mistreating inferiors and the folly of boastfulness or arrogance. But there may be many limited supermen, especially in the near future, and they will not necessarily have balanced judgement; some of them may be only strong, and not very sympathetic or wise. Still, at least two factors should tend to save the situation: heterogeneity and upward mobility.

If a sub-population is segregated geographically and culturally, as well as genetically, so that it is highly visible and enviable, then it has an explosive potential; but that is not likely to be the case. It will be more similar to the present situation of the wealthy: They are widely scattered, widely variable, and not, to any important degree, leagued together against the rest of us. At the same time, we all have some chance to become wealthy, not being excluded by any caste system; hence any envy or resentment tends to remain under control. Just so with supermen: they will probably be well mixed through the population, will not necessarily have any prominent stigmata, and will have little incentive to band together. At the same time, the techniques of improving people should be available to all —at a price, no doubt—and there need be no climate of envy or hate.

7

Morality for Immortals

*Didst thou not know that men prefer peace,
even death, to freedom of choice in the
knowledge of good and evil?*
—*Dostoevsky*

Now we must wrestle with our consciences, and win. The emphasis must now shift from superhumanity to immortality, from the third person to the first and second, from motivations to value and from aspirations to ethics. In particular, we must try to clarify the conflict between immortalism and traditional morality.

There is indeed, I think, such a conflict, on at least two levels. First, life extension will bring important practical changes in the effects of policies and actions; what may be "good" for a mortal may be "bad" for an immortal, because of altered perspectives and other changes. A few examples are offered.

Second, the very criteria of "good" and "bad" will change, especially in the related issues of selfishness vs. altruism, self-preservation vs. self-sacrifice, solitude vs. community, expediency vs. loyalty, pragmatism vs. principle, and growth vs. stability. The immortal superman, I believe—yourself and myself, day after tomorrow—will shift the balance substantially toward the first of each of these pairs, although with important qualifications. And again I hope to convey a feeling that these shifts are not only

142

probable but desirable, that after the wrenching changes our position will be more comfortable as well as more logical, that the gains will far outweigh the losses. But we must begin with some emphatic disclaimers.

The Need for Relatively Stable Values

It must not be imagined that there is much connection between immortalist morality and the "ethical relativism" or "situation ethics" currently popular in some quarters, or that immortalist morality is reflected in the decadent life-styles of some self-proclaimed *avant-garde* elements. The resemblances are superficial and the differences profound, as we shall gradually see.

Circumstances do indeed alter cases, and scarcely anyone now denies that cultural and individual differences bear on one's value system. But a sudden liberation from traditional values can have the same effect as "liberation" from a safety belt in a racing car. It is astonishing how few people understand the real rationale behind the rules against cheating and stealing, or the chief danger that premarital sex poses for most girls in contemporary society. I have never had a student give the answer which I believe is valid to either of these questions—viz., that these activities tend to corrode the personality and self-image.

To be sure, the notion of "natural law" is fuzzy and dubious, especially in the grotesque exaggerations of an Aquinas. Aristotle was not exactly on target in saying, "every ideal has a natural basis, and everything natural has an ideal development." Kant's "categorical imperative" has not been shown to exist. But men have enough in common, and psychology is sufficiently advanced, to make it clear that values cannot be tampered with lightly.

Maslow says, "The human being needs a framework of values, a philosophy of life, a religion or religion-surrogate to live by and understand by, in about the same sense that he needs sunlight, calcium, or love. . . . The value-illnesses which result from valuelessness are called variously anhedonia, anomie, apathy, amorality, hopelessness, cynicism, etc., and can become somatic illness as well. . . ."[111]

Weinberg writes, ". . . there is perhaps no more successful way of living than by carefully defining a value system, examining it from time to time, and upholding it. Among its numerous advantages, a code of ethics provides us with exemption from too great a dependence on other people's opinions of us. . . . Being stable would seem almost a requisite for mental health. . . . Whenever we undertake to change our personality, we must make ourselves unstable for a time. The disequilibrium we experience as anxiety."[176]

With these warnings soberly in mind, we must nevertheless prepare for change.

Some Effects of Longevity and Perspective

Some of the changes to be wrought by extended life and controlled personality are fairly easy to guess and to accept; let us tick off a few, both general and specific:

(1) Misbehavior due to weakness and stupidity will decline sharply, as we become less weak and stupid. Many affronts to society, and to oneself, are simple misjudgements or failure to take the long view. Crimes of impulse, rudeness, drug abuse, berserker syndromes, acts of desperation, short-end risks, naïve greed—all these should dwindle to a trickle when we are nearly all long-lived, informed, capable, and in control of our personalities.

(2) The Golden Rule should work much better for immortals than for humans, even as a mere tactic of expediency. Erich Fromm, although he seems to have fallen into the humanist trap about which we shall speak later, has written: "If the individual lived five hundred or one thousand years, this clash (between his interests and those of society) might not exist or at least might be considerably reduced. He then might live and harvest with joy what he sowed in sorrow; the suffering of one historical period which will bear fruit in the next one could bear fruit for him too."[56]

(3) Greater self-confidence and control of personality implies we should be less thin-skinned, leading, among other things, to more gracious giving and receiving. Aristotle considered it a mark of superiority to confer a kindness, and a mark of subordination to receive one; contem-

porary proverbs recount the resentment of the debtor for his benefactor; and today's militant minorities fiercely reject what is "given," prizing only what they can seize for themselves. All this touchiness is clearly neurotic and to be outgrown.

(4) Notions of dignity and honor, for the same reason, should become much more elastic in some respects. In Athens, a gentleman had to look and sound the part—sedate carriage, deep voice (!), measured speech, narrow norms of dress, etc. In certain circles of post-medieval Europe, a sidewise glance might be a deadly insult, to be avenged on the field of honor; the same thing is said to be true among some of today's motorcycle gangs. We are not likely to lose our need for formal courtesy, nor our sensitivity to insults—but our reactions should be under much better control, responding only to real threats, our egos being very hard to bruise.

(5) Tolerance of diversity, of individual idiosyncrasy and cultural pluralism, may increase while remaining responsible. (Much "tolerance" heretofore has just been a closing of the eyes and rejection of responsibility.) There is likely to be a strong tendency to live and let live, when psychopaths and neurotics are few.

(6) When we are immensely wealthy in material and inner resources, we should have greatly reduced need for outside help, encouragement, flattery, approval, or almost any kind of interaction; there may be many solitaries and a highly fragmented, loosely-knit society. This may lead, during a certain period of history, to a devaluation of some elements of morality. We may not exactly wash our hands of other people's troubles, nor refuse in all circumstances to be our brother's keeper, but may still tend to go our own ways, assuming the other fellow can take care of himself.

(7) Yet under some conditions there also exists the possibility of a much higher sense of community and greater *esprit de corps.* Paul T. Young has discussed morale in military forces, saying, "The impersonal threat of injury from the enemy, affecting all alike, produces such a high degree of cohesion throughout the unit that personal attachments become intensified."[185] Superhumans could de-

liberately create moral values analogous to this, with nature in the role fo the "impersonal threat", our broader perceptions and longer attention span allowing a lively and permanent sense of our beleagured position—a tiny speck of struggling consciousness, banded together against the cold and careless cosmos. This would not be a "brotherhood of man" in any syrupy sense, but a sober sense of duty born of practical necessity.

(8) There will almost certainly be a much higher price on human (or transhuman) life, for reasons obvious and otherwise. In certain kinds of industrial and construction work, costs may rise tremendously for a while because we will no longer tolerate the fatal accidents that always accompany current construction methods. We may accept great inconvenience in traffic for the sake of slightly greater safety. And a heightened sense of human dignity is almost certain to rule out prison or physical punishment for any purely financial or technical offense. (In current circumstances, however, talk of "human rights" vs. "property rights" can be very misleading.)

(9) Individual freedom may gradually come close to anarchy—and when freedom is abridged, the limits will be clearly recognized. (Is there anything more exasperating than the smug asseveration that service to God, or service to the state, is the "real freedom"? Submission may or may not be better than freedom, and one kind of freedom may or may not be consonant with another; but to say that submission *is* freedom is a mockery of language.) The freedom or "license" of one is not likely to be dangerous to others, because families should have ample resources to protect themselves against intrusion and their children against undesired conditioning. Freedom as a "moral" value is likely to be more exalted than it is now.

But now it is time to take a more systematic look at basic questions.

Classic Moral Philosophy

There are only two choices of basic moral guideline—to serve the whole self, or to serve society. (Erich Fromm's third criterion, that "revealed or postulated," is even less

146

distinct.) Writing in the context of humanity and mortality, the classic philosophers have leaned heavily toward society.

A few have taken a bold stance for self-interest, but the results, as in Epicureanism, have almost always been embarrassingly naive; the hog at the trough is no one's ideal. Nietzsche exalted pride over humility, but in the end nevertheless sacrificed the individual to a neurotic idealism. (He had some unusually forward-looking ideas, however, on the relation of biology and chemistry to temperament, speculating that the Asiatic outlook might derive from rice and the German from beer.) Spinoza purports to "prove," through logic, that self-preservation is man's primary motivation, but from this naive beginning he proceeds to the conclusion that supermen will free themselves from the individualism of the instincts and "desire nothing for themselves which they do not also desire for the rest of mankind."[160]

Most of the others came down heavily for the herd, often making explicit such principles as "The greatest good for the greatest number" or "Do as you would wish others to do." Immanuel Kant said, "We know . . . by vivid and immediate feelings, that we must avoid behavior which, if adopted by all men, would render social life impossible. . . . Morality is not properly the doctrine how we may make ourselves happy, but how we may make ourselves worthy of happiness." Plato said that morality is the effective harmony of the whole, that all moral conceptions revolve about the good of the whole. Thousands of years later John Dewey, the "modern," the "humanist," was still saying morality is in community—and acknowledging that in this community we seek a kind of immortality. The ecclesiastics offered essentially similar views, shored up by theology and tortured logic, culminating in the amazing St. Thomas Aquinas, who tamed logic to "prove" such propositions as the immortality of the soul and to investigate such questions as "whether one angel moves another angel's will."

There have been occasional oases in these deserts of thought, however—notably in William James, who emphasized pragmatism—"hanging loose"—and the value of the individual; he reminded us that the state is the trustee and servant of the interests of individuals, and promoted a philosophy that shall "offer the universe as an adventure rather than a scheme."[82] But these ideas must be elaborated considerably to be appreciated, both as to background and the new context.

The Natural History of Idealism

The idealist is about to become extinct, I believe, because the lies he lives by are no longer useful. The human race has always been psychotic, but now it is time to go sane and face reality. Being stripped of our delusions may be a little less painful if we are more clearly aware of their origins.

Until very recent times, dedication to a principle or cause was nearly essential both to society and the individual. Society required certain loyalties, even unto death, for military and disciplinary reasons; the individual needed just as much to commit himself, for a sense of worth and purpose in a world otherwise seemingly bare of both. (Our young, especially in changing times, have always been hollow with self-doubt, pathetically anxious for "identity" and eager to latch on to any apparent mooring; when old flags become too obviously threadbare, there is a desperate search for new ones.)

Among the lower animals the evolutionary necessity or value of certain types of behavior is obvious. The spider lays thousands of eggs, and some will mature without protection; in fact, about the same number would probably survive with or without parental protection. Hence parental devotion has no particular value to the species, and is unknown.

With birds, the case is different: the small number and early helplessness of the young means that parental devotion is indispensable for survival of the race. The mommy and daddy birds may or may not benefit from their protective feelings. If they could think about it, they would probably feel their attitude is "good" and "right," and would have only contempt for the selfish and uncaring spiders. (And the birds would have very reasonable explanations for their habit of forgetting the young beyond nestling age.)

Even higher orders of devotion are exhibited by some birds; in certain species, the individual who observes a fox may scream a warning to the flock, even though this draws attention to himself and reduces his chances to survive. His loyalty tends to improve the chances of the flock as a whole, including his own offspring; hence the trait is perpetuated. What avian odes might be warbled and screeched about the pluméd paladins of copse and cove!

Astronomer Fred Hoyle has remarked how the flower of civilization grows from a swamp. Imagine, if you can, the billions and trillions of lesser creatures, our subhuman predecessors, who lived in misery and died in agony that they might, bit by bit, blindly and unconsentingly, build to a higher species. The "shriek in the jungle," multiplied a trillionfold, reverberates down the bloody tunnels of time. Imagine the thousands of generations of our human ancestors who walked the tight-rope between cave and grave, maintaining always the necessary precarious balance between self-preservation and self-sacrifice. We can think of them with respect, and gratitude, but also with pity, and we can consider following a sharply divergent path—if our body chemistry will stand it. Of this, more later.

In the past, our actions had to pass several survival tests—for individuals, for families, for societies, for institutions. Those patterns of action, and hence those patterns of thought and feeling underlying the actions, tend to be perpetuated which favor survival and dissemination. Yet, it is apt to give us a very queer sensation to turn it around and reflect that, in effect, we were forced to think the way we do by a blind bookkeeper; many of our most important feelings and decisions arise not out of nobility, not even out of reason, but merely out of obedience to evolutionary laws of cause and effect.

Devotion to our children is a nearly universal trait among mankind. Yet rationalize it or idealize it how we will, it arose as an evolutionary adaptation; just so coldly unromantic is its basis. We are no better than the spiders, only perhaps unluckier in that the fewness and puniness of our offspring severely restrict our freedom of action. Are we better than the birds and bears, because these turn their children out when they can fend for themselves, and thereafter know them not? In fact, it is believed that in early human or prehuman societies the sons would kill the fathers, or the fathers drive out the sons, when the boys neared maturity; but the preservation of acquired wisdom, and the stability of clans, have survival value for the species able to deal in these complexities, and so our habits developed to a "higher" order. (Among royalty, however, the old habits frequently recurred.)

Why do we defend our homes and countries? Sometimes, of course, such defense is appropriate to preservation of self and family and property, and seems quite rational. But we may be just as vigorous in defense even when survival and well-being might seem better served by other actions; in particular, there might seem little logic in an individual accepting risk in a modern war—is not malingering often more reasonable? Clearly, a degree of idealism, of loyalty to causes and totems, has played a part in helping tribes survive and prevail; thus we are born with these loyalties, or the tendency to them, in blood and bone. (Many of our Vietniks were stayed from service, not by selfishness, but by a competing ideal.)

Robert Ardrey has written a whole book (*The Territorial Imperative*) on the thesis that man is a territorial animal, like many other species, and that he defends his stake instinctually—he just can't help it, and reason makes no difference.[3] Ardrey's ideas, although similar to some of Konrad Lorenz, have not been particularly well received by anthropologists, and the impulse to defend territory may not rest on a full-fledged biological compulsion, but on a biological predilection developed by culture. What does it matter? Whether it is narrowly the species preserving itself, or the society, or institution, is not the individual just as much a pawn?

Consider the soldier who falls on a hand grenade to save his comrades, or the mother who gives the last bit of bread to the children, or the priest who accepts celibacy for life, or (on another level?) the woman undressed in a burning building who perishes there rather than run

150

naked into the street. Are all of these serving noble and reasonable ends, or are some of them victims of poorly understood habits and social pressures misconstrued as ideals? Are they being sacrificed to a mindless machine— species, or state, or church, or culture—which has developed its own insensate but relentless techniques of survival?

Most of us will defend and admire the mother, and refuse to put her in the same category as the woman who feared embarrassment more than death. Americans will tend to respect and defend the priest—but Russians will think him deluded; and Americans will be inclined to rationalize the soldier's sacrifice only if he is an *American* or allied soldier, a gook being not a hero but a deluded fanatic.

One may ask, what does it matter the origin of our ideals, what does it matter the biological basis of our motivations? Are we not, in any event, stuck with them, and should we not, therefore, make the best and most of them? Whatever it was that made us men, are we not now committed to humanity?

The answer is negative: first, because our "humanity" consists of warring elements which cannot be reconciled; second, because times have changed, the old balances are out of kilter, and even the biological basis of our humanity will soon be a question of policy and deliberate change.

The Secular Religions

The flakiest forms of the traditional insanity—idealism—are seen in Eastern Communism and Western humanism, which are the principal secular religions. (A "religion" seems to be characterized mainly by *dedication* and *fellowship*, with a divinity and formal worship not essential.) These represent extremes of idealistic behavior which reveal the full degree of the aberration.

The Communist, and the humanist, may be thought "nobler" than the Christian or Moslem (*i.e.*, crazier) because they make their sacrifices without hope of personal reward in any afterlife; they labor, and if need be suffer, merely for the "holy joy of doing good" for the community, or for posterity. The very purity of this dedication reveals its absurdity.

They seldom ask *why* the state, or posterity, is so important. If they did, the only reasonable answers would be inadequate: the state has some importance because of its interaction with the individual and support of him; posterity has some importance because we are interested in the welfare of our grandchildren. But the Communist and humanist attach unquestioning and overriding importance to the state, or posterity, in their most extreme and sterile concepts, just for the mystic delusion of merging with the universal. An ideal of this kind represents a sanctuary, a haven from certain unpleasant thoughts and unwelcome responsibilities. It offers psychic safety, secure mooring, an apparently honorable place in some grand scheme.

In the context of modern dynamism and the new biology, the "noble sentiments" of the idealist become maudlin sentimentality. In the perspective of cultural and biological history, even the noblest sacrifice or grandest achievement is a drop in the tide, a snowflake in the storm, soon irrelevant and sooner forgotten. Institutions change and perish: will you lay down your life for a possible footnote in future histories, perhaps a derogatory one at that? The very genetic character of man will be transformed. Can you imagine that the supermen of the future (if you are not among them) will remember you clearly or gratefully, any more than we honor our simian and piscine predecessors? And even if they will, would that butter any parsnips?

These observations may be reminiscent of the tired views of cynics and hedonists, and it may seem that the answers of the traditional moralists apply. One such answer is that the cynic's argument, carried to its logical conclusion, strips life of all meaning and savor; that every loyalty becomes equally meaningless and arbitrary. Another answer, or perhaps a different form of the same answer, is that experience proves the sense of reverence is fundamental in man and requisite for mental health. But in fact, the new questions are not the same as the old questions, and the old answers have not retained their force, as I shall attempt gradually to show.

It will be helpful also to consider those sects with the full trappings of religion, including rituals and prayer. It has often been argued that such are essential for the full flowering of civilization; but it seems to me they lack any unique claim, and represent merely another example of idealism.

The social argument for church-sponsored morality has been summarized by Will Durant: "The Church believed that these natural or secular sources of morality could not suffice. . . . A moral code bitterly uncongenial to the flesh must bear the seal of a supernatural origin if it is to be obeyed . . . in the most secret moments and coverts of life."[41] Probably most ministers today maintain this belief, especially in the face of the challenges of "Godless Communism" and "decadent relativism."

But it is by no means clear that religious people in the United States are better behaved than irreligious ones—and if it were somehow found to be true, it would still be hard to separate cause from effect. Nor does it appear that standards of personal behavior are lower in atheistic countries; the Chinese, for example, seem just as decent as the Filipinos or Americans. In fact, one could make a case for the superiority of the Communist over the Christian, since the latter requires the carrot and stick of Heaven and Hell to make him behave. That the Communist so seldom cheats in favor of his own selfish interests is a tribute both to his character and his ideology; that the Christian so often sins, despite the dazzling promise and the blood-curdling threat, makes him all the more an object of contempt; or so a cynic might say. Furthermore, the cynic might add that the emphasis on faith rather than works for salvation tends to invite hypocrisy, the eyes raised to Heaven while the feet dance in filth.

Of course, such a cynic would be wrong—but why? One reason, paradoxically, is that the bulk of the faithful are not really all that Christian. They have frequent theological doubts, if they think about it at all; Heaven and Hell remain dim and distant; the actual, functional determinants of behavior are largely the same for them as for unbelievers, namely habit and social pressure, with an occasional flash of reason or impulse. As for those who have received the Christian vision in its full intensity (probably very few), they obviously are not just celestial bribe-takers; they are consumed by love of God (whatever they mean by that) and man (which is almost as unclear), and while they glory in their expected reward, they would serve just as wholeheartedly without it, or with a less explicit prize. After all, large numbers of Jews, and adherents of other religions as well, did and do travel what they conceive to be the high road for no reason other than to keep their feet out of the muck.

The main faults of the major denominations, it seems to me, are simply those they share with all ideals and utopias, which may be deceptive and baneful in several respects. First, they amputate abstractions from their roots in the individual and then invest the abstractions, rather than the individuals, with fundamental importance; put another way, they bloat the importance of a few (probably temporary) aspects of the individual's psyche at the expense of the rest, and even at the expense of his existence. Second, any vision of perfection or finality entertained by such lowly savages as we is nearly certain, in the perspective of history, to be a ridiculous and diminutive illusion. Third, the utopias have in practice been mostly of a dreary, negative character, concerned with nothing more imaginative than the elimination of sin or of what the Maoists would call "incorrect behavior." If we embrace these ideals we may remain lulled, and cozened, engrossed in our fumbling little games, even ascribing nobility and ultimate virtue to them, while all undiscovered the great world and limitless life are waiting.

The Quasi-Religions

There are many causes or ideals that rank lower than the formal religions and the major secular religions, but still have sufficient elements of dedication and fellowship to be characterized as quasi-religions; among these at present might be included, say the civil rights movement, the states' rights movement, feminism, and assorted varieties of nationalism. Since the taboos here are not quite as rigid, and since examples each with relatively few adherents can be found, we may be able to see more clearly the features of irrationality and counterproductivity. Today in America this is especially easy in connection with youth and the civil rights movement.

The saving grace of militant youth, according to the pundits, is its "idealism," which tends (they imply) to redeem and excuse obstructive and even destructive behavior, and which could be channelled into useful efforts. But it seems to me, once more, that idealism or quasi-religion—of the kind that creates martyrs—is basically insane and vicious, and that educators should aim not to harness it, but to eradicate it.

Certainly idealists have contributed much to the world, and when they do good we speak of "devotion" rather than "obsession." But a crusading Hitler or Torquemada would be seen from outside as at best a zealot, and more likely a fanatic. On the whole, idealists have probably done much more harm than good in the world, both to themselves and others, and the conditions of today and tomorrow particularly call for sober judgment and flexible attitudes, rather than ringing rhetoric and eternal principles.

Can an excess of virtue be a vice? Words are tricky, and differences are usually quantitative. There may not be much sky between "fanaticism" and "enthusiasm;" and one can, if he wishes, speak even of doubt and pragmatism as "ideals." (When we are supermen, our language will be more precise.) But the kind of idealism that creates martyrs is often easy to recognize, and its logic is as crooked as its effects are pernicious.

As an extreme example, consider the two young white men, Schwerner and Goodman, who were murdered in Mississippi while participating in a Negro civil rights campaign. Although those demonstrations were largely orderly and law-abiding, still the risk was substantial. Why were these young men willing to risk the supreme sacrifice?

Cruel as it may seem to say so, I think their motives were largely neurotic. Unsure of their own worth and purpose, they sought assurance and fulfillment through attachment to a Cause. The grandeur of the Cause, they probably felt, would lend dignity and value to their own lives—*irrespective of the outcome of their efforts.*

This is the insidious lure of any crusade: it is failure-proof. The valiant idealist need not win, and seldom even expects to prevail. Failure is easily excused, since (1) he is fighting an uphill battle against enormous forces of evil, and (2) victory for the Cause in the long run is assured, and he has made his contribution. Even to die is not to fail, but to become a martyr whose memory will inspire others, so that the fallen hero "lives on."

Does this mean that everyone who battles against odds for a principle is really copping out? Of course not. In the case of some—especially the leaders—there may be a shrewd assessment of opportunities, including personal benefit. (Most of the spokesmen for the oppressed do pretty well for themselves, in one coin or another.) Even for the humble spear-carrier, there may be an emotional history that absolutely demands this kind of commitment. But what may have been compelling for a Malcolm X is not impressive for a Schwerner or Goodman; they had better choices, under just slightly different conditions—and so do most of us.

Needless to say, the more obvious kind of cop-out is not restricted to racial minorities, nor to political liberals, but it *is* found most frequently among the young, who tend to value themselves too little and the world too much. There used to be a saying in Europe: "He who at twenty is not a Socialist has no heart, and he who at forty is still a Socialist has no brains." Traditionally, the young have had to learn, in the school of hard knocks, that providing for a family is both more important and more difficult than "saving the world."

A final word may be in order about the possible standing of cryonics itself as an "ideal;" I have been explicitly challenged on that score, and asked whether I would not sacrifice myself for this cause. The answer is no: I am interested only secondarily in saving my generation, and primarily in saving my own family and friends and myself, not necessarily in that order.

Even if we have succeeded in showing that the morality of community is empty and delusory, it does not necessarily follow that the morality of self-interest is valid, or even that the latter term has any proper meaning. We had better dot some *i*s and cross some *t*s.

We note that the doctrine of *enlightened self-interest* is well known, but seldom effectively applied or even made sufficiently explicit. As remarked elsewhere, *everyone* is *always* motivated by self-interest in the most direct sense; that is, we act as we do to please ourselves, or to please some aspect of ourselves (even if only to avoid a worse alternative). This is true even if unconsciously motivated behavior and of self-destructive behavior. Our errors lie in misjudging the effects of our actions, on the world and on ourselves, in comparison with the alternatives, and especially in failing to realize that our criteria of value change and can be changed.

There is nothing new, startling, or shocking in advocating selfishness, if it is viewed in this light. At the risk of some confusion, I can change the terminology and say the same thing with less offensiveness: obey your conscience, and train your conscience. The confusion here arises because "conscience" has come to have connotations of altruism, when really there is no such thing as altruism in any private sense; there are only various facets of one's personality, and more or less effective ways to satisfy their respective needs.

What some of these ways are, and how they may change, shall be touched upon presently, but there are immediate objections to be answered. For example, if every choice is properly only an exercise in mathematical decision theory, an attempt to maximize happiness, then does the word "morality" retain any meaning, beyond that of efficiency?

I think there are two useful and appropriate applications of the word "morality." First, one distinguishes between short- and long-term interests, between temptations and duties to oneself; morality lies in resisting the temptation to betray one's greater good. Second, one can continue to associate morality with intuitive ideas of "fairness," "justice," "right," and the other normative notions, while reminding ourselves that these are only working hypotheses subject to change. (And perhaps these normative ideas will include aesthetics, so that bad art or bad taste will be a form of immorality.)

There are also problems with our view of "idealism" and its origins. Does not life require convictons and enthusiasms, which could be called principles and ideals? And can these not have valid sources in our enlightened consciousness? Once more, the crucial questions are quantitative, situational, and personal. One will buy principles and ideals now and then, but his portfolio should be balanced, not over-invested in any one ideal; there should be substantial cash reserve and frequent review; and of course, the ideals in which he invests must be suited to himself, not to any other person, natural or corporate. "Idealist" can remain a respectable word only if its meaning is watered down and its connotations cleaned up. Moral ideals must not be associated with finality or perfection; they should be hypotheses subject to continuing reappraisal. With long life, this is feasible.

A Program for Reevaluation

The actual prescription for continuing moral reevaluation is not difficult to give in sufficiently broad terms. In reviewing or value system, we use three partly overlapping criteria: self-interest, internal consistency, and flexibility or allowance for growth. In contemplating a particular course of action three things need be considered: how it fits our current value system; how it may tend to change our values; and the respective weights of promise and risk—with an especially hard look at possibly irreversible changes.

In different words, once more: obey your conscience, and train your conscience. We want maximum growth, but a carefully controlled growth slow enough to keep one's emotional and moral identity reasonably stable and well structured at any given time. A sudden, hard blow might shatter the personality; but a steady push in the right direction may get us where we want to go, if we can figure out where that is.

More specifically, most of us probably need to reduce our institutional loyalties—a suggestion that will infuriate and confuse many.

Remember John F. Kennedy? "Ask not what your country can do for you; ask rather what you can do for your country." This solemn reversal of priorities is actually accepted, in varying degree, by allegedly sane people in a non-totalitarian country. What a cancerous overgrowth of the need for esteem and approval! The sane (selfish) person will always subordinate his country's interests to his own, or his family's, whenever there is a clearcut choice; but we must emphasize that, in practice, the feedbacks are complex and the choice seldom clear-cut.

We emphasize also that the recent deterioration of patriotism and national unity does *not* represent an anticipation of the recommendations outlined here. This deterioration does not represent valid efforts to improve value systems, but merely the substitution of different totems for the flag, or else a simple disintegration. There have been many periods in history when one set of false values decayed, to be replaced by another set equally fraudulent. Despite some superficial resemblances, immortalist morality has made only a tiny, nearly invisible beginning.

What about those too brittle, still too committed to "universals," to entertain the notion of "betraying" one's country? If he is capable of recognizing the validity of self-interest on an intellectual basis, then he may gradually bring his emotions and conditioning under control with an oblique approach, by first abjuring loyalty to less-important institutions, such as organized charity. For example, if he has been buying Care packages for an Asian country, he might quit, as a little light exercise in applied selfishness, softening up his conscience for remolding. But this suggestion, again, has important qualifications.

Force-feeding our sense of self-interest need not necessarily wait until we are superhuman, but the external and internal results of such meddling are hard to predict. For an amateur to attempt to adjust his own psyche is a little like trying to perform brain surgery on oneself with a mirror and a hacksaw. It is a *little* like that; yet nearly all of us desperately need to change, and I for one intend to keep whittling on my tumors.

Despite the repeated qualifications and disclaimers, some will still think we are advocating a simplistic, hoggish-type of selfishness, and that we are ready to forego all the warmth and support of human community and loyalties. Not so. Man—let alone superman—operates on several levels and can learn to shift gears rather easily. The woman who enjoys operating complex machinery can still also enjoy a simple stroll; the more sophisticated adult can on occasion delight in childish horseplay and atrocious puns; a cynical San Franciscan can watch a band of itinerant mercenaries and still take pride in "his" Giants when they win a game; and we all know how to bask in the reflected glory of distant relatives and remote ancestors, while quietly disassociating ourselves from their failures and crimes. So it goes; there is nothing wrong with a little doublethink, so long as everyone understands the game. When community serves, enjoy it; when it gets in the way, stomp on it. Just don't be *sneaky* about it, because then you will probably be disliked by everyone, including yourself.

To recapitulate and summarize, I envision the following protocol for a person of reasonably normal and stable personality. First, one makes his world-view as explicit as possible, and examines as carefully as he can the structure of his personality. In so doing, he will find certain elements of inconsistency or conflict; typically, he will discover himself the victim of institutional conditioning, with disproportionate emphasis on the altruistic and communal aspects of his conscience. (But some will find they have not given enough attention or respect to the traditional wisdom.) He will then—gingerly and gently, with frequent critical review—attempt to modify his emphases, or the shape of his conscience, probably in the direction of reduced altruism and a more carefully calculated self-interest.

Whether we can really climb this spiral staircase—

whether, in the long run, this growth-and-feedback process will prove viable in a community, or even in an individual—remains to be seen. The enormously hopeful factor, the gloriously novel element, lies in the prospect of immortality and transhumanity, which provides the elbow room and motivation which have never been present in all the ages of men, until now.

Priorities of Loyalties

To get down to cases, my examples so far having been few and well-hedged, just how should we allocate loyalties, and how far should they extend?

As a first approximation, loyalty attaches primarily to those people, principles, and institutions closest and most important to us. Crude and obscure as this rule may be, I think we can get some mileage out of it.

Casual application of this principle would seem to tell us that the people claiming our loyalties, in descending order of priority, are oneself, immediate relatives and close friends, more distant relatives and friends, fellow citizens, and finally foreigners; and our actions and feelings often do acknowledge this sequence—charity begins at home and all that. Most of us would and do go to much more trouble to save inconvenience for a friend than to save the life of a starving Pakistani; and I think this attitude is correct—it simply isn't feasible at this time, for most of us, to worry overmuch about those mountains of misery in distant places.

But intuition is by no means a reliable guide. A trivial and well-known example is that of the husband who berates his wife just because she has slightly embarrassed him, through some gaucherie, in front of a waiter or clerk or other stranger. Of course, he is not subordinating her to the *waiter*, but either (1) to his own vanity, or (2) to an unmanageable sense of propriety; but he can still redeem the situation and avoid recurrences by reminding himself that his wife is very close to the inmost circle. Similar remarks can be made about those (very many) who habitually are more polite and considerate to strangers than to their own families.

This crude rule of thumb—a kind of psychological inverse square law—has other easy applications as well, for those reasonably stable and self-confident. One does not ordinarily accept dares, play "chicken," or volunteer for hazardous duty. A young woman does not forego marriage to care for her invalid mother. Parents support their children against the community, and even against the law, if that appears truly in the children's best interests. When misbehavior and alienation reach a certain point, parents may disown their children.

Remember—we said the conclusions above would be drawn by someone who recognizes our priorities, and who is "reasonably stable and self-confident." Some parents would refuse, say, to help a son convicted of manslaughter to escape to South America; usually this would show, I think, that they were unduly under the influence of social conditioning. But this is not the only possible interpretation; perhaps social sanctions, rightly or wrongly, are near the core of the parents' personalities, and the son is estranged, so their refusal to help him is properly selfish and correctly calculated, at least for the short term.

Let no one be misled by hypothetical questions involving physical risk and emergency situations. Most of us would risk our lives to save someone near and dear in a crisis, and this is possibly correct and necessary for a long time to come, for self-respect and mutual esteem; but there are some very relevant things easily forgotten. For one thing, in the conditions of modern life, the question of physical self-sacrifice or even risk seldom arises. (Children sometimes agonize over hypothetical questions of this type: "If Mom, Dad, and Sister were drowning, whom would I save first?" "If I were a prisoner of the Viet Cong, would I let them cut off my testicles rather than give military information?" And so on.) In the hard practicalities of everyday life, there are indeed limits on the sacrifices we will make for those near us. Friendships are sometimes more cherished and valued than family relationships, even though there is no question of loyalty "unto death." Those who are cowardly or timid may still be capable of giving and receiving love. And those who imagine their near ones are indissolubly bound to them are living in a fool's paradise; have they never heard of divorce?

Superman will doubtless prize himself and his potential above everyone and everything else; but this does not mean he will be a cunning, slavering hyena, treacherous and cannibalistic, or that such a future will be cold or cruel or lonely. Our skins may grow in subjective value, but not to infinity, for obvious reasons; our courage, when we reach transhuman estate, can be expected to overtower current standards, but to serve the more fully self-conscious self, not quaint or grotesque totems.

At present, we typically give blind allegiance to various ideals—yet often the quality of our service is not high. The traditional American was a strong patriot, but he did not always treat his neighbors well. In the future we can expect coolly to limit our allegiances, but to imbue them with vastly more value, the casual friendship of a superman being warmer and more useful than the blood oath of a human. If everyone understands exactly how far a given loyalty extends, and does not expect more, there can be no betrayal.

Each of us must be capable of standing, in the end, alone, if need be. But such a grim necessity should be a far, far more remote contingency among us as supermen than it is today.

8

The Penultimate Trump

It's no disgrace to be poor, but it's no great honor, either.
—Tevye, *Fiddler on the Roof*

When the trumpet of medical science calls us frozen patients back to active life, we shall see great and splendid things—almost as great and splendid as the Christians among us expect after Gabriel's Last Trump. Yet there is a psychological problem, a certain ambivalence of potential immortals toward that world of the awakening. If it is pictured too much like the present, it isn't very attractive: "Once around is enough." If it is imagined too *different* from the present, that's bad too; we are weakened by hesitance, trepidation, and a sense of unreality. Hence we must build half-way houses in our imaginations—not simple-minded utopias, but down-to-earth visions of a near future in which "superhuman" will still have the accent on the *human*.

Predictions of the near future are in many ways the most difficult. Again, there is no attempt to be comprehensive or even completely consistent; these "predictions" are intended mostly as casual—although not irresponsible—looks at some of the possible avenues of change and new conditions of life. Most of these avenues require solid gold pavement, and the new conditions can exist only atop enormous mountains of money.

164

In Al Capp's comic strip, *Li'l Abner,* one of the more engaging institutions is the Billionaire's Club, which has a sign in front to warn the riff-raff: *Millionaires, Keep Out.* Well within the next century or two, if exponential growth continues, that sign will be discarded, and the club disbanded, because not even in the most dismal pockets of poverty—not even in Dogpatch—will there remain any such pitifully disadvantaged wretch as a millionaire. One reason for determining to extend our lives, then, is clear: we simply can't *afford* not to stick around.

At least, this would have seemed a reasonable expectation to almost everyone just a few years ago, since it embodies the traditional American outlook: bigger and better, faster and cheaper, onward and upward forever, excelsior! Many of us still have this outlook, but at the moment optimists have to be a little defensive. At any rate, we will concede that the possibility of unbounded economic progress is not self-evident.

The historical sources of increasing wealth are three. The first is the use of surplus wealth to create more capital goods; the growth of capital from savings is *compound interest.* The second is the discovery of better methods in economic tasks and the invention of labor-saving machinery, which we can typify as the use of *robots.* The third is the discovery of *new bounty in nature, e.g.,* virgin lands or outcroppings of native metal or a medicinally useful plant. Can we depend on these in the indefinite future? Do they have limitations? Can wealth increase without limit?

Even the sober limits posed by serious students for the near future offer considerable scope. Herman Kahn and Anthony Wiener estimate that for the Year 2,000—a scant three decades hence, when most people living will still be within their "natural" lifespans—the Gross National Produce per capita in the U.S. will be $10,160 (in 1964 dollars), compared with $3,557 in 1965.[87] They guess that the typical member of the "Postindustrial Society" might work 4 days per week, 39 weeks per year, with

13 weeks vacation per year in addition to 10 legal holidays. And this is only the beginning.

Of course, extrapolations can be dubious. We recall the statistician who noted that American girls were marrying ever younger, the average age declining by a year every four years, and who predicted that by 1999 the typical bride would be eleven years old. The economic growth curve will doubtless have some queasy squiggles in it, and maybe even dips, but material goods should, in the long run, increase without bound. Such wealth depends, after all, only on *matter, energy,* and *organization.*

Matter, including soil to walk upon, is in virtually inexhaustible supply even without leaving the Solar System; when necessary and desirable, we can anticipate manufacture of earth-like environments out of the other planets and planetoids, and perhaps one day out of the stars. Energy is no problem either: there is a vast store of fission (atomic) energy in the granite hills, and a still vaster supply of fusion energy in sea water, when we learn to extract it; beyond that, again, the stars can fuel us. And organization should fairly soon reach its climax in the form of self-reproducing, self-improving, thinking and actuating machines capable of turning out almost anything desired in jig time and in any required amounts. We expect not to find our djinni in a bottle, but to design and build him ourselves, and thereafter to let him continuously redesign and rebuild himself. The humblest citizen then (if any remain humble) would have wealth to glut a million sultans.

Such optimism may seem glib and airy, although to me it reflects the clear trend of history. This is not the place to defend it in detail, but it does seem prudent briefly to answer the doom-criers, especially the sectarian ecologians and conservationists.

Pollution of the Mind

Rapid growth in industry and population has brought serious problems, including depletion of certain resources, loss of some natural beauty, and the release of poisons into air and water. At the same time, changing habits and weakening institutions have undermined the personalities and confidence of many. But the backlash almost threatens to outdo the frontlash at the moment, with the ecology freaks (as they sometimes call themselves) and the wild-eyed conservationists often substituting evangelical zeal for rational inquiry and useful programs. They tend to regard every problem as a doomsday crisis, and every loss as irreversible; furthermore, some of them equate material gain with spiritual loss.

In April of 1970 I was scheduled to lead off a "teach-in" at Highland Park College as part of the national Earth Day rites. At our school the program was cancelled because of the annual spring riots, but I learned a good deal about the radical ecologists, one of whom suggested we might meet the following disasters before 1980: (1) the death of all the fish in the ocean; (2) the collapse of agriculture in the underdeveloped countries; (3) the near-extinction of bird life; (4) smog suddenly killing 200,000 Americans; (5) a permanent drought producing a desert in the midwest; (6) the reduction of American life-expectancy to forty nine years or less—all from pollution or disturbed ecology.[43]

I am convinced such threats are grossly exaggerated, and that almost all the trends decried by the eco-faddists are very much slower than alleged, or reversible, or both. After all, the eruption of Krakatoa caused more pollution in one day than world industry does in a year, and so probably do routine natural disasters such as forest fires. Lake Erie, loudly mourned as "dead," still has as many fish as ever, although it will cost a lot of money to restore the balance of species we desire.

Even where the eco-freaks regard their arguments as indisputable, they are not. "Extinct" species of wild-life, for example, are *not* lost forever; leading biologists expect that one day it will become possible to grow new animals from scraps of fossil tissue.[17] Talk of "spaceship Earth," with its hints of an eventual "steady state economy," is full of loopholes; many experts believe it will become feasible to expand beyond the earth, as well as into it.[42] (Yes, there are knotty problems meanwhile, and I hope to be forgiven if I don't have an answer for every one.)

The flavor of thought of some eco-crusaders can be

sampled in these fragments from *The Environmental Handbook*.[31] "Americans might be happier with fewer automobiles." "(We) had better learn how to live the Simpler Life." "The 'massive American housing shortage' is a myth." "Less emphasis on acquisition and material wealth as any measure of anything good." "Let man heal the hurt places, and revere whatever is still miraculously pristine." "Instead of being anthropocentric *you have to care equally about all earth creatures.*"

The emphasis was mine in the last quotation, although its absurdity scarcely needs emphasis. Fishes and flowers are fine, but whoever equates their welfare with that of people is a little confused; and a back-to-nature philosophy would simply bypass most of our present problems and altogether close out our future possibilities.

If someone chooses to live in the "natural" forest—or in the equally natural malaria swamp or alkali desert—it's a free country. But let him not pretend that this will feed the underprivileged, or educate them; and *especially* let him not imagine that anything other than an intensive industrial-technological civilization can provide modern medical care. Unless he is rich to begin with, his bucolic idyll will come to an abrupt end with the first serious illness in the family—unless he succeeds in throwing himself on the mercy of the welfare institutions of the city folk. And for the longer term, the outlook is even clearer: the immensely improved and complex medical technology needed to provide extended life demands great wealth, hence can *only* arise from an industrial base and habits of work and competition.

It is needless (I hope) to say that I am not defending every aspect of modern life; among other things, the motorboats that stink up our lakes disgust me. No more than anyone else is the cryonicist in favor of more smog or planetary paving; no less than anyone else do we enjoy quiet and open places. But one of our mottoes is *"first things first."* We do not delude ourselves. Immortality costs money: to make it as individuals, we must earn and save substantial amounts; to make it as a society, we must increase the GNP, and rapidly. The notion that we can enjoy the fruits of labor without first laboring is a pollution of the mind, and it is *this* pollution which is the greater threat.

Enough, for the moment, of the fretful present; let us take out our trusty rose-colored glasses, and look at a few facets of the relatively near future.

There is a striking relationship between "mere" wealth and gadgetry, on the one hand, and on the other, one of humanity's loftiest ideals—that of justice under law. Regretfully restricting attention to just two aspects of guilt and punishment, I shall demonstrate the possibility of enormous improvement in our current barbaric customs—improvements which, as far as I know, have not been proposed by others.

For a period, crime will remain a problem, and we must end the disgraceful prevalence of crime without punishment, and punishment without crime. A giant step in this direction will be the elimination of the guilty-innocent dichotomy, substituting instead a finding of *probability or percentage of guilt*.

In our present criminal practice there is a presumption of innocence, with conviction requiring proof "beyond a reasonable doubt." In civil cases, on the other hand, the finding is based on a "preponderance of evidence." The arithmetic in both cases is very grim indeed.

In criminal cases, let us assume that the probabilities of guilt of a suspect run smoothly between 50% and 100%. Let us also assume (grim laughter) that the judges and juries assay the evidence scientifically, and return convictions whenever the probability of guilt is greater than 95%. We then have the following situation:

10% of the suspects are convicted.
90% of the suspects are acquitted or dismissed.
75% of the suspects are (in fact) guilty.
72.5% of those released are guilty.
83% of the guilty are released.
2.5% of those convicted are innocent.

In civil cases, on the other hand, if the "preponderance of evidence" rule is interpreted to mean that a judgment is returned on a 75% probability, and if we assume, in those cases tried, a smooth distribution of probabilities from 50% to 100% in favor of the plaintiff, then we have:

75% of those complaining have cause.
75% of those defending are in the wrong.
50% of those complaining receive judgments.
50% of those defending have to pay.
87.5% of those receiving judgments have cause.
62.5% of losing plaintiffs were in the right.
25% of justified complaints cannot get into court.
12.5% of the judgments are unjust.
62.5% of absolved defendants should have paid.

Perhaps the most shocking injustice and danger here is that, in the criminal cases, 83% of the guilty are necessarily acquitted, and even so 1 out of 40 convicts is innocent. Remember, also, that this is the *ideal* situation, assuming probabilities accurately calculated, whereas in fact our antiquated, sloppy system mangles the probabilities and makes the real situation much worse than this. We often say, with naive pride, that we would rather free one hundred guilty than jail one innocent man; but with this setup, even idealized, out of every thousand accused we free over six hundred who are guilty *and* we jail two or three who are innocent.

Notice that there is no way out in the framework of the existing system. Even if we rationalize our procedures of evidence evaluation, even if we educate our juries and give them explicit instructions on the calculation of probabilities, even if we avail ourselves of the best computer services, we shall still reach the above situation as a ceiling or optimum; it is the *best* we can do on the basis of guilty-innocent, as long as there are doubtful cases. If we raise the required probability, say from 95% to 98%, this will cut down the number of innocent men convicted, but will increase still further the number of the guilty who are acquitted. If we reduce the level from 95% to 90%, we shall convict more of the guilty, but also many more of the innocent.

In the civil cases, the picture is in some respects even worse: counting those cases which do not get into court, one-eighth of penalized defendants are wrongfully punished and *more than two-thirds of the legitimate griev-ances are not redressed.* Is this not intolerable?

The remedy, as intimated, is to eliminate the dichoto-mies and make the disposition of the case reflect the prob-abilities. For example, an accused found to have a 50% probability of guilt in a robbery case should not be jailed—but neither should he go scot-free, since there is a substantial chance that he is a danger to society. Instead, he might be put under close probation, of a kind not yet economically feasible, *e.g.*, required to carry an electronic signal allowing his location to be monitored at all times. If the probability of guilt is 75%, he might in addition be re-quired to make restitution of part of the stolen money. There would also be indemnities payable by the state to the convict, if it later could be shown that the penalty was unjust or excessive. The exact determination of the appro-priate levels and penalties will occupy large numbers of sociologists continuously for a long time and will cost a great deal of money, but it seems almost self-evident to me that, if we are to become civilized, this is the direction we must take.

In what we now call civil cases, or generally in money disputes between private parties, similar reasoning would apply: if there is only a modest "preponderance of evi-dence," then the amount of the judgment would be corre-spondingly reduced. Even if the defendant is more likely right than wrong, he might be required to pay something, *e.g.*, if his probability or degree of error is 40%, he might pay somewhere between 20% and 40% of the maximum judgment. This would improve the over-all picture, reduce the likelihood of *severe* miscarriages of justice, and make everyone more circumspect. Possible abuses—nuisance suits, etc.—could be minimized in various ways, and there would doubtless be a cut-off point; perhaps the minimum accountability might be at the 25% level. The troubles created by the new approach should be of a better class than those eliminated.

Our second point concerns reforms in punishment, which should fit not only the crime but the entire situa-tion, including the families involved. Some of the vast im-provements foreseeable are available right now.

Suppose a crime, or a criminal, is so vicious or else so uncontrollable that even close supervision (with radio tracking) is not deemed sufficient protection for society: is there then any alternative to prison? Several possibilities suggest themselves. A confirmed, stubborn pickpocket might have a finger or two surgically paralyzed; a rapist might be given female hormones. These alternatives might be made optional with the convict himself to eliminate any accusation of cruelty; my guess is that many would prefer such a solution, and would benefit from it. If the procedure, besides being optional with the offender, were also reversible, there could scarcely be any objection.

(It is not asserted that such solutions would invariably work; we realize that the pickpocket might turn to another, equally offensive trade, and the rapist's personality might still seek cruel expressions, but these avenues should not be closed.)

Another possibility, once suspended animation is perfected, would be to us anabiotic preservation in the case of the most serious crimes and the most conclusive evidence. The convict could simply be stored until a later age when a wiser court, with more resources, could review the case. This would be cheaper than prison, and would offer society complete protection, while still leaving the offender the potentiality of a full and normal life some day.

A Public Trough for Every Hog

The vastly greater complexity of the machinery of justice, intimated above, provides also a clue to another important aspect of everyday life—the nature of our daily work. I think that in the interim period we are considering—when wealth and technology are enormously improved, but we are still essentially human—that most people, most of the time, will do work related to government or politics.

When automation becomes highly developed, very few people will be required for ordinary tasks of production and maintenance—what is now the chief economic business of the world—and all ordinary merchandise can be extremely cheap. Automobiles or their equivalents could be free in the same sense that drinking water is free today. Just as today you would give the most casual guest a drink of water, next century you may just as easily give him a Chevicopter if he needs one—and never think of expecting it back; municipal supply would routinely keep your garages full, presenting a small quarterly bill. We could likewise expect food to be free, in ordinary quantity and variety, as well as clothing (if we wear any), furniture (if we continue to make it, rather than grow it), and most other kinds of "merchandise." . . . . But now the confusion that exists in some minds about who will pay for all this must be cleared up: how everybody can be rich without doing honest work.

The kind of system hinted at here does not require revolution or communism; far from being un-American, it already exists in the United States today, and need only be carried to its logical conclusion. It is a system in which a small fraction of the people are responsible for the production, but almost everyone shares its fruits.

Consider the barber, who a few years ago in Spain, I was told, would cut your hair for five cents, or fifteen cents if he came to your house. In Detroit today the barber gets three dollars plus a tip, and *the difference* is *unearned*. The American barber produces not a whit more than the Spanish barber—but he demands, and receives, his share of our generally higher production, which is almost entirely due to our businessmen and engineers. And any good union man will tell you that you do not *work* for money: you *vote* for it and you *strike* for it. (Little sarcasm intended; within reason, this is just as it should be.) Our capitalist state has gone a long way toward realization of the communist ideal—from each according to his ability, to each according to his need.

In a very real and important sense, then, the barber (like most of us) is living on a kind of public dole to the extent of at least 90% of his income. Put more tactfully and fairly, we implicitly recognize a *basic dividend* to which citizens are entitled, merely for breathing. This will probably be formalized before long, possibly under the name of *negative income tax*, which has been much discussed. When automation makes most types of work superfluous, perhaps only big businesses and unusually wealthy people will pay positive income taxes, the average citizen living (luxuriously) on his negative income tax, supplemented by investments and the occasional sale of artistic work or personal services. But our souls may still yearn for work, and work there will be.

That we require work for our mental health is reasonably clear. Freud seemed to think so: "Laying stress upon the importance of work has a greater effect than any other technique of living in the direction of binding the individual more closely to reality."[55] Keynes also: "If the economic problem is solved, mankind will be deprived of its traditional purpose ... I think with dread of the readjustment of the habits and instincts of the ordinary man, bred into him for countless generations, which he may be asked to discard within a few decades."[91] There are some counter-examples and arguments, but perhaps most would agree that we need at least some serious, challenging, goal-directed activity if we are to avoid alienation, disorientation, and a generally sick spirit. This activity could be primarily bureaucratic and political.

Problems of legislation, administration, and adjudication are growing ever faster, and are unlikely to be met soon by technology alone. We can expect heavily increasing demands for service on juries, drain commissions, election boards, regulatory agencies, boards of arbitration, social service administrations, watch-dog committees, advisory panels, municipal councils, civic welfare agencies, lobbying associations, special interest caucuses, and so on. In these activities, the common man can make two vital contributions.

First, his run-of-the-mill skills can fill the gap, probably long extended in time, when there is a great deal of work too ill-structured for robots, yet well below the level of human expertise. Second, his native *suspicion* and *conservatism*, his well-founded distrust of the technocrats and professional politicians, will be desperately needed. He himself, John Doe, must review new policies; he, in person, must verify the books and bank accounts to keep the thievery in check; he must snoop the laboratories to verify what the scientists are up to. He must, in short, be the final custodian of the custodians.

This is a big order, but not impossible. To understand the broader features of policy, to review budgets, to verify accounts—these things require some intelligence and training, but as long as the experts are available as consultants, a professional level is not needed. To ferret out wrongs and peculations and perils—this demands mainly persistence and determination and a nose sensitive to rotten smells. To maintain structure, morale, and vigor in political parties—this needs primarily a sense of community and an instinct for survival.

The ordinary, no talent citizen, then (in the pre-superman period), is likely to be a government employee or amateur politician. The work may not be arduous, but for the conscientious it will always be challenging, continuing education being a must. And far from being a parasite on the big brains, the little man can continue to be the bastion of freedom, holding tyranny and anarchy at bay ... at the same time enjoying a grand life, some aspects of which are speculated on below.

Tissue Farming Foods & Fabrics

There has been much talk in recent years about farming the seas to feed our growing populations, and in particular about growing algae which can be processed for food. One hears of algae disguised as steak, hamburger, and other foods. Maybe so; but it seems more likely that *tissue culture* will largely replace animal husbandry, and perhaps much of plant farming as well. Instead of growing cattle, we will be able to grow steaks. Limited success in tissue and organ culture dates back several decades. Nearly everyone has heard of Carrel's chicken-heart culture, which grew chicken-heart meat for many years and had to be constantly trimmed. Fairly soon, we ought to know enough about control of development so that any part of an organism can be nurtured separately.

For meat culture there are at least two obvious advantages, economy and humaneness, and at least one less obvious, versatility. It is wasteful to grow a whole steer when

175

just a few select parts are preferred, and when the steer's activity while growing is sheer loss of food energy. It is also inhuman, and undermines our morale to treat other mammals so brutally, imposing a life of slavery ending in slaughter. At present, tissue culture is enormously more expensive than ordinary farmer's methods, but eventually growth of chicken muscles *in vitro* may be a bigger step forward in economy than the use of batteries over barnyard flocks. (The raising of poultry in "batteries," or ranks of tiny cages with automatically regulated feeding etc., was responsible for dramatically reduced prices; chicken, formerly a luxury, is now one of the cheapest of meats and poultry.)

Along with economy, the new versatility promises to be equally remarkable. Instead of having to breed a new variety of cattle to gain different or better meat or hides, one could merely adjust hormone and nutrition balances in the culture tanks to produce meat finer-grained or coarser, fatter or leaner, red or white; choice would be quick and cheap. Hides for leather could be designed thick or thin, stiff or supple, porous or impermeable, and of course with a full range of color options. And all this would be only merchandise, with no conscious entities born or dying: just grow a few more pounds of sirloin, slice it off, and package it.

Even more impressive savings might result from applying culture methods to such luxury items as mink pelts. To raise a mink for its skin is *very* roundabout and wasteful, minks being carnivores that demand expensive food. Growing the skins only, in culture, would allow furs of much greater variety as well as much lower price; we could develop every imaginable type and combination of hair and hide, for furs ranging from gossamer types fit for underdrawers to rainbow-hued and patterned sables and ermines. In fact, the individual customer, at no extra charge, can have his fur custom-made, his requirements being fed into the culture-computer which will set the growth parameters accordingly.

With plants the likelihood is not so clear, since the opportunities for economy are not so great; but even here, the versatility of tissue culture is so great that this may be the deciding factor. Being bound by the fixed heredity and development of a few standard plants is unsatisfactory, and we will probably insist on a system that permits the greatest flexibility in control and experimentation.

The Arthropods Among Us

Genetic engineering's most sensational impact will concern the modification of humans; but it will have other uses as well. Some of the "robots" that will serve us will need to be nanominiaturized or picominiaturized and this can perhaps be accomplished better organically than electronically.

If we can design sufficiently complex behavior patterns into microscopically small organisms, there are obvious and endless possibilities, some of the most important in the medical area. Perhaps we can carry guardian and scavenger organisms in the blood, superior to the leukocytes and other agents of our human heritage, that will efficiently hunt down and clean out a wide variety of hostile or damaging invaders. Possibly they can even be programmed to remove the scale from blood vessels and the fat deposits from those who tend to obesity. This remains to be seen. But it is known that very complex responses can be carried in beasties the size of small insects; hence the arthropoda may constitute the cheap labor of the future.

Consider the sweeping-scrubbing-dusting-waxing aspects of housekeeping. Possibly these could be delegated to an appropriately designed species of small bee. The bees would enjoy the work, just as they presumably enjoy nectar-gathering today. They would be less nuisance than machinery (provided bees don't bug you) for several reasons: they would require no supervision, would be subject to no breakdowns, and would be less obtrusive, patiently waiting for you to move your feet before attending to that spot.

The bees do not have to understand the work, of course; they only have to feel a desire to do it. Existing bees feel an urge to gather and store nectar; certain ants and termites feel the urge to gather grains of sand for their mounds. Our tidy bees would be content to seek out grains of dirt, in a certain range of size and composition, and

177

remove them to the disposal place. They need not work in a particularly orderly way, any more than modern bees in clover; but they would keep coming back, and scouring the territory until it became clean. Appropriate signals—whether odors or colors or radiations or what-not—could delimit the territory. Landing to rest could be permitted only in the hive, and there could always be a shift on duty; breeding would be regulated by an instinct to keep the hive at optimum population.

Economically, the savings would be impressive. (Yes, we billionaires probably will still be concerned with efficiency and thrift; didn't Lyndon Johnson keep turning out the lights?) Bees are self-repairing and self-reproducing. (Our machines will be too, but they are likely for a long time to remain great, clumsy things, with voracious appetites for rare metals and energy.) Bees demand only simple, cheap fare. The beautiful aspect of the symbiosis is this: we can gather or make food more efficiently than bees, but bees can gather small particles of dirt more efficiently than we, or even machinery.

Let us look at some numbers. What happens when a housewife vacuums 300 square feet of carpeting? It may consume a half-hour of her time, and between the pulling and pushing, shifting furniture, etc., 50 (kilo) calories of her food energy; worst of all, it probably bores her. The vacuum cleaner itself may consume 0.2 kilowatt hour of electrical energy; depreciates perhaps 3 cents worth, and tends to wear out the carpeting with all that dragging. If the vacuum cleaner becomes fully automated, then the housewife is saved effort and trouble, but the machine becomes even more expensive to buy, operate and repair, is bulkier to store, and more subject to breakdown; it may also impose stringent requirements on the design of the house, if it is to operate automatically, as long as robots are relatively stupid and cumbersome. And all this expenditure—the cost of the machine, the electrical energy, the repairs, the housewife's effort, the wear on the carpet—all this is merely to move perhaps an ounce of dirt from the carpet to the trash bin.

Tidy-bees will do better and cheaper work. The carpet will *always* be clean, not just periodically. A hive of bees can gather several pounds of nectar in a day, ranging up to a mile or more. Thus, if your estate includes clover or other flowers and perennial blooms—and whose will not?—then the bees can gather their own food, and do the cleaning chores in addition, just by making the colony a little larger than otherwise would be self-sustaining. (However, your staff of multi-purpose bees may be too large to be self-supporting in this respect, with added chores mentioned below.)

Admittedly, there are other solutions to the housekeeping problem of dirt. The building could be hermetically sealed, dust not permitted to enter; and already moderately successful dirt-repellent fabrics have been developed. But these are probably incomplete answers; we may prefer open windows and a more natural mode of life. Who wants to be a stranger to the outdoors? Who wants to live in a submarine?

The tidy-bees could keep the outdoors clean too, acting as gardeners, scavengers and vermin-hunters. They could cut and remove weeds, carry off certain kinds of debris and rout unwanted rodents and pestiferous bugs. In these chores they could, of course, be aided by genetically-engineered species of other classes and even phyla. Birds could be built whose principal pleasure in life is hunting mosquitoes and house-flies. This recourse would have many advantages over the increasing and increasingly dangerous use of poisons.

Certain possible difficulties suggest themselves, naturally. They are not ecological: our pest-killing birds will not depend on the pests for food, but only for sport or work, hence we need not tolerate any substantial pest population; there can be a very large ratio of predators to prey. But if the vermin-killing instinct is strong, and there are few vermin, will the birds become neurotic? Can they be psychologically stable? There are many affirmative answers to this; I leave it to the reader to supply some of his own.

Finally, let us note that the indoor tidy-bee could even be given chores of personal hygiene. Why should he not have sharp mandibles, a gentle touch, and shave you while you sleep? Trim your toenails? Remove your dandruff? His soporific buzzing will be better than a sleeping pill, and he will enjoy the chores you detest. To bee or not to bee; there is no question at all.

To convey adequate appreciation of our future lives seems, in most areas, nearly hopeless, because the changes beyond the very near future will be profound, awesome and bewilderingly complex. But if we look at sports, perhaps we can get some notion of the color, variety and sheer fun in store for us. In particular, let us toy with some of the implications of *reduced weight,* as found for example on the moon or (apparently) in the oceans.

Near the surface of the moon, a body's weight is only one-sixth that on earth; that sounds like fun, and astronauts Armstrong and Aldrin and their successors have already reported that indeed it is. (We saw them bouncing around on television, bundled and burdened though they were.) When we have colonies in natural or artificial caverns on the moon, we could have a wild variety of new games and modifications of old games.

Plain and fancy jumping might alone be fun for even a jaded spirit. High-jumping and pole-vaulting will be dreamlike experiences with slow-motion artistry. Probably we will run faster (leaning forward more), but how much faster seems uncertain. We will jump higher, but the new high-jump record will not be anywhere near 40 feet. (The high-jumper on earth, who clears a 6 foot bar, raises his center of gravity only about 3 feet, which means that, if he could get the same spring on the moon, he could clear about 21 feet.) The platform diver will be in the air roughly 2½ times as long as on earth, before hitting the water, thus having time for the most beautifully intricate convolutions. (Time of fall is inversely proportional to the square root of the gravitational acceleration.)

Tennis will require a whole new set of responses. Serves, of course, will start higher, since the server can jump higher. The ball will travel in flatter trajectories; it will rise and fall more slowly, while the horizontal motion remains unchanged. In volleyball, also, trajectories will be flattened; this does not mean the net will be much higher (which would merely produce a slow, boring game), but that the ball will seldom be hit upward to any degree, nearly always horizontally or downward. Billiards, on the other hand, will be affected scarcely at all.

Swimmers will go much faster. You will not float any higher in the water, since the water's weight is reduced as much as yours; but using swimming strokes to raise yourself partly out of the water will be much easier, and therefore swimming will be faster. It is even possible that, with a good deal of exertion, you could "walk on water," *i.e.*, tread water so energetically that you are immersed only to your knees or so.

Even more exhilarating than these games, however, will be a completely new one—flying. Not gliding, or parachuting, or powered flying, but using your own muscles to activate wings attached to your arms, like Icarus. (See also Chapter 4.) This is impossible on earth, because the muscular strength and the energy requirements are far beyond the ability of the strongest man; but with weight reduced by a factor of 6—with a 180 pound man weighing only 30 pounds—it should become feasible. (If necessary, the air in the flying cavern could also be made denser than one atmosphere, to make the flying easier.) What fun, and what a whole new world of sports in three dimensions! If professionals play these games, or zealous amateurs, they could be more dangerous than ice hockey, with damaged wings causing falls from dangerous heights. (And uninjured teammates will make daring power dives in rescue attempts, etc., etc.)

Back on earth, under the seas, there will likely be another new world of sports and adventure, again in three dimensions, predicated on radical new developments in underwater adaptation. Perhaps we will submit to biological modification that will permit us to use oxygen with extreme efficiency. We may learn actually to breathe seawater. Or we may just develop miniature gadgets that will protect us from the water and extract oxygen from it. In any case, the feeling would be one of naturalness and freedom. Diving to the murky depths, rising to the sparkling surface, roaming the forests of seaweed, exploring the canyons of coral, hunting the shark and the squid—here, alone, excitement enough for an ordinary lifetime!

Relative to our billionaire status, meat will be cheap. Even *human* meat will be cheap. (Yes, there will probably be "cannibals;" some will try, and like, human flesh grown in culture; but this isn't what I am getting at.) Not only tissues, but organs and even whole bodies will be reasonably priced as replacement parts. (The brain, of course, cannot be entirely replaced without creating a new person.) This opens up interesting possibilities in aggressive sports.

So long as the brain is protected, one could indulge in occupations, including sports, of any degree of roughness, including "fatal" injury. Karate could become a spectator sport—real karate, not throws but blows, intended to kill or maim quickly. The death suffered by the loser would not be as permanent as it would be now, but it would be just as painful.

Will some of us actually accept risk of dreadfully painful injury, even the physical experience of "death?" Certainly—for kicks. Fairly large numbers of people might be involved, not just a few masochists and sadists. The reason is obvious: many of us need the kind of stimulation and catharsis to be found in fierce physical combat. At least occasionally (especially when life is long and safe) we may need to "get back to nature," to test our muscles and reflexes and nerves, to rejoin contact with the hunter, the warrior, the beast of prey.

One can only speculate as to the degree of indulgence in mortal combat, and the social institutions that could grow up in connection with it. As already indicated, it would partly be involved with spectator sport—and the champions may become trillionaires. Again, there may be whole subcultures centered around combat, as there are now around drag racing and surfing. And it may even permeate ordinary society in the form of a duelling code.

Many years ago Robert Heinlein wrote a novel about a future society, *Beyond This Horizon*.[73] He postulated a duelling code for two reasons: to enforce good manners and to breed people with faster reflexes. The latter notion seems silly in terms of cost and alternatives, but there is something rather charming about the former idea. The idea has many obstacles and defects, but it has flourished in the past in various places, and persists to this day to some extent. (There are many places where public rudeness invites a rap in the mouth.)

It should not be thought that, just because permanent death is not allowed, combat will lose its challenge. It will take real courage to fight to the "death." After all, ordinary fist-fighting involves scarcely any risk—one seldom suffers anything worse than a black eye or a broken nose—and yet most people are rather timid about fisticuffs. Saber-duelling, as at the German universities, risks only some superficial cuts on the cheek, and yet many lack the nerve to engage in it. When it comes to having your arms broken, or your testicles crushed, or your eyes gouged out—well, the polo-playing millionaires of today will seem like small potatoes.

Wall-to-Wall Grass & Homes Without Houses

The word *cybernetics*, coined by the late Professor Norbert Wiener, refers to communication and control, and especially feedback, in mechanical systems—organization of a type which frequently mimics aspects of living organisms. But it will also often be useful for life to imitate art, for living organisms to be designed that copy certain features of mechanical systems or that are subject to mechanical controls. Certainly biological machines can be extremely flexible, and can utilize a degree of miniaturization not yet even approachable in any other way.

One of the obviously desirable features of many utilitarian devices is the capacity for self-repair, which is typical of living things. Your carpet, for example, will never wear out if it is a surface of living grass; it could be designed to grow just fast enough to compensate for wear, and only in those places where wear occurs. As for luxury, is there any carpeting of wool or silk or synthetic fiber that can compare with a lawn of bent grass?

Your indoor lawn, your living carpet, might also have features of flexibility and adaptability not to be found in the products of Persia. For example, each blade of grass could be given a different color, changeable at will, which means the pattern could be altered as frequently as you wished. At one stage in history, designing patterns for grass-carpets (and for clothes, furniture, walls, etc.) will become too complex for the home computer, but will be individually available, at a moderate fee, from a commercial computer. For a small monthly charge, your commercial designer could send periodic instructions to your home computer, which in turn would implement the new carpet art. Each day, if you wished, you would be pleasantly surprised at the change in decor.

This decor could be chosen to carry further the garden theme consonant with the carpet of grass. Living, growing flowers could be permanent indoor features, again with characteristics of extreme flexibility. You could sleep, if you liked, in a bower of roses; you could awaken, if you wished, to the smell of mint, and go to sleep, if you liked, to the scent of honeysuckle. Making the necessary radiant energy available for the growth of these neoplants, and the required nutrients, would be a matter of detail that would certainly offer no serious obstacle.

With grass and flowers all around, the indoors would seem a good deal like the outdoors. We can go even further, in view of our coming control over weather: we could leave off the roof, and *be* outdoors, snug in our own pocket of metered and controlled micro-weather. We could allow rain to fall just beyond the rooms, and lull us to sleep. If we have enough room or gadgets for privacy, we could even forget about walls, and give our living areas an outward look of open gardens. Compared with this, the flossiest of present mansions will seem no better than a stinking cave.

The House Dutiful*

Ways will probably be found to make the micro-environment extremely sensitive and responsive to us; the

---

*This term is due, I believe, to William Tenn.

home, in particular, will be a wonder of care and solicitude on many levels.

In the present primitive state of affairs, although the best homes have some degree of flexibility, active and conscious control is almost universally required. Occasionally a door has sense enough to move aside when someone approaches; virtually all other functions demand either individual control or adjustment of automatic parameters. Room air is sometimes controlled by thermostats and humidistats, for example, but these stupid gadgets maintain the same temperature and humidity regardless of your changed feelings or inclinations, and you must actually make a decision, walk over and reset the control if you want a variation. There exists a type of glass that darkens when the sunlight on it is brighter, so that roughly the same intensity of light is transmited at all times; but the idiotic glass pays no attention to whether your eyes are open or closed, let alone to what you are thinking or feeling. How barbaric!

The future run-of-the-mill billionaire's home, and the computer at its core, could have capabilities several orders of magnitude higher, and a built-in sense of mission. The effect would combine elements of a super-efficient staff of servants, a faithful dog, a Jeeves, a maiden aunt, a genii, a physician, a bodyguard and a psychiatrist. It would react not only to what you and others do, but to what is said, thought and felt; and it would not only take orders, but would make suggestions and take initiatives.

Beds and chairs, for example, could contain sensors for reading your physiological variables and referring these to the computer for diagnosis. (There already exist diagnostic machines and diagnostic computer programs.) Depending on its estimate of the kind and degree of dangers, the house might make suggestions, slip something in your drink or in your air, refuse to give you another drink unless you actuate the override, or call for help. Speculative writers have sometimes imagined homes that could also go berserk, make love, and so forth; but I shall ignore such possibilities.)

Adjustment of such factors as temperature, humidity, electrical charges in the air, sub-threshold or super-threshold background noises, would be made through responses to make subtle signals. The super-home could easily sense the amount of perspiration on your skin, for example— in fact, the *pattern* of perspiration on your body—and would correspondingly adjust the composition of the air in various places and the design of the room's breezes. But it could also pay careful attention to the pattern of your behavior, reading carefully all the small clues in your shifts and twitches, to deduce the existence and nature of any discomforts or desires. Furthermore, it would hear your subvocalizations and monitor your brain waves, which would make it very nearly, if not fully, a mind reader.

Such ideas may seem decadent and repulsive to some. Do we really want to be cradled and massaged, pampered, and coddled? Do we want to be hovered over by a simpering servant? Is not life more than lying on perfumed couches, waiting for the peeled grapes to drop into our mouths?

Certainly there are individuals, and there have been whole cultures, having the belief that vigor and virtue demand a rugged way of life, or at least a simple and frugal way of life. It is also true that ease can lead to sloth, and sloth to disaster; but this is not *necessarily* true. We would not improve ourselves by exchanging our mattresses for beds of nails, and it is unlikely that the Japanese owe any part of their success to wooden pillows. On the contrary, ease and comfort at the appropriate time almost certainly tend to increase general efficiency and the capacity, again at the appropriate time, to work hard and fight hard.

We must remember that the super-home would not be just a "house," and the central computer would not have the attitude of a Madam pandering only to sensual desires. It could have whatever attitudes you and your advisers build into it, and it would look out for your larger interests. So long as you permit, it could give you an argument when your welfare seems to demand it, and take over some of the wifely functions of prodding and nagging; to a considerable extent, it would be a kind of prosthesis not only for your hands and brain, but for your conscience. How far it can go in these directions, and how effective it can be, will naturally depend on the rate of development of artificial brains; as in all else, there will be constant change and improvement.

The Era of Self-Sufficiency

The greatest of all inventions, in many respects, will be the self-improving (and, if desired, self-reproducing) robot, the machine with no fixed limits to its intelligence or to its physical capabilities. A source of potentially limitless power and improvement, it will pose profound problems of several different classes, only one of which is now considered here, viz., that of the self-sufficient individual or family.

Automation and robotics will reach their culmination in the all-purpose thinking and actuating machine, which will supply its owner with endless merchandise, advice and services. (The merchandise, whether ermines, artificial hearts or spaceships, could be made from any materials at hand, even plain air, soil, and water; the advice might take such forms as improvement in the owner's mentality and the services could include the surgery that might be necessary to implement that improvement.) One of the results, clearly, would be the emancipation of the individual (or family) from dependence on society, at least for most purposes. How far will this independence extend, and will it be good or bad?

(I bypass the question, considered elsewhere, of why the machine should remain subservient to its owner, remarking only that one possible solution is for the machine, or certain aspects of it, to be an extension of the owner, integrated with his mind through suitable links).

Individuals, couples, families, or communities of any size will probably be able to isolate themselves—by distance, physical barriers, or simply by rules—and go their own way, and there is much good in this; it provides nearly the ultimate in freedom and diversity and eliminates many sources of conflict. (You are unlikely to quarrel with someone if your paths do not cross, although the American Indians did seek each other out, on a nearly empty continent, to make war.)

One can build an idyllic picture of countless free spirits, each the owner of wealth to glut a million sultans, each a master of a genii of bottomless resources, each the king of his castle and the ruler of his realm, yet each a gypsy, not rooted in any turf, whose star-wagon can carry him over the gulfs of space as across the chasms of the mind.

Answers—of a sort—are to be found for every objection. Does a king require subjects? Not necessarily, for his mastery can include his own psychology, and he may excise, by psychological or even physical means, any unhealthy leanings; or, alternatively, he could create suitable robot subjects, with desired responses, possibly even including intelligence, but without genuine feelings. (There will probably be both kinds of automata—those with self-awareness, which would be "people," and those without.) Or a family, or small community, might for a time find a stable set of relationships which would harmlessly allow a pecking order; when the order begins to chafe, those who are uncomfortable, presumably would be allowed to have their own general-purpose robots built, and strike out for themselves. Anyone who insists on his prerogatives as the head of the family or community can always raise another family—and even design the desired traits—although it is difficult to imagine a personality that would require that kind of satisfaction indefinitely.

Is there a danger to the larger human community in allowing such freedom to individuals? Might not some instruct their machines to concentrate on growth and weapons development, with a view to conquest? Does not the welfare of children—and even of all citizens—require some degree of government and paternalism? And would not such splinter-isolationism border on chaos, with even newsgathering reduced to haphazard gossip and progress to a random walk?

Such questions cannot yet be answered with any degree of confidence, because the answers depend sensitively on parameters still unknown, on the historical development of culture and human biology. My own thinking—wishful, as usual—is that sense, prudence, and empathy will prevail, and that we will indeed be able to combine nearly complete freedom with a suitable degree of cooperation and intercourse. Such a culture would represent very nearly the ultimate our minds can presently conceive in any detail; beyond this, the outlines of destiny will depend on discoveries and concepts still in the future.

9

Tuesday in Eternity

What do you do in Heaven on Monday morning?
What do you do on Tuesday afternoon?
—Rabbi Sherwin Wine
Birmingham, Michigan

While short-range, mundane speculations are both pleasant and important, certain *whithers* and *whys* of our Long View remain to be clarified, and if possible to be reconciled with religious philosophy.

Since I have no religious beliefs or training, it may seem insincere or presumptuous to offer theological opinions and religious advice. Yet I intend to do so, in appropriate places, for reasons which should become obvious if they are not already, and which I hope will be acceptable.

The Cryogenized Christian and the Gelid Jew

Since Christianity and Judaism are life-affirming religions, it is not surprising that initial clerical reaction to cryonics has on the whole been friendly. For example, when Professor James Bedford, a cancer victim, was frozen in 1967 and stored at first in Phoenix (symbolism coincidental!), several clergymen in that city were interviewed by Marie H. Walling, religion editor of the *Arizona Republic*. According to the Associated Press, ". . . most of the theologians were generally in favor of the experiment."

The Reverend Howard McBain, minister of the First Baptist Church, said, "If he were later revived, I would regard it as one of the many miracles God works through medical science." (There was also some understandable skepticism: another Baptist, the Reverend Wesley Darby, said, "I have never had a funeral that failed.") Catholics and Jews have expressed even fewer reservations than Protestant clergymen; as remarked elsewhere, on at least one occasion a cryocapsule was actually consecrated by a Roman Catholic priest, with the approval of the bishop.[32]

To be sure, this climate may change when the cryonics movement becomes larger and its deeper aims more apparent. When clergymen begin to comprehend that we are seeking to shed not only our mortality, but also our humanity, they are likely to become much more uneasy. Superman may not threaten God, but he does threaten the church, primarily by questioning its relevance. The main weakness of the churches—beyond the philosophical level of the grade school—is not that they fail to make Heaven and Hell understandable, but that they fail to make sense of the world.

Although "relevance" is a popular topic these days in church circles, for the most part only its trivial aspects are discussed, e.g., whether ministers should become involved in politics or race relations. Such questions show only the penumbra of the deepening shadow over modern theology, especially Christian theology. The umbra, the core question, concerns the ultimate worldly mission of man and of men.

What is the goal of the human race. What is the duty of the individual? What is the purpose of life? What is Christianity for? The more naive Christians, taking a narrow view, consider the answers pat: humanity's goal is to achieve Christ's kingdom; a man's duty is to lead a devout and respectable life; earth is the testing place of souls: Christianity is called to save souls. More highly educated, thoughtful Christians are less assured. But there remains a pervasive reluctance to ask the hard questions or to face the hard answers.

Specifically, the churches have concerned themselves almost exclusively with short-term, negative goals. They want only to eradicate sin, not to fabricate greatness; they perceive good principally as the absence of evil. They focus on transient social problems—poverty, war, bigotry, and so on. They seldom ask: After the Global Great Society—what? Will the only remaining significant task be the conversion of unbelievers? And would success in this task signal the end of history?

It is obvious that there is more to life than most Christians recognize. We need merely ask: What does the "folk Christian" do after his soul and his own community have achieved peace? (After all, many believe they have come to terms with God, and many small communities are reasonably serene.) Do you play canasta until death and reward? Are your further activities no more than hobbies? Does the secular world consist only of tinker toys? Or are there other roads and different horizons apart from traditional religion? In short, is Christianity (as narrowly conceived) all that is really important in life, or is it only a part?

In slightly different terms: Is it enough to "lead a Christian life?" Would a collection, say, of Amish communities constitute a Christian utopia? Can we settle for peace, faith, and virtue, and forego the stars? Can we rest content to be good men and relinquish or subordinate the drive to become supermen?

My own belief is that we cannot. Is it conceivable that God created the awesome galaxies just for scenery? Were our cunning brains, clever hands and restless glands designed to no purpose beyond the plow and altar? Can homo sapiens be the realized image of God? No and no, assuredly not.

The Paradoxes of Radical Theology

The obvious weaknesses in traditional Christianity, some of them recited above, have always tormented theologians, and lately have forced some into paths nearly parallel to the cryonicist's. The radicals include the "Christian atheists" and death-of-God theologians, although some of their ideas have already passed the zenith of fashionability and appear inadequate in any case.

Several years ago, William Hamilton and Thomas Altizer were making waves as leaders of the "death-of-God" movement, and if the waves have subsided it is not so much because they shocked the traditionalists as because they have simply run out of steam. How quaint it seems already to read Professor Hamilton's statement, "One of the most pressing intellectual responsibilities of the Negro student and minister today is that of working out some of the ethical and theological clues that the Negro revolution is teaching him and us all."[67] How easy it is to sympathize with the condescending recent dismissals of "mood theology!" Surely the meaning of religion cannot shift with every political breeze! And yet, there does seem to be something authentic in "Christian atheism."

On the Christian side—distinguishing them from ordinary atheists or agnostics—is a will to cling to Jesus, to Christology as distinct from religion and God, and also a residual longing or hope or faith that somehow, some day, God will reveal himself and "live" again; it seems almost a mysticism devoid of content, little more than a wistful ache. Yet these nearly inchoate yearnings are not altogether without force or direction.

In fact, they tend to provide psychic fuel and compass (however wobbly) for the "atheistic" or humanistic aspect of the movement, which is a commitment to the world and a groping forward, a search for growth and meaning in the here-and-now. In some respects this is closer to the cryonicist feeling than is humanism, because it contains a vaulting aspiration that the plodding humanists seem often to lack.

Other modern theologians, more "respectable" than the death-of-God people, are hardly less radical—Niebuhr, Karl Barth, Rudolf Bultmann, Dietrich Bonhoeffer, and the German expatriate Paul Tillich. If the average parishioner or "folk Christian" does not revile Tillich, it is only because he does not read or does not understand him. Tillich retains use of the Gospel and of Christian mythology and symbolism—but he rejects literalistic interpretations of the biblical witness, he rejects any distinction between the sacred and the profane, and he rejects the notion of "eternal law" in favor of situational or evolutionary ethics.[169] For Tillich, there seems to be only one world—this world—and religion boils down to a sense of "ultimate concern;" again, aside from labels and phrases, radical Christianity seems to come very close to humanism.

The difference is that the radical Christian, while sometimes vaguer and more muddled, is also gutsier, more vital; he is charged with a higher voltage, and shares with the cryonicist—or with other cryonicists—a vision of something higher, something qualitatively different. If I had to choose one or the other as companion or colleague, I should much prefer the radical Christian over the humanist. The latter, limp and pallid of spirit, typically pays lip service only to radical change, and has sold out cheap: settled for humanity, with minor improvements. The Christian, while perhaps nearly indistinguishable in his actions, is always goaded onward by the inner conviction that somewhere there is meaning, sometime there will be greatness, somehow man can find the means to transcend himself.

But the road of cryonics is wide, and it is our hope that humanists, almost every stripe of Christian, and indeed nearly every mother's son can walk it with us. There will be quarrels along the way; it remains to be seen how much conflict, in practice, will result from the philosophical clash between Christian morality and the ethics of self-interest. The important thing is that our initial goals lie in the same general direction, which is pointed out below.

The Purpose of Life

At last one of the central questions can be dealt with: What is the purpose of life? Answer: To discover the purpose of life. This is not a play on words, but a recognition of the obvious truth that since ultimate answers are not within view we must make do, for the foreseeable future, with uncovering and pursuing a succession of intermediate goals, and that this requires a program of growth and development.

The universe is vast and mysterious, its qualities and values hidden either in distance, smallness, complexity, subtlety, darkness or dazzlings that bewilder eye and mind. To attempt to fathom its depths in the manner of the traditional philosopher is a task which may be likened to that of a dog trying to build a bridge over the Mississippi. To begin with, he needs tools; working only with jaws and paws, he finds the job hopeless. But even if he had the tools and could handle them, he would not live long enough to make a dent in the task. And even if he had greatly extended life or the help of many others, he could neither handle the tools nor organize the work. In short, he must fail simply because bridging the Mississippi is not a job for a dog.

Just so with the philosopher. To begin with, one cannot unriddle the world simply by reasoning it out, as the Greeks thought; one has to go out into the world and tinker with it; one needs tools—microscopes and telescopes and oscilloscopes and spectroscopes and much, much more that we have yet to imagine. Nor is it other than arbitrary and unreasonable to suppose that an ordinary lifetime could suffice for the work; much more likely, millenia of effort by the entire race will be required. Finally, it seems also arbitrary and unreasonable to imagine that merely human intelligence can operate at the required levels; instead, we shall probably have to improve the very physical structure of our brains before we can expect to make important progress. We must, in fine, become immortal supermen—not to gloat over our accomplishments and strut among the stars, but simply to do our work, the only work there is.

Super-Christian

Such perspectives are unsettling even to sophisticated theologians, many feeling that Christianity is put on the defensive or elbowed rudely aside. Their forebodings may to some extent be justified, especially if religious leaders take a reactionary stance. Yet it seems to me, although I am not a theologian or a Christian, that there are many intimations in Scripture and tradition that would allow embracing the larger view.

For example, most churches have accommodated themselves to Darwin's theory of evolution. Dr. E. C. Messenger has written, "... many think there is good reason to suppose that the 'dust of the earth' of the Scriptural text need not and should not be taken to signify that the immediate source of the first human body was in fact inanimate matter. They see no reason why, on the contrary, the first human body may not have been fashioned by God from some animal organism, and this hypothesis has now been officially recognized by the supreme authority in the Catholic Church as open to discussion."[121]

There is every reason to think the churches can also accommodate themselves to the idea of *future* evolution, natural or "artificial." In fact, it seems to me, they must, since it were surely blasphemous to assert that present-day man is made "in the image of God," whether that "image" be taken as physical or spiritual. We obviously have a long way to go; man is still being created; he must *develop* into the image of God. And did not Jesus say, "Greater things than I have done, shall ye do"?

For those committed to Scripture, yet prepared to interpret it liberally, there are also many other possibilities. The teaching of "resurrection of the body," and eternal life for the resurrected, need not conflict with cryonics. Perhaps our medical revival *is* the promised resurrection, at least for some, and Heaven is not a different realm, but *this* world after we have improved it and ourselves. Somewhat similar doctrines, mundane interpretations of *Revelations,* have already been espoused by the Jehovah's Witnesses and others.

Such ideas have been entertained, at least tentatively, by some clergymen of the major denominations; and some have preached or written in favor of cryonics.[126] Perhaps the most vigorous "Christian immortalist," however, seems to be A. Stuart Otto, a maverick who has written a book, *How to Conquer Physical Death,* and publishes *The Immortality Newsletter.*[134] The book seems to reflect Christian Science as well as cryonics influence, and to contain major errors; but it also shows remarkable insights and interesting biblical interpretations. Mr. Otto advocates a double-barreled attack on death, spiritual and physical, and stoutly maintains that "Death is not a friend but an enemy and must be overcome . . . Jesus made no mention of resurrection after death as having any part in the new birth. The new birth is a change that comes here and now . . . 'The world to come' (mentioned in Mark 10:30 and Hebrews 2:5) is the world of tomorrow—*this* world as it is to be."

There are still many who worry about the sin of pride and about the futility of dreams of heaven on earth. But most of us who intend to go forward do not dream of any simplistic heaven on earth; indeed, we explicitly recognize that mere material comfort, even universal peace and good will, constitute only a starting point, not by any means a final goal. We go forward into the unknown because there is nowhere else to go. Is the past so beautiful that we should dust it off and wear it? Is the present so precious that we should preserve it in amber? Shall we walk with downcast eyes in circular ruts? For us this is not possible—and some of us are Christians.

We aspire to be supermen not necessarily because we are vain and arrogant; rather, our dissatisfaction with present endowments and attainments reflects a realistic humility—we are painfully aware of our shortcomings. The Christians among us are not rebelling against God nor aspiring to equality with him (if such a thing were conceivable); they seek rather to become his more effective tools, his worthier stewards. Neither do we seek endless change just for the sake of change; we pursue intermediate goals on what we hope will be an ascending road, a road perhaps some day leading to the Celestial City—wherever and whatever that may be.

Does not Christianity need supermen? Can any *but* a superman be a complete Christian? Can the highest spiritual merit be built on less than an adequate intellectual substrate? We have got to grow, and growth requires more than formulas or incantations; it requires changes in the biological structure, changes which in all probability those of our generation will not experience except after freezing, storage, and revival.

If one construes biological engineering as a threat to the churches or to the peace of mind of individuals, he must be careful not to misdirect his resentment. The threat comes not from any person, or even properly from any school of thought, but from the world itself, which is to say from unresolved contradictions in the threatened churches and philosophies. At one time Moslem conservatives held that the Koran contained all wisdom and that to read or write another book was blasphemous; this ostrich attitude succumbed not to the malicious attacks of unbelievers but to the incontrovertible facts of life. Likewise, religion today must regard the biological revolution not as a threat, or even an annoyance, but as an integral and extremely important part of God's gift and continuing revelation—mind-wrenching though such a change of view may be for some.

The Long View vs. Alienation

Superman and the Long View are needed, among other things, to cure the alienation so celebrated in current American and Christian life—the malaise that afflicts even affluent segments of our society and our younger generations, the lack of adequate feelings of identity and destiny. This disease is not restricted to unbelievers or backsliders; many pastors are close to panic in their failure fully to reach their people, in their inability to make religion satisfying.

The issue is obscured by the fact that the alienated often turn from the institution that has disappointed them, only to seize uopn another and perhaps even less promising ideal. The despairing Christian may become a Communist, and vice versa; the switch may be from a liberal to a conservative denomination; or a Marxist may turn to anarchism. This is like the restless and vacant man or woman wandering from one lover to another, when the real problem is another realm altogether. The real problem of alienation is that the traditional institutions—Christianity, Judaism, Marxism, and humanism, in particular—would be unsatisfactory even if they succeeded in all their ambitions—*especially* if they succeeded in all their ambitions. That the institutions sometimes betray their own credos is only a secondary problem.

It should be obvious that Christians also require mundane challenge and secular purpose, that religion as narrowly conceived is not enough, that earth must be more than the anteroom to Heaven. There is a very simple reason why many parishioners are impatient or bored with constant preaching against sin, viz., in many communities most individuals are already honest, decent, and pious, even though there is room for improvement. It may not be to the point to overemphasize various social problems, since most parishioners may already be doing about as much as their talents and resources permit. If the average, decent Christian is to improve himself and his contribution to any notable extent, it is not likely to be by nagging exhortation but by a complex process of education, growth, and biological change.

As already noted, it is not only the churches but other institutions as well that are missing the point. Among the other institutions are those quasi-religious bodies, the communist states, which to instill spirit and assure support rely on that old standby, the martyr syndrome. This gives the individual both happiness and usefulness—but the happiness may be brief and illusory; the usefulness may accrue only to a false ideal. (It should not be necessary to elaborate on the possibility of "illusory happiness," in which category I would include, for example, that of the contented cow, the euphoric acid-head, and the kamikaze.) In parts of the more advanced communist countries such as Russia, where material wealth has increased and revolutionary fervor subsided, idealism is failing to satisfy the restless young, just as Christianity is failing here. (The "Jesus freaks," even aside from their small numbers, can scarcely be counted successes.)

The necessary change in outlook cannot and need not be either sudden or universal. Many will lack the time or the flexibility to modify their philosophies; presumably God's mercy will provide for them, as for the nameless myriads throughout pre-history. But those able to understand the questions and vigorous enough to accept the duty must face the issue.

That issue is whether Christianity (and the other religions) will be universal and evolutionary or narrow and static. Merely to phrase it so nearly removes any choice; a narrow and static religion can end only in impotence and decay. The practical question is whether Christians will be followers or leaders, whether they will sullenly and grudgingly submit to change or eagerly and gratefully seek to guide it.

The Ultimate Ecumenism

That traditional religion should adopt the Long View and welcome superman is a disturbing suggestion for theologians, but it will not panic even the conservatives among them; they are very canny, tough and shifty customers. They will soon see that we are really asking for an ultimate ecumenism, a final rapprochement between science and religion. I think such a rapprochement is possible, and that its necessary condition—an end to religious dogma—can be made acceptable to the churches.

Most of the supposed conflicts between science and religion have been resolved or left behind. The twentieth-century scientist is less confident and more puzzled than his predecessors, and so is the contemporary theologian, who is very respectful of science. Typically, the philosopher of faith not only acknowledges his duty to interpret religious doctrines in accordance with "scientific facts," but he also tends to apply the critical standards of the scientist to his own work—even though often protesting, all the while, that his realm is entirely different and apart from that of science.

This is a major cause of confusion: the tendency to smile at the scientist's supposed concern only with those things that can be "seen and felt, weighed and measured," the tendency to ask such questions as: Can you put beauty under a microscope? Can you put love on an oscilloscope? These people have been misled by the fact that the scientist does indeed, when feasible, prefer to work quantitatively, and by such dicta as that of Lord Kelvin: ". . . when you can measure what you are speaking about . . . you know something about it; but when you cannot express it in numbers . . . you have scarcely advanced to the stage of *Science*. . . ."

This kind of attitude, combined with the diffidence of most scientists in the face of truly slippery problems, has produced the widely credited notion that science and religion have different "provinces," that they do not share the same "universe of discourse," that they meet only tangentially and that, fundamentally, one is irrelevant to the other. Nothing could be sillier.

The fact is that when a scientist cannot find accurate data, he makes do with less accurate ones; and when he cannot define a concept sharply, he works with a fuzzy one, applying, nevertheless, all the honesty and resourcefulness at his command. These, in the end, define the "scientific attitude": honesty and resourcefulness. Paul W. Bridgman, the eminent physicist, has made this explicit by saying that the most important part of the scientist's procedure is simply "to do his utmost with his mind—no holds barred."

In this larger sense, then, clearly the province of science is universal, not excluding art, human relations, or religion. But while this statement may at first seem both vague and innocuous, it packs a punch. Now comes the crunch.

The gut issue, to use the current argot, concerns the validity of "spiritual insights." The argument from such insights is presented in crystalline purity by Billy Graham, who says, "I know God exists . . . I have talked with Him . . . I have walked with Him." That is, he has experienced a direct perception, and needs no further evidence; he feels only pity for the blind man who has not seen, and who requires mountains of indirect evidence to allay his doubts.

But if Dr. Graham were scientific he would acknowledge the well-known fact that there is such a thing as delusion, and entertain the possibility that his "insight," convincing as it seems, may nevertheless be delusory. Many others—possibly most others—do entertain this possibility. Pierre Teilhard de Chardin, to cite an eminent example, occasionally voiced such doubts. The root question is how much weight to give to personal visions, and how much to other kinds of evidence.

Most theologians, I believe, have the scientific attitude in some measure. They make every effort to be reasonable, and they admit the possibility of error. After all, absolutely convincing visions have frequently occurred under grossly discrediting conditions, *e.g.*, through the use of drugs, as well as through diverse faiths.

Perfect faith is only for perfect fools. It requires the most foolish arrogance to assert, "I cannot be mistaken." To be sure, those who say this will assert that they are humble, not arrogant, and their claim is that *Jesus* cannot be mistaken; but this is specious.

It will be only a partial digression here to comment on the remark often made by Dr. Graham and others, to the effect that "faith" is necssary in everyday life—that all of us must have faith that our spouses are loyal, that the food in the can will be fit to eat, etc. The error is profound: there is a world of difference between "faith" on the one hand in the sense of a reasonable degree of confidence, based on experience, and on the other, the kind of religious faith that brooks no questioning of dogma.

Many theologians, even of conservative denominations, come rather near being scientists and monists, rather close to agreeing that essentially there is only one kind of truth-seeking and one set of rules; the well-known Dutch Dominican, Eduard Schillebeeckx, speaks of "truth without adjectives." But the churches as institutions mostly fall much farther from the mark: they tend to emphasize conformity rather than honesty for the rank and file, and they tend to make exaggerated claims as to the certainty and finality of their "answers;" yet in this they differ only in degree from the recognized branches of science. While a full discussion of this aspect of the church would have to be lengthy, I believe the churches could purge themselves of their taint of irrationality without losing much of substance.

My principal suggestion, then, is that the theologians recognize themselves as scientists, and accept the discipline of science. Such a "one-world" movement would not necessarily be one-sided: for example, while the theologians might learn something about discipline, the natural scientists might learn something about responsibility, and stop pretending that their only duty is to their sense of curiosity. This would be ecumenism with a vengeance—but could it work?

The premier case of contemporary religion without dogma is one that many will regard as a horrible example. The Unitarian Universalist Church is considered by many conservatives to be no church at all. Unitarians, the old joke goes, believe in one God—at most. Certainly they impose no doctrine on parishioners: their aim is "not to think alike, but to walk together." Their services, judging by the few I have attended, are rather pale and unimpressive. Church attendance appears casual, and ties loose.

Nevertheless, this church is large, widespread, and apparently vital. Its members enjoy fellowship and display dedication, which seem to be the only universal characteristics of religion. The dedication, to be sure, is somewhat vague and diffuse, relating mainly to seeking and to social consciousness, but it seems to suffice. Apparently, religious liberalism can be carried to its extreme without destroying a church.

The Jewish faith, also, seems to hold little of dogma. Even in its Orthodox branch, with its emphasis on strict adherence to custom and ritual, there seems little attempt to regulate thought and belief; I have never heard of a heresy trial in modern Judaism. In particular, there seems very little interest in the hereafter and rules for entering it. Yet, without promise of Heaven and in the face of unfriendliness and even persecution, the tenacity of Jews in their religion is well known. It may be argued that the ethnic element makes this a special case—but Jews include very diverse peoples; the community created the "race," not the race the community.

It is also possible to straddle the fence on the question of dogma, in either of two ways, one exemplified by the Communist "religion," the other by the thinking of *avant-garde* Roman Catholic theologians.

The Communist approach is formally to eschew dogma, but in substance to impose it. Marx and Lenin are admitted to be humans, and idealism is spurned, supposedly; but in practice Marxism-Leninism is exalted to a jealously guarded ideal. This approach, viewed from the standpoint of a churchman, has some merit: it makes change difficult, but not impossible; the "revisionist" is reviled, but usually not burned at the stake, and revisions can make some headway if they have enough to commend them.

The approach of some Catholic theologians is in a sense the reverse: in theory, at least some elements of dogma are insisted upon, but in practice virtually unlimited change is gradually permitted. Consider, for example, some of the comments of the German Jesuit, Karl Rahner, concerning the recent Constitution of the Church (Vatican II) and the conciliar decree itself:

> "Our imagined Christian (of the future) will be living as a member of the little flock in an immeasurably vast world of non-Christians ... our future Christian will read with pleasure in the conciliary decree, 'God's salvific will also includes those who (without having yet received the Gospel) acknowledge the Creator.... For those who through no fault of their own do not know Christ's Gospel and Church but seek God with upright hearts and so in fact under the influence of grace seek to do his will, made known by the dictates of conscience, can attain eternal salvation.'
>
> "Of course the passage quoted is not easy to harmonize with the absolute necessity of faith, of revelation and the necessity of the Church for salvation, which cannot be denied either. In order to show this compatibility a very subtle theology of the possibility and existence of anonymous Christians would first have to be worked out....
>
> "That conciliar statement also comprises atheism of the troubled, inquiring and seeking kind, within the scope of the grace of God."[142]

Of course, Rahner is far ahead of the "folk Catholic," or the average parishioner, or perhaps even the Pope; some of these still insist that every atheist must burn in Hell. But the direction of the march of history seems reasonably plain, and its relevance to the question of dogma seems fairly plain too. If the substance of dogma is evaporating anyway, why retain the name, with its opprobrium?

What the believers must see clearly is that the abandonment of dogma need not enervate the churches. No one pretends he is a Republican or Democrat by virtue of divine revelation, yet the political parties are full of vitality. When we go to war, there are not many claims that it is a holy war, we admit the issues are cloudy—and yet the soldiers lay their lives on the line. Likewise, a church need not prove to its adherents that it is in any sense perfect, but only that it is good.

We must also admit that giving up dogma, putting on the cloak of humility, may still entail some danger for the churches. There may still be some individuals who cannot be satisfied by anything less than assurance up to the hilt, whose insecurities are such that they will crumble at the least sign of weakness in their spiritual leaders. But if this is the price, I think it will have to be paid. In any case, the ultimate decisions will be based on principle, not short-term politics, and the new breed of scientific theologians will be standing on the firmer ground.

10

Copouts and Dropouts:
The Threat of Immortality

Because of lack of interest, tomorrow has been cancelled.
                                        —Anonymous

What fools these mortals be!
                                        —Puck

Today Shakespeare might have Puck say, "What fools they be, who *choose* mortality!" This foolishness remains nearly universal; almost everyone rejects his chance of extended life, as well as his chance to become superhuman, for reasons we shall now discuss further, with some naming of names.

Certainly I am not pessimistic about the success of the cryonics revolution. Human stupidity is formidable, but not invincible, and sooner or later most of us will set our sights on immortality and transhumanity. Patients who have "died" will be routinely stored in coolers or freezers to await help. Only a few would-be martyrs will insist on their right to rot. The nastiest four-letter words in the language will be "melt" and "thaw", and the vilest epithet will be "mother-melter".

The trouble is "sooner or later" may not be soon enough for many of us, and despite a great deal of activity of many kinds, the actual score in frozen patients is far from impressive. In 1971, seven years after the publication of *The Prospect of Immortality*, the score in the United

States seems to be roughly: Grave, 14,000,000—Freezer, 14.

Most peculiar! Somebody must be crazy. Even if the idea were pure crackpot, it should have had more success than that. People can be found to try yoga, vegetarianism, astrology, naturopathy, or almost anything else that promises more or better life. To be sure, the proponents of LTA—low temperature anabiosis or latent life, a term suggested by Professor G. J. Gruman—do not *promise* anything, but only point out that a real chance exists, and this may be part of the trouble: we are not rabid enough. Even so, there is in one sense nothing to lose by freezing after death—at worst, you will merely remain dead—and it might be thought that many a rich man, at least, would bet part of his estate on a chance at a long and fascinating future life. In fact, there were alarmed predictions that the project would instigate countless swindles, with hysterical millionaires showering money on freezer salesmen and with sick people changing their wills in favor of anyone who held out any hope, however slim, of cheating death. "Die now, pay later" was seen as a potent lure for the suckers.

Please Kick the Tires

Nothing even remotely like this has happened, for a variety of reasons, almost all of them psychological rather than logical. In one large class of resisters, the diagnosis is plain: they are rigid because they are frigid; their minds are frozen by fear. They are, sometimes literally, scared to death. What is it they fear?

In a sense, they fear the prize itself: immortality, or indefinitely extended life, and its concomitant, the outgrowing of our humanity. They see this not as an opportunity, but as a threat. The threat is mainly to their peace of mind, and this can seem fearsome indeed.

Ordinary people are often frankly petrified by the prospect of the great journey: they won't buy our vehicle, or even kick the tires, but simply announce after profound thought lasting in some cases for as much as a minute and a half, that they intend to go when their "time comes."

To such, one is tempted to give a snotty answer. Goodbye. So drop dead already. We'll try to get along without you. You have a right to rot. You'll soon be rotten and forgotten. Good; that will leave more room for the rest of us. We'll give your regards to Broadway. It's a free country. Suit yourself. Who needs you?

But of course these aren't real answers, only expressions of irritation. We certainly have a moral duty to try to persuade these people: for being a little slow, the death penalty is somewhat severe. More than that, we do need them. If the cryonics program is to be efficient—if the cost is to be within the reach of all, and if help is to be quickly available at every place and time—then it must be a large scale project. We do not need everybody, or even a majority, but we do need substantial numbers.

The illogic and shabby psychological defense mechanisms so often observed in the man in the street are displayed a trifle less blatantly by the intelligentsia, who frequently outsmart themselves in rather slick and plausible-sounding ways. It will be worth our while to mention a few by name, and I hope they will forgive me for being used as horrible examples. Their usefulness lies in the very fact that they are brilliant men; if they can err so grossly, then the average man need not be ashamed of his own obtuseness and can change his mind without humiliation. Let us begin with the least extreme example.

Alan Harrington

Writer Alan Harrington is not one of life's dropouts, not one of the apologists of death; on the contrary, his book, *The Immortalist,* is built on the theme that "Death is an imposition on the human race, and no longer acceptable."[99] Yet after this brave beginning, after many flourishes and gallant aphorisms, he emerges a copout; he appears to be not an immortalist, but only a talkative dilettante.

Incredible! Consider, first, how deftly he dissects the old myths, how shrewdly he pulls the scabs off our psychoses:

The disguised message in the Tower of Babel story is that if we get together and talk in one language we *can* erect a structure that will reach heaven—in other words, become gods ourselves and attain immortality.... We created the Devil to express our most radical and dangerous intent. Through history he has been the host, the standard-bearer of man's aspiration to become immortal and divine....

(The) habit of doubt creates habitual reservations about entering fully into any emotional life that might be possible—because in the end there is death. And unfortunately a negative reflex comes into being; that the only way to hold off death is to refuse to jump into the life that leads to it. If you don't buy death you may refuse to buy life....

Purchasing eternal life has become increasingly common in our supposedly enlightened time. This is done, for example, by starting a foundation and giving it your name....

All mass-action, for good or ill, gives members of the crowd an illusion of being immortal and vaguely godlike....

The devout Chinese Communist running around and waving his little red book of Mao's aphorisms, may appear psychotic to me. Yet he is less conscious of death than I am, closer to 'the All', much farther from death and less afraid of it, safer, and secure from cosmic anxiety....

To be sure, his arguments are often weak and loose. Surely he goes far beyond the evidence when he asserts that the " 'problem of alienation' ... derives from a single cause: the fear of aging and death ... feelings of isolation; aggressive behavior toward one another; massive paranoia, and the common inability to believe, commit, or care—derives, going back to the beginning, from a single cause ... the fear of aging and death."

Again, his phrasing of the goal seems ill chosen—to become "divine," "deities," "gods." This phrasing brings unpleasant and inaccurate connotations, such as a desire for worshippers and a static utopia. This last, especially, is astonishingly shallow and short-sighted.

Harrington visualizes a "utopia beyond time," an "immortalist state" in which we—or our descendants—will be periodically roused from sleep or hibernation to "pursue lost dreams and careers, becoming doctor, space explorer, artist, athlete, scientist—fleshing out in free play all of the myths that have ever occurred to mankind. . . ."

What a dwarfed and puny vision! Essentially, Harrington seems to see a future not much different from the present, except bigger and better—eternal variations on the same old themes. This is not only unrealistic but uninspiring, playing into the hands of the thoughtless who say they wouldn't want "another time around."

The worst, however, is that finally Harrington's nerve fails him. He acknowledges, "The frozen casket does hold out a faint promise, and currently the only promise of survival." But his ultimate conclusion is that ". . . members of the transitional generations will almost surely not live to experience the immortal state (but) . . . through our efforts we honor the human species by helping to turn it into the divine species. We may fairly consider ourselves the heroes and heroines of the evolutionary process. . . ."

What a splendid conclusion! Our descendants will conquer aging: this is news? We will find solace in the nobility of martyrdom: this is different? It is nothing more than the same old humanist copout, the same sick delusions that Harrington himself has gone to so much trouble to debunk. What it amounts to, then, is that Harrington is just another "futurist," someone who enjoys mental games, talking about the future with no intention of participating. He shares, in the end, the common paralysis of will.

Or so it would appear from reading *The Immortalist*. In mid-1970 the grapevine had it that Harrington had become actively involved at least on the fringes of cryonics. Perhaps he will turn out to be an immortalist after all.

Joshua Lederberg

If the universe has no malice, neither has it mercy; it accepts no excuses, and a miss is as good as a mile. The rarest genius has but to take one misstep in New York City traffic, and the universe will judge him incompetent and sentence him to death.

Joshua Lederberg, a Nobel Prize winner, is a professor

of biology at California Institute of Technology. Despite his acknowledged genius, Professor Lederberg appears a little too confused to survive.

Pondering the puzzle of identity, of the nature of soul or self, he has written, "The whole issue of self-identification needs scientific reexamination before we apply infinite effort to preserve a material body, many of whose molecules are transient anyhow."[99] Someone who loves him should take him gently by the hand and tell him, "Dear Joshua, it is not a question of 'infinite effort,' which is impossible in any case and was doubtless just an unscientific slip of your scientific tongue, but of *moderate* effort; and your poor material body, of which I am quite fond, transient molecules and all, is almost certain to break down long before you solve the profound and subtle riddle of identity, thus assuring that you never will know the answer, and leaving me desolate besides. There is always time to choose death, but you have very little time to choose life. Please choose life, while you still can; *then* we shall see."

Such men as Professor Lederberg may not be manifestly frightened of the future, not obviously intimidated by the magnitude of the immediate personal challenge; what I would ungenerously describe as paralysis would be seen by many as an understandable dubiety, a prudent hesitation, indeed a virtuous sense of cautious responsibility. But it all comes to the same thing, in the end, and his end will soon come.

Furthermore, one begins to understand a little more the *actual* reasons for opposition, in listening to those who feel they must do more than shake their heads and mumble, who feel obliged to offer "positive" reasons for negativism.

Isaac Asimov

Dr. Isaac Asimov is a very well-known writer of popular science and science fiction, formerly a biochemist at Boston University, a man of prodigious knowledge and towering IQ, who has spoken and written about the cryonics program several times. In a magazine article early in 1967 he allowed as how: (1) no one would want to live more than five centuries at most because by then he would be bored to death; (2) greatly extended life (through freezing or other means) would petrify society because it would perpetuate in positions of influence a bunch of old dogs who can't learn new tricks and who have already contributed whatever their potential included; and (3) even our species must die eventually, but that's all right if the evolutionary process is allowed to produce a new and better species first. "Surely, if the species must die, let it die while leaving behind a greater species that can take up more effectively the eternal struggle with darkness, and stride to the kind of victories we can't even imagine. Properly viewed, such a death is no death at all, but another step toward the only worthwhile immortality—that of life and intelligence in the abstract."[6]

How wonderful! "Properly viewed," says he, death is not death. This man apparently would die happy—almost any time, one supposes—if only he could be assured that, a billion years from now on a planet of Antares, a race of giant spiders would discover a way to spin more beautiful webs. Can he really mean it?

And consider the blandness of the implication that, since we would grow bored within five centuries anyhow, we may as well die now, or at the end of our "natural" term, especially since we are only barnacles on the ship of state. By my arithmetic, five centuries is considerably more than 75-odd years, even if I agreed that life would be boring beyond 500 years; in fact, the difference is 425 years, and I say *vive la difference*. Can Asimov be so weak in computation?

Furthermore, the very notion of boredom within a few centuries is absurd, even for a human, let alone a superman, given health, wealth and opportunity. There are endless avenues of exploration and achievement, even in a world like the present. Normal curiosity and appreciation could scarcely be exhausted in a mere 500 years.

Finally, and most puzzling, he has implicitly taken a stand of the most rigid conservatism on the question of individual improvability. If we, in our adult persons, can by various techniques be changed and improved in the course of time to become not just immortal, but immortal *super-*

men, then obviously the questions of boredom and mental stagnation do not arise; and there are many indications that this improvement will be possible. It is true that nothing is guaranteed, and the senile rigidity problem may indeed be a tough nut, conceivably harder to crack than that of physical immortality. (On the other hand, despite popular notions, it is far from clear that old age, even now, necessarily causes a decline in adaptability and creativity.) But this is just another problem in our bulging bag; we may solve it, or we may not—but why give up in advance? Why surrender before we are beaten? Why sacrifice our lives, and those in our families, just because one or another problem *may* prove insurmountable?

Since all these weaknesses in Dr. Asimov's arguments must be obvious to a mind as sharp as his, I conclude that his real reasons for opposition are not the ones he adduces. What some of these real reasons may be, we can begin to guess by considering one of the more extreme reactions to the cryonics proposal.

Russell Kirk

Russell Kirk is an educator, writer and well-known commentator on a wide variety of subjects. That he is politically and religiously conservative is *not* the point; plenty of right-wingers are friendly to cryonics, and many left-wingers icy. But the vehemence of his reaction exposes rather plainly the nature of the threat many people feel, and the workings of their defense mechanisms.

In a syndicated article, "The Iceman Cometh," he attempted to dissect the "mentality of the Shakespeare-hater" and roast the abominable iceman.[94] To prove the insanity of cryonic interment he quotes a minor passage from *The Prospect of Immortality*.

I am convinced that in a few hundred years the words of Shakespeare, for example, will interest us no more than the grunting of swine in a wallow. (Shakespeare scholars, along with censors, snuff grinders and wig makers will have to find new, perhaps unimaginable occupations.) Not only will his work be far too weak in intellect and written in too vague and puny a language, but the problems

213

which concerned him will be, in the main, no more than historical curiosities. Neither greed, nor lust, nor ambition will in that society have any recognizable similarity to the qualities we know. With the virtually unlimited resources of that era, all ordinary wants will be readily satisfied, either by supplying them or removing them in the mind of the individual ... competitive drives, in the interpersonal sense, may or may not persist; but if they do, it will be in radically modified form.

Kirk then comments: "What a charming prospect! ... thawed out after some years or centuries of cryogenic interment, we shall be as gods, for Science will have remedied all ills ... thinking machines will perform all the work ... motherhood will have been abolished—good riddance to bad rubbish—by ectogenesis.... And how very happy and very different we defrosted survivors from quasi-Shakespearean savagery will be! ... Mr. Ettinger, in fine, smilingly advocates what C. S. Lewis called 'the abolition of man.' ... How very tidy would be the future world of cryogenic interment and resurrection! How very untidy, how nastily human Shakespeare is! Blow, O blow, ye winter winds: freezing's the way to dehumanized Elysium."

We need not belabor the *non sequitur* aspects of Kirk's arguments, *e.g.*, that I am a "Shakespeare hater" merely because I predict that man, if he survives, will become superman and naturally outgrow all current literature; or the hilarious notion that *my* predictions about the future should affect *Kirk's* decision on attempting to extend his life. Of more concern is the psychopathology which cherishes the "untidy" and the "nastily human," which wants to perpetuate weakness, vice, suffering, and stupidity because without them we would be "dehumanized."

There is nothing especially mysterious about it, of course: essentially, Mr. Kirk is already frozen—frozen in his convictions, frozen in his world-view—and being frozen is brittle and vulnerable. While I have not actually attacked Mother, God, or The Flag, I have made it plain enough that I do not hold them sacrosanct, but regard them (like everything else) as subject to continuous reappraisal and improvement; this raises the hackles of ice-cubical people as a conditioned response.

Hard as their heads may be, I feel some hope that, if we belt them repeatedly with the crude club of logic, perhaps we can pound in some sense. Why, for example, should anyone object that "motherhood will have been abolished" in the sense that gestation will be in an artificial womb? To "carry" and bear a child *is* uncomfortable and inconvenient, and also (for some people) a bit nasty; and it is scarcely conceivable that mother-love should hinge on it, since father-love does not. (Not so long ago, self-appointed defenders of traditional "humanity" complained bitterly about the wrongness of using anaesthesia in childbirth.) In any case, if I am wrong on this small point—or if my view is the wrong one for some individuals—then I will stand corrected; but I will be corrected by *relevant* information, and not by some vague feeling of loyalty to an outworn tradition.

The Nervous Nellies also feel that God is threatened, or that their own notion of God is threatened. Indefinite life seems to dim the luster of Heaven and pale the fires of Hell; the audacity of the would-be superman seems to say to the ice-cubes, with insupportable condescension, "Your Kingdom of God was indeed a noble vision of Utopia—but we intend to seek beyond Utopia."

The Gulfs of Fear

And here again we really have it; once more we name it, the chill blast that penetrates to bone: it is agoraphobia. This is what the little people are afraid of—the vast black spaces, the mysterious open reaches, the vertiginous depths.

Hardly anyone has tried to look into these spaces, these reaches, these depths. Almost all our prophets, in this the dim dawn of the race, have been concerned with beating back the jungle to protect the garden, not with building the city. Virtually every visualized Utopia has been a mere negation of vice and not an affirmation of aspiration in any positive sense. But when sickness and sin are cast out,

215

when everyone is filled with loving-kindness, when men walk in universal affluent brotherhood—what then?

Then comes our real task, the continuing exploration, exploitation and transformation of the internal and external universe. The achievement of a planetary Great Society is only getting the vessel ship-shape and seaworthy; the voyage is yet to come. And small wonder it is that many shrink and shudder before the prospect of this voyage, over seas not only uncharted and certainly dangerous but possibly endless. This is what is so frightening—the casting loose, the abandonment of moorings.

Most of us by early maturity have wrestled with angels and devils—if I may change the metaphor again—and finally established some kind of shaky truce; the horrors, dangers and mysteries of the universe have been shudderingly faced, and a creaky *modus vivendi* developed, a tolerable world-view constructed. This world-view, however grotesque and rickety, may be the individual's most precious possession, and he may strike like a snake or run like a rabbit if it is threatened. It is a sad syndrome, easily understandable in retrospect, even if not fully appreciated in advance. The demolition of one's world-view can entail many terrible things. At the least, it may mean a wrenchingly difficult readjustment, an "agonizing reappraisal;" but it is not only a matter of effort and inconvenience. Other kinds of menace are also involved.

One of these is the stab of "betrayal." The proverbial "woman scorned" is hellishly furious because her offering was belittled and her trust misplaced; naked and tender she proffered herself, only to be left cold, bewildered, and alone. Being ignominiously dumped seems to prove, she thinks, either that she is worthless or that her former love object is villainous—a pitiful dilemma. In a somewhat similar way, one may feel betrayed and besmirched if his painfully established convictions and commitments are called in question. If you attack a man's most cherished beliefs, you are attacking *him,* and he may have no effective recourse other than a blind frenzy of counter-attack or a sullen withdrawal.

A slightly different aspect of the threat is the potential loss of status, the diminution of the values that may have

216

informed one's life and of the achievements on which one would like to rest. Who wants to be told, at a comfortable and respected age, that he must get out of his armchair and take up a new and perhaps endless apprenticeship, that his accomplishments are not substantial and finished but trifling and preliminary? How can a Successful Businessman or an Eminent Statesman admit that he is only beginning life and has yet to find and prove himself? How can a dedicated partisan acknowledge that Racial Justice, or the Crusade Against Godless Communism, or the Revolution Against Predatory Capitalism, is only a minor episode in the Long View? If you dare tell a man that his crusade is little, this seems to imply that he is less than little, he is nothing. How does a man face the fact that he has given his heart and soul to a side issue? Imaging trying to interest Herbert Marcuse or George Wallace in the cryonics program!

Related to these problems is the threat the prospect of immortality brings to one's ideas of his own "usefulness." Many people have such deep feelings of insecurity, worthlessness, and timidity that they cringe from any idea that they may be other than ants in a hill, good little helpers in some Great Design. They feel safe only as toilers in the vineyard, working pluckily and loyally for Humanity or Posterity or The State or some other absurd or distorted phantasm.

And this prepares us to state, more clearly and explicitly, the character of the principal threat, the *reason* we fear the gulfs. It is this: the prospect of becoming an immortal superman deprecates every work, ideology, and manner of life as uncertain, unfinished and unsatisfactory, and hence imposes the nearly intolerable burden of total responsibility.

Decision-making is the hardest and most nerve-wracking kind of work, and most of us will do almost anything to avoid its necessity. Many of us settle the large questions, and "solve" the problem of personal survival and meaning, by self-abnegation, by the tacit admission that institutions and ideas are more important than self. While this admission forfeits much—even life itself—it also gains much, viz., the calm of surrender, the luxury of rest, the relief from responsibility and the delusion of virtue. A creed or a cause bestows the comfort that one's actions are of limited importance: the individual may fail, but he will have done his bit and others will carry on and the cause will triumph; to put forth the last ounce of personal effort is heroic but unnecessary.

Every potential immortal, on the other hand, must take Harry Truman's famous reminder for his own: the buck stops here.

Reactions and Crises

The reactionaries, in their muddled thinking, cherish a delusion as dangerous as it is pathetic, viz., that somehow by rejecting biological improvement and extended life for themselves, by choosing humanity and mortality for their families, they can stay the tide of history and assure the perpetuation of their quaint and squalid little world. The danger lies in their reaction when it gradually dawns on them that they are only consigning *themselves* to oblivion in what is a quite needless and thankless sacrifice, that their descendants will neither emulate nor admire them. What will be their dismay, what their fury, when they perceive that they have cast themselves on the rubbish-heap of history, that they will soon be one with Australopithecus!

In particular, a major crisis of history may occur when it becomes unmistakably clear that Homo Superior is being born, and perhaps officiating at his own delivery. Any or all of four events will signal this condition: (1) fully perfected freezing and thawing methods will make revival of the dead a virtual certainty and not just a debatable possibility; (2) new medicines or techniques will greatly extend the maximum life span; (3) genetic engineering will allow great improvement of succeeding generations; (4) new medicines or techniques will permit substantial improvement of normal, living, mature individuals.

Quite possibly these events will be so well heralded that they will be almost anticlimactic, with nearly everyone prepared and eager; this, of course, is my hope and a reason for my writing. But one or more of them could just possibly occur suddenly and very soon, perhaps provoking an hysteria of reaction among the lovers of the "nastily human," a frenzied effort by the agoraphobes to drag us all back into the cave to avoid the view of the vaulting sky, a murderous and suicidal spasm of hate and terror.

The fearful man will be faced with a bewildering and maddening prospect: his mythos a dead letter, his creed a curiosity, his God a superstition, his institutions relics, his community a backwater, his ideas irrelevant, his power evaporated, his influence attenuated, his presence only tolerated, his person shamefully debilitated. With what insane despair might not such a one lash out!

The depth and pity of his predicament may perhaps be seen a bit more clearly by analogy with a case once presented to one of the newspaper agony columns—Dear Abby or Ann Landers. A woman wrote about her problem with her husband, who wanted normal married love while she—although, she said, she loved her husband in other ways—regarded sexual intimacy as disgusting and degrading. Her question was only how to persuade her husband to demand less; *she did not want to change herself.* Given the premise, this was logical; could one of us, if assured that homosexuality, say, or drug addiction was pleasurable, want to become a homosexual or addict? It is impossible to demand of someone that he deliberately alter emotional attitudes that are close to the core of his personality.

At least, it is impossible if the demand is direct and sudden; but if the approach is subtle and gradual, something can be done. There is nothing subtle about my approach, but its gradualness has been excessive, and unless things are speeded up the signal of emergent superman may trigger a paroxysm of destruction.

What form this destruction might take is hard to say. It might be simply an explosion of the smoldering East-West controversy—because of plans in the East to breed or build super-soldiers; or just because totalitarian regimes could not afford to allow their people immortality. Or it might be multiple civil wars between New and Old. Or, without much bloodshed, it might be a ruthless clamping

219

down on all progress, resulting in a universal frozen totalitarianism approaching those of the social insects.

The foregoing picture, of course, has been painted in deliberately dark shades of gray; the outlook is not quite that bad. The freezer program has begun and is progressing (see Chapter 11 for a report of the current situation). The survival instinct, while in most practical situations less potent a motivation than social pressure or simple laziness, does yet exert some influence. Familial love, while weak and scarce enough to justify cynicism, can still betimes provide a mighty driving force. And the cryogenic and biological revolution, terrible threat to some though it be, will probably take place so gradually and so well within the framework of existing laws and institutions that effective opposition will be impossible.

Nevertheless, there exists the possibility of public crisis, and the certainty of private crisis. In planning to meet these crises, it is already late.

11

Cryonics and the New Meliorism

It should be amply clear by now that the immortal superman represents not just a goal, but a way of life, a worldview only partly compatible with today's dominant ideologies. We might call this fresh outlook the *new meliorism*, of which the *cryonics* or people-freezing program is an important current element.

The old meliorism, it will be recalled, flourished in the eighteenth and nineteenth centuries; it maintained the optimistic view that indefinitely sustained *progress* is possible by human effort, especially through science and technology; it is the traditional American outlook. However, it focused primarily on social rather than biological change and many of its goals proved elusive in the short run. In the twentieth century the bewildering zig-zags in science and the piling up of calamities produced a psychological backlash and the rise of dark and gloomy philosophies such as existentialism.

Nevertheless, I believe the meliorists were essentially correct, and wrong only in their emphases and time scales. The new meliorism will shift the emphasis away from the herd and social change, toward the individual and biological change, and it will entail more subtlety, wariness, and scope, while retaining the basic elements of optimism and scientific orientation.

My main task has been to show that optimism is not just an accident of body chemistry, but that it has rational foundations; that is what this book is about. I now conclude the effort by laying down the cornerstone of optimism, and then briefly reviewing the history and status of cryonics.

The First Theorem of Hope

Many people, before and after Gautama and Mary Baker Eddy, have thought themselves blessed with insights worth sharing, insights which illuminate or transform life. In most cases, the "insights" are defective or even delusory, as perhaps mine also will prove to be. Nevertheless, I also have a Message of Cheer, a Word of Comfort, which seems to me to have certain elements of freshness, but in any case is worth passing on to my family and friends. In particular, I hope my children will never forget it.

Like many other messages—the Lorentz transformation equations of special relativity, for instance—this one can be expressed in a few words or symbols, *but not conveyed.* In order really to understand and appreciate it, one must (1) follow the derivation or proof, and (2) attend or work out numerous specific examples; otherwise the import simply does not sink in. In these few pages I hope then, to state the theorem, prove it, and flesh it out a little.

The theorem itself can be stated in many equivalent ways, of which the following is perhaps as good as any: *It is always too soon for despair.*

This doesn't sound like much, but stick around. It is not merely a slogan, but a theorem, and is not merely asserted, but will not be proved; then its versatility will be displayed.

As preliminary to displaying the proof, a few words are in order concerning ambiguities of language and the character of mathematical and logical proofs. On the first score, we note the uncertainties of language, or even of logical relationships, do not necessarily vitiate a statement; for example, Newton's laws of motion were at first couched in slippery language, and there are still disputes as to whether the Second Law is a definition or a discovery, but there is no question that Sir Isaac said something very important. On the second score, we remind the reader—or admit to him—that in the last analysis "proof" is subjective; one uses certain (permissible) tactics to persuade the reader, and if he isn't persuaded, that isn't necessarily because the proof was wrong, just as his agreement doesn't necessarily validate the proof. Usually, in mathematics, all competent readers will agree, but occasionally there will be a protracted wrangle. (I bypass the question whether it is possible, in principle, always to frame a proof in terms which can be verified by a computer.) I think my theorem will pass the critical tests, but perhaps not easily.

Theorem: It is always too soon for despair.
Proof: We do not know our fates.

Admittedly, this theorem will (for many people) require interpretation, and the proof, explication. First I will elaborate on the proof, with examples.

Despair is founded on the assumption that one knows his fate, or at least knows that it will be tragic. Yet in fact, no one does have such certain knowledge. Even if the world is not more mysterious than it has appeared to be, there is always a chance that one has misjudged the situation. The cavalry may be riding to the rescue and may momentarily appear over the hill; a disease may show spontaneous remission; the pistol pointed at your head may misfire, or its wielder may have a heart attack, there may be a shakeup in the administration; your own personality may suddenly improve, through a variety of causes; etc., etc. In addition, there are countless possibilities of delusion or illusion in your state of mind and estimate of the situation; it is even possible that you are dreaming.

We tend to forget the simplest and most obvious lessons. This is especially true in a state verging on despair, since this is often more a matter of mood and psychology than fact and logic. (In fact, we are in the process of proving that it is *always* a matter of mood and psychology, rather than logical estimate.) Despair derives not just from situations, but from our reactions to them. As a crude example, the onset of nuclear war should be

223

the cause of despair for many—but some would rejoice, seeing not the end of the world but the beginning of God's kingdom. New insights and radically altered viewpoints have occurred suddenly, again and again, to men great and small, and if the individual, bordering on despair, can discipline his mind to marshal the lessons of experience, he must always come to the same conclusion: hang in there a little longer, because the picture may yet change.

From a slightly different viewpoint, we need only recall that history—both personal and community history, micro- and microhistory—is characterized, in the first instance, by largely unpredictable *change*. Things get better, things get worse; things look better, things look worse. Like the stock market, fortunes wax and wane. We hope, on the whole, the trend is upward; in any case, it is not monotone, and anyone who is *sure* the future will be no better is a fool.

(My favorite optimist is the medieval con-man who was sentenced to hang by the local king for a swindle. He begged the king for a year's stay of execution, promising to teach the king's horse to fly. The king grudgingly agreed, but under stringent conditions that would make the year no easy one. When another servant asked why he made such a ridiculous promise, why it wouldn't be easier to take his medicine and get it over with rather than live with hard work, fear, and tension for another year, he shrugged. "A lot can happen in a year. Perhaps I will die of natural causes, and avoid hanging. Perhaps the king will die or be overthrown, and the new regime will be more lenient. Or—who knows?—perhaps the damned horse will even learn to fly." Some will say, of course, that the con-man only conned himself, but that is part of the art of life.)

The above reminders are banal and trite, although none the less true and relevant. But there are other references in the proof less obvious and more closely related to modern developments. We see one example in the narrow application of cryonics: contrary to very recently prevailing opinion, clinical death is not necessarily irreversible, nor is biological death, and if you are frozen after death you may some day be rescued, rejuvenated, and transformed into a superman. Although the problems of mind and identity are still obscure, Dandridge Cole, for one, thought it not beyond hope that even people dead, buried, and rotten might still be resurrected by a variety of scientific techniques.[26] It has also been frequently speculated that only the *pattern* of the personality is decisive in determining identity; this would leave always open the chance that someday, by accident or design, you might be reincarnated. (This is not my view; see reference 45.) The crucial question is *How likely* is it that some saving grace will be found, that will turn seeming doom into life and hope?

Precisely here is where most people are betrayed by their narrow experience and curdled imaginations. They suppose that hypotheses at variance with orthodoxy and everyday experience are remote ones, threads too slender to support one's hopes. Their uneducated guesses make the palpable world the dominant one, and the alternatives highly improbable—even collectively.

How wrong they are! Any single hypothesis, alternative to the prevailing world-view, may have debatable probability; but the alternatives *collectively* far outweigh the apparent reality. This is obvious from a reading of history. Until relatively recent times, our knowledge of man and the universe was only a fraction of what it is now. In physical nature, nearly *all* the currently-known laws of physics and chemistry were beyond the veil; the workings of man's body were almost completely mysterious, even to so simple and fundamental a fact as the circulation of the blood, while the conscious and unconscious minds were scarcely admitted as possible subjects of investigation.

Think of the surprising jolts delivered to science in the memory of living men. Near the end of the nineteenth century nuclear radiation was discovered, with the overthrow of the supposedly sacrosanct laws of conservation of matter and energy (in the forms then accepted). Shortly after, Einstein's special relativity turned common sense topsy-turvy, for example, proving false the "self-evident" proposition that two events either are simultaneous or not. (They may be simultaneous in one frame of reference, while not in another.) Later, the quantum theory seemed to admit a random factor in the world, shaking Newtonian and Laplacian determinism. In the last decade we have seen serious consideration of the idea that signals can be transmitted faster than light.[52]

Reputable scientists are working on a theory (the Everett-Wheeler-Graham theory) of multiple worlds or parallel universes, with each quantum event producing a new splitting or branching so that realms of existence proliferate in stupendous numbers; thus another old notion of science fiction is being tentatively reduced (or expanded) to mathematics, if not yet to hardware.[36]

There is no sign whatever that we are near the end of the road; some scientists conjecture that reality may consist of an infinite number of layers, each more subtle than the previous one and conferring greater powers of manipulation, so that we will learn more and more, but will never know everything.

In view of the number of surprises we have already received, and the rapidity with which they keep coming, it is only prudent to suppose that the outer darkness is far vaster than our little circle of light. The ancients considered it only remotely possible that reality was other than it seemed; but we must conclude the reverse—it is extremely improbable that our present notions of the world will stand up. What we now see is only a small facet of the world, and our interpretation even of that facet we must assume to be dim and clumsy. We can have confidence only in this: the world is *not* what it appears to be. Hence there is never ground for despair, which is the complete abandonment of hope.

But is this the proper definition of despair. As a matter of psychological—as opposed to logical—reality, an extremely slim hope may be equivalent to none. Furthermore, despair may in some sense be a benefit; some may embrace despair as a way out of their troubles—give up and avoid further responsibility. It is for just these reasons that I have been at pains to show that it is not merely possible, but nearly certain, that our present outlooks will be radically altered by new discoveries. Not only will we discover new things, but startling new interpretations of old things, and we shall surely find ways to take comfort from some of them without delusion.

It is a strange irony that despair requires a kind of arrogant self-confidence, the assurance that one knows all the important factors, while hope can stem from humility (or realism), the recognition that hidden factors may still operate to save us. How fortunate then is our generation, in this also, that we have so many recent lessons in humility, on which to build our structure of hope.

None of the foregoing is new, in its individual elements; but there is some degree of novelty in the overview, in making explicit and cohesive what has heretofore been implicit and fragmented. In particular, I am not aware that there has been any formal recognition of the implications of recent lessons in the unreliability of world-views, *in terms of individual outlook and behavior.* No one really seems to take seriously the lessons of history outlined above; our "philosophers" are dilettantes only, who talk a good game sometimes but never play it.

Those who learn the First Theorem, and some of its many corollaries, would be advised to adopt the cryonics motto, not just as it pertains to physical death, but for all situations where one is tempted to fundamental despair: *Never say die.*

Emancipations and Revolutions

Now some loose ends need to be tied together, not through a full-dress exposition of cryonics—which was the work of another book—but by a brief review of its origin and status, including recent developments.

As of 1971 at least fourteen "dead" people have been frozen in hope of eventual rescue—*i.e.*, restoration to active life, health, and even physical youth. The human cold-storage concept first received wide attention in 1964, and the first human was frozen in 1966; now there exist physical facilities and organizations for this purpose in a score of states and foreign countries, and many leading experts in low-temperature biology have given at least tacit approval.

Two obvious questions come to mind. (1) How is it that so radical a notion, so outrageous a proposal, so shamelessly ambitious a project has had relatively so much success so soon, so little active opposition? (2) How is it that the greatest hope of all the ages has met so much passive resistance and so little enthusiasm, especially among scientists? The following discussion provides at least preliminary answers to both.

Cryogenics is an old word referring to low-temperature technology; *cryonics* is a recently coined word pertaining to human cold-storage or "cryogenic interment"—and, in a large sense, to all of the life extension sciences. The purpose of cryogenic interment is nothing less than our emancipation from the ultimate bondage of death. (How ironic, that writers often refer to people being "freed" by death!—when in fact death is the complete, the absolute absence of freedom, since both power and will are reduced to nil.) The emancipation from death, seen as an historical process, in some way resembles an earlier and lesser emancipation, that of the slaves in America.

Every great controversy sees people of intelligence and high principle on both sides, even though later ages may view one side as entirely in the right. For example, when the abolition of Negro slavery was a political and social controversy, the abolitionists were considered radical; they were extremists. From our standpoint in history, we regard the abolitionists as having been altogether in the right, and those who wanted to preserve slavery as completely unjustified. But for a long time the weight of prestige and the influence of many great and good individuals was all on the side of preserving slavery, or of slowly modifying it.

Every revolution, every radically new program, encounters massive resistance at first, even if only the resistance of inertia and indifference. It is well known what Semmelweiss went through with regard to the use of asepsis in surgery—how important that revolution was, how slow it was in making headway, and how great was the opposition of tradition.

Laymen almost always feel compelled to accept the consensus of "expert" opinion; but when there is a sharp break with tradition, and when the issue is laden with heavy emotional freight, the appeal to authority is virtually useless. The individual, whether scientist, physician, clergyman, or layman, has the onerous duty of evaluating the evidence as best he can and deciding for himself. In the military field, by way of partial analogy, we do not blindly accept the advice of the experts on all occasions; in fact, the Commander-in-Chief of our armed forces (the President) and the second in command (the Secretary of Defense) are both civilians. They accept the responsibility of passing military judgment, and sometimes overrule the experts. Despite their lack of training and detailed knowledge, they acquire enough information about specific large issues through study and argument to consider themselves—and to be—competent to pass judgment.

To gain perspective we must also remember that, in emotional issues, much seems to hinge on subtle nuances of psychology, on shades of meaning and turns of phrase. Those who bristle at the blasphemous notion of "resurrecting the dead" may be perfectly agreeable to "saving life." Those who are repelled by the thought of "another time around," or "imposing themselves on the future," may be attracted by the idea of new opportunities for adventure, growth, and service. Only an imperceptible shift may be required to transform the pessimist who sees the door of opportunity as nearly closed, into the optimist who sees it beginning to open.

This shift is occurring. The climate of opinion, as I know from frequent public contacts, is steadily improving. But the change is still too slow; the same tired misconceptions and spurious objections are hanging on much too long, and repeated efforts are necessary to put the program and issues in focus.

As a prelude, for the benefit of the latecomers and the partially oriented, I will very briefly outline the history of cryonics.

Cryonics Precursors

Faint and distorted intimations of our thesis have been around a very long time—perhaps almost as long as man

229

himself. Certainly the ancient Egyptians attempted to preserve the bodies of the dead with the thought of resurrection, and the astonishing thing is that they may not have been far wrong. Mummies thousands of years old sometimes show much soft tissue partially preserved, including brains.[17] Recently, scientists have suggested that it may become possible to extract the genetic information from mummified animals, including humans, and grow organisms—"twins" of the deceased—from the cultured material. While this is very far from restoring the individual himself, still it would be most impressive.

About a century ago, C. A. Stephens tidied up the Egyptian notion and wrote, "Have your own body embalmed at your death in the hope that ere many decades death will be vanquished and the resurrection be brought within scientific possibilities."[60] Benjamin Franklin had similar ideas still earlier. Stephens was over-optimistic as to the pace of progress, but the basic idea has not been proven wrong.

In the 1930's, Neil R. Jones wrote a science-fiction story about a Professor Jameson who arranged to have his body placed in an artificial satellite for perpetual frozen storage. (Jones apparently believed, mistakenly, that the "temperature of outer space," even at the earth's distance from the sun, is near absolute zero.) After millions of years, however, with humanity extinct, a wandering spaceship happens by, carrying aliens of such advanced accomplishments that they are able to revive his brain and endow it with indefinitely extended life, placing it in a mechanical body. Oddly enough, Jones (and his readers) never seemed to realize that what aliens might do, we might also—someday—and that this offers hope for everyone.

Meanwhile, stories about "suspended animation" had become common, going back at least as far as Edmond About in nineteenth-century France. These usually focused on freezing as the means of biostasis, but they seldom linked suspended animation to extended life, and they always seemed to assume freezing before clinical death, by non-lethal methods.

In 1946 Jean Rostand first reported the protective effect of glycerine in freezing animal tissue, and this might be said to open the modern era of cryobiology (low-temperature biology) and put anabiosis on a footing of more than vague hope.[147] Rostand himself made part of our thesis explicit by predicting that one day the incurably ill would be frozen to await the time when technology would be equal to their needs.[148]

Ideas about the relativity of death were also being deepened and broadened in the first half of this century, with thousands of people revived after clinical and legal death.[129] It was becoming clear that life is a set of complex processes, and that death—the cessation of life—is not necessarily sudden, or complete, or irreversible. Rather, it is usually gradual, incomplete for a protracted period, and dependent for reversibility on the state of medical art; absolute criteria of reversibility, if they exist, are still unknown. These remarks apply, it is important to note, both to the organism and to its individual cells. In short, death may be regarded as a disease, not necessarily fatal.

Equally important, although less generally recognized, was the gradual emergence of the idea that deterioration with age may not be an inevitable consequence of living, as Bernard Strehler noted.[163] Senile debility itself may be regarded as a disease, since it is a "deficiency relative to a desired norm," which is Joshua Lederberg's criterion.[99] This disease—the most insidious of all—may one day be preventable and even curable, allowing indefinitely extended life.*

Despite the complex side issues in sociology, religion, economics, law and philosophy, the basic proposition re-

---

*In 1947 I began to rediscover, integrate, clarify, extend, and develop these ideas. First publication was in a fiction story in 1948.[50] In 1960 I selected a couple of hundred names from *Who's Who in America,* and tried to interest them by letter, but the very small and weak response made it clear that a convincing presentation would have to be of book length. The preliminary version of *The Prospect of Immortality* was privately published in 1962, and the expanded Doubleday edition in 1964.[45]

mains simple. The patient (we do not regard him as a cadaver, even if his death certificate has been signed, and even after he is glass-hard we prefer not to call him a "stiff") should be frozen or otherwise preserved, as soon as possible after legal death, by the best available methods, even if these are "lethal" by present criteria. He will suffer, in general, six kinds of damage, due to (1) the fatal disease or injury; (2) the early stages of the dying process; (3) the crude freezing techniques (in the near future); (4) old age (since most people die old); (5) the effects of long-term storage; and (6) the effects of thawing. But deterioration in liquid nitrogen, once cooling is complete, is thought to be negligible[119], and no one will be thawed until these techniques are fully perfected, as proven by animal experimentation. (If, nevertheless, an error is made, and revival is not fully successful, he could be popped back into the freezer until our resources improve sufficiently.) Hence, if it turns out that the first four kinds of damage are reversible—no matter how far in the future this is accomplished—the patient may one day be restored to active life and physical youth.

These ideas were beginning to stir in several minds in the early sixties, and probably occurred to many people independently. Evan Cooper also published a book in 1962[27] and Lawrence N. Jensen was preparing to write one.[84]

Recent Events

It is not yet time, and this is not the place, to attempt a detailed tracing of the modern history of cryonics. A partial history is available in *We Froze the First Man*, by Robert F. Nelson, President of the Cryonics Society of California. Let us just note here a few highlights of recent years, and the situation as of this writing.

At least fourteen people have been frozen, although only eleven of these remain frozen; history, alas, has already seen its first mother-melter. Perhaps the best-known names are Professor James H. Bedford[11], Marie Phelps Sweet, Steven Jay Mandell[110] and Mrs. Ann DeBlasio.[82] There have also been persistent rumors that certain wealthy and famous people have been quietly frozen, notably Walt Disney, but so far as I know, these are false.

Non-profit organizations active in the program have a probable membership of between one and two thousand. The Cryonics Society of New York was formed in 1965 as a result of a schism, over activism, within the Life Extension Society, headed by Evan Cooper. The leaders of C.S.N.Y. are attorney Curtis Henderson and editor Saul Kent; they, together with Bob Nelson, have in recent years been the chief sparkplugs of the Societies, and someday historians will pay adequate tribute to their qualities of leadership and determination. Anatole Dolinoff, the principal European leader, has similar qualities.

There are now about a dozen Cryonics Societies in the United States, Europe, and South America.[29] There are also many "cryonics coordinators" laying the groundwork for additional Societies. At least four of the Societies—those of France and, in the United States, New York, California, and Michigan—have physicians and morticians as members or in cooperation, and have substantial physical capability, including specially constructed equipment, e.g., mobile emergency units (special vans analogous to ambulances) and permanent storage units or cryonic suspension modules.

Led by Frederik Horn and the St. James Funeral Home (Long Island, N.Y.) and Joseph Klockgether in California, several morticians have given active cooperation; and the National Funeral Directors Association has moved, in the course of six years, from cautious hostility to cautious approval.[155] Colleges of mortuary science have repeatedly invited our speakers, as have medical colleges. The list of cooperating physicians is headed by Dr. M. Coleman Harris, first chairman of the Bay Area Cryonics Society (San Francisco).

The first permanent storage units, or cryocapsules, were made by Cryo-Care Equipment Corporation of Phoenix, Arizona, headed by E. Francis Hope and his partners. These could be described as giant dewars or thermos bottles, with an inner cylinder of aluminum or stainless steel (which does not become brittle at very low temperatures), an outer cylinder of steel, and a vacuum space between for insulation, with multiple radiation barriers of aluminized mylar. These units, varying in design, are about ten feet long, four feet in diameter, and weight 1,000 pounds empty; a charge of liquid nitrogen lasts several months. They sold roughly for $4,000, and reportedly required $300 to $500 annually for liquid nitrogen. It was the pictures of Ed Hope's capsules, big and solid on many magazine pages and TV screens, that began to convince the public that cryonics was more than talk.

In August 1969 the first of the large cryogenics firms entered the field when Minnesota Valley Engineering Co. produced a new unit for vertical storage. (Society members can now say we are so stubborn that when we die we not only refuse to rot, we won't even lie down!)

Religious objection to cryonics has been minimal, with most major denominations showing no hostility to "God's frozen people." When Mrs. Ann DeBlasio was frozen there was a Roman Catholic funeral, with the approval of the priest and the bishop, and the capsule was consecrated by Father Saverio Mattei in a formal ceremony. In connection with Steven Mandell's cryonic suspension there was an Orthodox Jewish ceremony. Many clergymen have written favorably.[126] Others have objections or reservations, but these seem to be mainly sociological rather than strictly theological.

There has been at least one instance of formal legal recognition: Bronson LaFollette, the Attorney General of Wisconsin, has written that in his opinion cryonic suspension is lawful in that state.[98] A committee of attorneys of the Cryonics Society of New York has prepared suggested legal documents—to be modified for the individual and the jurisdiction—intended to give reasonable assurance that the patient's wishes will be carried out.[62] There have been several papers in legal journals.[76]

The first two storage facilities have ceased to operate, but the patients have been transferred to others that are intended to be permanent. Cryonic Interment, Inc. has two facilities on land purchased in cemeteries, one near Los Angeles and one in Butler, New Jersey.[29] Cryo-Span Corporation has a facility on Long Island.[29] Cryo-Crypt

Corporation has purchased a small cemetery on Long Island, and built an installation there.[29]

To some extent, there persists a chicken-and-egg problem: the potential customers do not know where to buy a complete package of cryonic services, and, therefore, cannot make the demand known; in the absence of a proven large-scale demand, the people best qualified to provide the services hesitate to enter the field. This vicious circle has been cracked at several points, but it remains true that no well-integrated and well-financed organization exists. The societies and the new firms are trying hard to remedy this.

Advances in Research

Meanwhile, cryobiological research has advanced somewhat in recent years, despite the scant support it receives and despite the almost total lack of full-time workers in this field. Gains are being made in the understanding of freezing damage.[89] Although supposedly knowledgeable people are repeatedly quoted in the press to the effect that we still cannot successfully freeze "even a single organ," there have been several successes and partial successes. Ralph Hamilton and Herndon Lehr have frozen a segment of dog small intestine for a week at liquid nitrogen temperature, with full restoration of function after thawing.[66] N. Halasz and colleagues have reported the long-term survival of dog kidneys after freezing to below $-50°C$; and the kidney is a very complex organ with many functions.[63] More spectacular, although less unequivocal, were the results of Professor Isamu Suda and colleagues at Kobe University; the brains of several cats were frozen, one for over six months, with a fairly good corticogram—brain wave tracing—after thawing.[166] The brain is, of course, by far the most important organ, being the principal seat of the personality and memory; in fact, many physicians advocate using the encephalogram as the main indicator of life or death, so that one could make a case for saying we have already achieved suspended animation!

In fact, the Cryonics Society of Michigan in 1970—following a suggestion a couple of years earlier of Dr. M. Coleman Harris—began investigating the legal feasibility of "mercy freezing"—freezing a terminally-ill patient before clinical death. The three main advantages are obvious: (1) the patient will be less deteriorated if the present incurable illness is not allowed to go its full course, and therefore fully successful revival will be more probable; (2) even more important, perhaps, the freezing will take place at a selected time and place, under optimum conditions, whereas ordinarily it is extremely difficult to make an accurate prediction of the date of death, so there is usually a delay after death before the team can reach the patient; (3) suffering and expense will be reduced.

We may go to court and seek a declaratory judgment that will allow freezing before death, under carefully specified conditions, arguing that it is *desirable* because it improves the patient's over-all chances, and it is *permissible* both for this reason and because the patient—in light of Dr. Suda's experiments—may still be "alive" after freezing. Needless to say, if the patient has official status as still living after freezing, this again offers many legal and administrative advantages, along with endless puzzles and difficulties.

(In April 1969, at the Second Annual National Cryonics Conference, at the University of Michigan, the Cryonics Societies of America presented Dr. Suda with the first cash award for outstanding research in cryobiology.)

Another important advance in research was announced at the Third National Cryonics Conference in Los Angeles, in May 1970, by Dr. Peter Gouras, referring to his own research and to work reported by Hossmann and Sato in Germany.[80] Briefly, they have debunked the myth held almost universally by physicians and scientists, that the brain suffers "irreversible" damage after eight or ten minutes without blood and oxygen.

Cryonicists, of course, have always pointed out that the word "irreversible" refers to *existing techniques*, and that *absolute* criteria of irreversibility, if any, are unknown, so it is always wrong to give up. Now we have been vindicated in another important specific instance. It turns out that the mammalian brain (the work was done with cats) can stand *at least an hour* of total ischemia (lack of blood) at body temperature and recover completely. Apparently, previous failures resulted from inability to re-establish circulation, because of swelling in certain tissues. The remedy is extremely simple: raise the blood pressure to force the renewed circulation despite the swollen tissues. "Irreversible" indeed!

In light of these and other successes, it is clearly time for the scientist to examine his conscience, if he has not already done so.

The Scientist's Double Standard & Probability Theory

How is it possible that in spite of growing support and an unimpeachable logical foundation for our thesis, so many men of intelligence, good will, and expert knowledge are still cool to cryonics? The answer is manifold, since the scientist has many facets to his personality and cryonics touches on every nerve and gland; the root cause, in most cases, lies in neurosis, in irrational pathways of fear. But right now I want to look at the shortcomings of these scientists as scientists.

The ugly central fact is that many of them have simply been irresponsible, making offhand statements about our program that they would never dream of making in a technical journal.

There have been many public statements to the effect that if someone is frozen by present methods, the chance of revival—ever—is "negligible" or "remote" or "vanishingly small." Well, if someone says the chance is "negligible," that merely means that *he* is willing to neglect it. But if someone says the chance is "vanishingly small," he is simply lying. The proof is easy: ask him the simplest and most direct questions. How do you know? What is your proof? *Where are your calculations?* These "experts" have no answers to such questions; they can only point out, lamely, that the repair job will be exceedingly difficult— *measured against their estimate of future capability.* But our knowledge of the nature and extent of freezing and thawing damage is limited, and anyone who thinks he can estimate the limits of scientific capability in the indefinite future is an idiot. No one, to my knowledge, has even *pretended* to make such an estimate on any rational basis, let

237

alone succeeded. This is hard for a layman to appreciate, but should be easy for a scientist.

Perhaps some of these men suffer more from ignorance than irresponsibility; maybe they know a lot about biology, but little about probability theory. Yet a little reflection should convince them that the probability of revival is not small; it is simply unknown, which is not at all the same thing.

It is possible, in principle, to make a calculation of probability for any event, past or future, repetitive or not. Yet in many cases the sequence of reference experiments—roughly corresponding to the *kollektiv* of von Mises—is so vaguely indicated or so limited that the uncertainties make calculation virtually useless. This is our situation with respect to the event, "future technology will allow repair of injury inflicted by present freezing methods." We want to minimize risks and maximize chances by every means, but we cannot actually assign a number to the probability of success with even moderate confidence.

Some eminent cryobiologists have actually asked us something like this: "If you have so much faith in future technology, why bother with freezing? Why not just embalm these people, or preserve them by some other cheap method? Will they not still be eventually rescued?" Incredible, that people calling themselves scientists should seriously ask such questions! *Gegen die Dummheit, selbst die Götter nicht kämpfen Können*. Although we cannot explicitly calculate the odds with any confidence, it is crystal clear that our chances are better with freezing than with embalming. There is evidence that, under favorable circumstances, most of the cells survive freezing; this is not true of embalming. Mammalian organs have survived freezing, but not embalming. We do not have "faith" in future technology; we simply observe the outlines of history and play the percentages, determined to give ourselves every possible advantage.

Judging a Gamble

The reluctant scientist can, and often does, take final refuge in his "feelings;" he cannot prove the chance is small, but nevertheless feels it is. The giveaway is his frequent use of the word "negligible," which just means, as already pointed out, that he is a pessimist. There are two sore points here, both related to value judgments.

First, it is clearly not cricket for the scientist, if he happens to value extended life lightly, to use his prestige *as a scientist* to browbeat laymen. (Harold Meryman, for example, is a cryobiologist who has deprecated the chance of revival, and who also has admitted that he *hopes we do not learn how to extend life indefinitely*.)[120] Personal values must be kept distinct from scientific judgments of this sort. This is especially true when his professional competence is in question—and no one is competent to make confident predictions about the distant future. The appeal to authority is almost completely spurious.

Second, the deprecator can easily obscure another vital point; the worth of a gamble depends not only on the chance of success, but also on the value of success; in fact, the positive term in the "expected value" is just the product of these two members, the probability of success and the payoff. Even if the chance of revival and repair were minuscule—which I do not concede—the prize is so enormous, in the view of some people, that the effort would still be justified. Although there is not—I emphasize, not—a very close parallel, we can draw a partial analogy with the Irish Sweepstakes.

The probability of success in the sweepstakes is very small; yet the prize, for many, is attainable in no other way. Unless they buy tickets, they feel *sure* of dying poor, whereas the chance of winning brightens drab lives. Hence it is not necessarily wrong to participate, even though the expected value is negative, since the positive term is less than the cost of a ticket. In the cryonics sweepstakes this is emphatically not true; the expected value may be tremendous, both in dollars and in the intangibles. An interesting sidelight is that the Irish Sweepstakes generate money for hospitals; there is a good parallel here—the cryonics program is generating money for research in cryobiology and gerontology, with potential benefit to everyone.

So very many scientists are so very confident that this or that will "never" be accomplished! They are unaware that they are revealing childish egotism! They are saying, in effect: "I cannot imagine how this thing could be accomplished; therefore nobody, even from the vantage point of a later era, will ever be able to do so." What sublime conceit! What historical illiteracy!

We need not agree that "anything is possible." In fact, the things that are possible are probably of measure zero—to use mathematical jargon—compared with the things that are not possible. Just the same, every generation of scientists is surprised to find that the end is not yet. Regardless of lip service to radical change, every generation, with the exception of a few hardy souls, seems to think that all the revolutions are past, and that only minor refinements are left.

We have mentioned some of the ludicrous failures of nerve and imagination so frequent among distinguished scientists in the past, including the recent past. Even professional visionaries have been comically short-sighted. H. G. Wells, in 1902, said, "I do not think it at all probable that aeronautics will ever come into play as a serious modification of transport and communication ... Man is not an albatross."[177] Such examples could be multiplied.

Certainly the optimists have also frequently been wrong; great expectations have often gone unfulfilled. For every successful visionary, there are probably hundreds who are not vindicated. But there is one crucial difference between the optimist and the pessimist: it only takes one success to prove the latter wrong, while any number of failures can only prove the optimist is wrong *so far*. When the Wright brothers took the air at Kitty Hawk, all the hundreds of previous failures to fly, all the thousands of years of negative results, in that minute became irrelevant.

In any case, the "experts" are nearly the worst people to ask about future prospects—for example, of reviving someone frozen by crude methods. They are so familiar with the difficulties, and so impressed by them, and so devoid of any present ability to cope with them, that they naturally tend to pessimism. And although there is a pleasant legend that great men tend to be humble, my experience suggests the contrary: the more exalted the expert, the more rigid he is likely to be in his insistence that what he cannot conceive, now, no one can accomplish, ever.

Two Extreme Views

Until very recently, in fact, the experts clustered near the extreme lower boundary of pessimism or conservatism, which is the recommendation that no one be frozen until success is assured. Idiotic as it sounds, this view is actually expressed by many scientists and physicians. It means, presumably, that we must wait until someone has been frozen, stored, revived, rejuvenated and lived forever. More seriously, it means that we cannot place any reliance *whatever* on future advances in repair; we must assume that damage not reparable now will never be reparable. (And we must lump in thawing damage with freezing damage.) Such an attitude cannot be explained in terms of logic or biology, but only sociology or psychiatry.

The view at the opposite extreme—in which I concur—was expressed by Professor Gerald Feinberg of Columbia University: "I believe ... a good first approximation for ... predictions is to assume that everything will be accomplished that does not violate known fundamental laws of science, as well as many things that do violate these laws."[51] In other words, if something is possible in principle and if we want it enough, it will be achieved in practice, sooner or later, regardless how formidable the difficulties appear; and even if it is now thought to be impossible in principle, it may nevertheless turn out to be feasible, through changes in the "laws" or in their interpretation.

Through no coincidence, Dr. Feinberg is a member of the Cryonics Society of New York. He is also the author of a paper in the *Physical Review*, the world's leading journal of research in physics, which stunned the scientific world and may revolutionize both science and industry, as previously mentioned.[52] In this paper he showed, contrary

241

to the previous opinion of almost every scientist, including Einstein himself, that the theory of special relativity does not necessarily preclude the existence of particles traveling faster than light *in vacuo*. His hypothetical "tachyons" have also been discussed in many lay periodicals.

If the existence of tachyons is verified—and university laboratories in the United States and Europe are spending substantial sums of money looking for them—there will be staggering theoretical and practical consequences; it will amount to a fourth major advance in physics, comparable to those of the Newtonian era, relativity, and quantum theory, and Professor Feinberg will take his place among the giants of history. But even if tachyons do not exist, the electrifying shock to scientists is scarcely diminished. It has been shown, once more, that things may be achieved which were thought to be not only improbable, but downright impossible. This new lesson in humility is sorely needed.

Cryonics and Medical Ethics

Like the scientists, most physicians remain pessimistic and noncommittal. Let us consider the ethics of their position.

Apparently tending to justify reluctance is the tradition that rejects the use of any but proven methods on human patients; and this principle fits well with the natural inclination not to exert oneself or expose oneself to criticism. This combination, in fact, dominates the thinking of most physicians (with some notable exceptions). In addition, there is a school of medical thought that recommends, in principle, against extraordinary efforts to save "useless" patients. (There was a well-publicized scandal in England a few years back about the notation "NTBR"—"not to be resuscitated"—on the beds of elderly patients in event of heart failure.)

Yet the vital core of the medical ethic is that the patient comes first—not society, not the family, and certainly not the physician's convenience, but the patient—and that even heroic measures are justified in the attempt to prolong life, especially if the patient requests them. Furthermore, there is wide recognition that desperate cases justify desperate measures: unproven remedies are permissible if the patient has no other hope.

The latter viewpoint was publicized in the fall of 1967, when Dr. Christiaan Barnard appeared on American television after the first heart transplant. He had been criticized for using an insufficiently tested technique, but calmly pointed out that the patient had no other chance. If this reasoning is valid, as most seem to agree, then it applies even more forcefully to cryonics. After all, Dr. Barnard actually killed his patient, in a sense, since he cut his heart out, and the net result *might* have been to shorten his life, whereas the cryonics patients are already clinically dead and have nothing at all to lose.

Another point with a close parallel in cryonics was made on the same TV program by an American participant, the celebrated surgeon Dr. C. W. Lillehei. Dr. Lillehei pointed out that Dr. Barnard's operation gave hope to countless other heart patients, and therefore constituted a therapeutic achievement in itself, regardless of the outcome. Just so, and more so, with cryonic suspension! The patient "dies" with an extra measure of hope, and the family's grief is mitigated; these are substantial benefits, whatever the medical sequel. This is not guesswork; we have firsthand reports that the patients, and their families, were comforted. After young Steven Mandell was frozen by the Cryonics Society of New York in July of 1968, his mother, Mrs. Pauline Mandell, said: ". . . there is so much less feeling of loss when there is a flicker of hope . . . there is a light at the end of the tunnel."[110]

Needless to say, the feeling of hope does not by itself justify unusual medical measures; if it did, every con artist and fakir could make a case for himself. But when it can be shown that the hope is rational, then the other benefits, such as stimulus to research and reduction of grief, become bonuses.

Understanding is slowly increasing, and medical participation in our program is also. The early fears of scandals and ostracism have proven empty; there has been no hysteria, and the medical and other professionals who have assisted in cryonic suspension have not suffered. But nei-

243

ther the growth of awareness nor the degree of awareness is adequate to the challenge, so far. The minimum moral requirement has been expressed by theologian Robert Johansen, Crozer Theological Seminary:

> "Doctors and ministers who, by not at least *explaining* the freezer program, are actually making a decision about the lives of their followers without even consulting them. Whether or not one favors cryonic suspension, it is my belief that it should at least be made known as an option. That is to say, even a chance of success offers enough merit for close examination by all those who are honestly concerned about life."[85]

By acquainting his patients with the opportunity, the physician is not putting himself out on any limb. After all, there is no problem of availability of a new drug, of learning an esoteric technique, or of legal permission. The physician does not have to perform any physical services, if he prefers not to; Cryonics Society personnel or associates will take over, if appropriate arrangements can be made in time. The minimum asked—and the minimum the patient has a right to expect—is that the opportunity be made known in time. In this case, silence is not golden, but perhaps the blood red of negligent homicide.

Research and Cryonics

There is one more foible of many scientists and physicians important enough for separate attention: the notion that we should spend our money on research, not on cryonic suspension. This is nonsense on its face, and on the record.

To begin with, as repeatedly emphasized, those now dying cannot wait for more research, but must be given the benefit of whatever chance current methods offer. Most of us, if we are in our right minds, have limited interest in abstract humanity or remote posterity; we are primarily concerned with those near us, and cannot forgo their probable physical benefit and certain psychological benefit. But even on their own terms, those who complain that research should come first are wrong.

244

Cryonics does not divert money from research, but channels money into research, and it is the *only* likely source of such funds in large amounts. Those who speak of using the funds for research "instead" of cryonics are out of touch with reality: these are not the alternatives. This is scarcely even arguable; it is a matter of record.

Cryobiology has always been ill-supported, and in recent years support seems actually to have dwindled, partly because of a cutback in NASA funds. And private efforts to raise research money have had very little success.

In contrast, organizations growing directly out of the cryonics program have donated money to cryobiological research without the help of a single big name: these include the Cryonics Societies of America, the Harlan Lane Foundation, and the Bedford Foundation. The sums involved have so far been very modest, but they will grow with the Societies. Note, for example, that Professor James Bedford, not a very wealthy man, left $100,000 of his estate for research in cryobiology and related areas, because he was planning cryonic suspension for himself.[10] Does it require much imagination to see how this research will fare when people are being frozen by the thousands or by the millions?

The can-rattling approach to fund-raising, and appeals to a vague and diffuse altruism, are unlikely to produce more than small change. The community will not support many "March of Dimes" campaigns. But a dynamic cryonics program will mean personal involvement and emotional commitment, and the will to apply *major* resources to research. Note carefully, once more, that this is not conjecture: it is happening. I personally know many individuals in our societies who are devoting major energies to the program and making many sacrifices to assure their families' preparations.

We in the cryonics societies intend to extend and systematize our efforts to support research in cryobiology, gerontology and related disciplines. The measures contemplated include a routine allocation of a percentage of all funds, and organized solicitation of foundations and individuals, as well as lobbying. (The latter activities will be important only in the short run; the program itself, once it reaches critical mass, will generate all the money the biologists can possibly absorb.) Needless to say, our efforts will depend substantially on the support we receive from the scientific community. A positive feedback is involved; cryonics and biology need each other, and to speak of either as coming "first" is nearly meaningless.

The Scientific Advisory Council

In 1968 a breakthrough was achieved in relations with the scientific community. Until then, very few scientists, especially in biological and medical disciplines, had been willing to associate themselves with us publicly, although many had given informal expressions of sympathy. But by the middle of 1968, through a protracted communications effort, I estimated that a full half of American cryobiologists had come around to a position at least of tolerance or passive approval. In forming the Scientific Advisory Council of Cryonics Societies of America, we did not insist that the members fully endorse all of our positions and programs, but that, in addition to assisting us in areas of common concern, they give formal recognition to the principle of free individual choice and to the fact that the probability of revival (after freezing by present methods) is not small but only unknown. This was done, and the Council now includes important names in cryobiological research, as well as in other areas of science and medicine. While the work of the Council will only develop slowly, as money becomes available, it is hoped that its existence and its activities will benefit all parties. The current list will be sent on request. The latest recommended freezing procedures are available to members of the Societies, and to others at our convenience.

Among the large majority of scientists who have not been asked to join the Scientific Advisory Council, and have not volunteered, there are many who show a considerable degree of sympathy, and even in nominal opponents there is evidence of decided ambivalence. Audrey U. Smith, for example, the grand old lady of cryobiology, has often expressed disapproval—and yet she has written:

246

Recently, our ideas about what is possible in human surgery have been shaken by the transplantation of hearts into patients who would otherwise have died from incurable diseases of their own hearts. Several of these patients have actually returned home and even resumed some of their activities . . . We must therefore hesitate before stating that anything is impossible . . . There is (however) *little* chance that a whole body frozen several hours or *days* after death of the animal could be revived either at the *present* time or at any *foreseeable* time in the *near* future. . . .[158]

The added emphasis in the above quotation provides an interesting contrast to the more categorical statements she makes elsewhere.

Stanley W. Jacob and Ralph D. Robertson, surgeons and cryobiologists at the University of Oregon Medical School, wrote in their excellent 1968 review article, "Now, recent successes in freeze-preservation offer a glimmer of scientific hope for negating death." They also made explicit a point that has always been emphasized by cryonicists: "Organs frozen and thawed with present technics may not be irretrievably damaged; it is possible that the organ is lost because technics of resuscitation are inadequate. Present knowledge of the effects of shock on the mirocirculation may offer fruitful clues to both the pretreatment and the resuscitation of frozen organs."[144] (Earlier in this chapter a similar cryonicist viewpoint concerning "irreversible brain damage due to ischemia" was shown to have already been vindicated in the laboratory.)

Finally, to cut the list arbitrarily short, there has been a degree of support from a surprising source. Professor Vladimir Alexandrovitch Negovskii is a member of the Academy of Medicine of the USSR and Director of the Experimental Physiology Laboratory for Reanimation of Organisms in Moscow; he is one of the world's acknowledged authorities in resuscitation techniques. In August 1971 he invited and received Anatole Dolinoff, President of the *Societe Cryonics de France,* and was most cordial, expressing his continuing interest in cryonics and his belief that it *might* work. The general opinion in Russia, according to M. Dolinoff, is that cryonics, although scientifically not impossible, may not be useful and reserved only for a few capitalists; nevertheless, Professor Negovskii promised to come in person to Paris for the formal founding—expected in 1972—of the European Cryonics Corporation. (A French municipality, *Beauvoir-sur-Mer*, has already donated land—or more precisely, sold it for one franc—to allow the new corporation to build a permanent storage facility.)

In short, while the scientific establishment still is not exactly warm toward cryonics, a definite thaw has occurred and continues.

The Sociology of Life Extension

Volumes could be written—and doubtless will be—about cryonics as a social phenomenon. At this point a brief summary of certain aspects may be useful.

Some of the obstacles to cryonics are obvious, the first being simple *inertia* of individuals and institutions. One of the charter members of the Cryonics Society of Michigan, Dr. Ronald Havelock, is a social psychologist at the University of Michigan whose *specialty* is the study of the dissemination and utilization of new ideas, and *he* doesn't know how to overcome this inertia in any quick or easy way.

Two of the more obvious and direct methods of overcoming inertia would be to incite fear or desire. But in modern circumstances few people can be moved by fear of death or of senility: not many have quit smoking, not many wear seat belts, and I know from personal experience that even in war it is often hard to make soldiers dig in—they would rather rest than improve their chances of survival. As for the potential rewards of extended life and personal improvement, these remain to almost everyone dim, distant, and unreal; this book is one part of the intended remedy.

Another major obstacle, touched upon in Chapter 10 and elsewhere, is the *threat* to value systems and ideologies implicit in an open-ended and activist outlook. In particular, a philosophy of self-interest seems to outrage every ideal based on self-sacrifice or fanaticism. Partly

248

related to this is the unwelcome *burden* of total responsibility the cryonicist must accept.

These general principles are obvious enough, but certain particular conclusions may not be. For example, what kinds of people have joined the program, and why have some "obvious" candidates remained aloof?

To begin with, the surmise originally made by some— that primarily those with an abnormal fear of death would be attracted to cryonics—has emphatically been proven false. On the contrary, they tend to be bolder than average: Curtis Henderson, the attorney who is President of the Cryonics Society of New York, flies his own plane, as does W. C. Gaines, President of the Cryonics Society of Kentucky; and Robert F. Nelson, President of the Cryonics Society of California, is a scuba diver and former prize fighter. (But they also tend to be prudent; Mr. Henderson has a blast shelter under his house, and the percentage of shelters among our members runs unusually high.)

The very elderly and the very ill are poor prospects, which surprises some people, but the reason is simple. Those who are suffering, or who have low vitality, typically are not afraid of death, but only of pain and the demands of others. They just want surcease. Young people are usually not the best material either, because their interest is mainly intellectual and they tend to have a short attention span, as well as limited financial resources. Our strength—such as it is—with some notable exceptions is in the middle-aged group, for whom the reality of death and the value of life are becoming serious questions, but who have the vigor and resources to help themselves and each other.

Very rich people apparently are not survivor types either. Alleged millionaires and billionaires are always nosing around, professing either a personal or business interest in cryonics, and we talk to them politely, if not enthusiastically; but they never seem to grasp the nettle. Many well-known personalities, including a considerable number in the entertainment business, have expressed a seemingly substantial degree of interest, only to fade out again. The reasons, I believe, are several: (1) they are too busy; with all their time already committed and pet projects coming out of their ears, they can only be caught at strategic moments; (2) they are afraid of being suckered in some way, and protect themselves with layers of advisers who, in turn, protect *themselves* by taking the most conservative possible view; (3) they are vain, and tend to avoid areas where leadership has apparently been preempted, or where their business and social peers are not involved.

These difficulties can be resolved, but not easily. My own policy has been to ignore the rich and eminent (and their swarms of greedy relatives) in the main.

It is ironic, too, that the very character of the typical cryonicist—individualistic, nonsacrificial, nonfanatic—makes organizational success difficult. Most of the problems of the cryonics societies are simply the problems of *organization*, irrespective of goal or ideology, problems shared by every business, every club, every fraternal group, every political party. Those who do the daily work, if not motivated by money, are in other organizations looking for companionship or for a focus for zealotry or rebellion. Perhaps we need more inflammatory types, who will do the right things for the wrong reasons; or perhaps we need more charismatic leaders. Or perhaps, on the contrary, we are fortunate to go slowly (except for those who die unfrozen), since we may be building a more solid foundation and undermining potential opposition. It is true, at least, that early warnings of swindles and hysterical stampedes have fallen completely flat, and few now seem to doubt that the movement, whether right or wrong, is at least sane and sober.

Despite the foregoing there is still some disapproval, even within the movement, of commercial activities; For example, Evan Cooper, one of the early leaders and an important contributor, abhorred commercialism and indeed hoped the program would be taken over by the United Nations. Most of us agree there is room for both nonprofit and commercial organizations, and that large-scale success will come only with profitability; after all, even physicians and pharmacists work for profit. The profitability, in my opinion, requires nothing more than any other successful business—competence and adequate capitalization. The tentative ventures to date have been grossly undercapitalized, and there has never been a professional marketing campaign. The cryonics societies, of course, are strictly nonprofit and the major ones have federal tax-exempt status.

There is one commercial avenue that could have some pitfalls: cosmetic freezing, cryogenic interment at relatively high temperatures and without special preparation, merely to preserve the *appearance* of the deceased in a way superior to embalming. Pitfalls or no, one firm has already entered this field; freezing with ordinary electrical refrigeration is much cheaper than with liquid nitrogen. Some people may become confused about the difference between cosmetic and prophylactic freezing, and again we may see the right things being done for the wrong reasons, or vice versa.

One of our current efforts to improve both the image and the impact of cryonics concerns a clear understanding of its *scope*. We are not just abominable icemen; we do not see heaven in the shape of a giant refrigerator. Someone has said: the only thing worse than growing older is *not* growing older. Saul Kent, Secretary of the Cryonics Society of New York, often says that the only thing worse than being frozen is to die and not be frozen. We don't want to be frozen; we are trying strenuously to avoid it. A soldier digging a trench in expectation of a bombardment would much rather be doing something else, and the foxhole is not his goal in life; in a similar way, we are obliged to focus on freezing for the present, but we have larger interests, involving all of life and its extension and improvement.

A dramatic instance of life-saving without freezing occurred in the summer of 1971, when a Canadian child of eight years was apparently dying of cancer that was destroying her second kidney. A large Montreal hospital had given up on her case and her parents were told it was hopeless. Her parents remembered a Canadian television program on cryonics, and in particular our van (mobile emergency unit) with "Cryonics Society of Michigan" on the side; they reached us by phone to arrange cryonic suspension. After discussion of then available storage facilities, the child was taken to California—but the Cryonics

Society of California people did not merely wait for her to die; they had her admitted to a first-class Los Angeles hospital for reevaluation, and the prognosis was reversed. By removing her second kidney, treating remaining traces of cancer with chemicals and radiation, putting her on dialysis (kidney machine), and awaiting opportunity for a kidney transplant, she could probably be saved! At this writing she is back home, much better, an in-and-out patient at another Montreal hospital. A happy by-product of this episode was the discovery that, contrary to the current impression most people have, dialysis machines are *not* in short supply everywhere; in Michigan and California, for example, there is a surplus.

Perhaps this child will *never* have to be frozen. Within her "natural" lifetime, maybe we shall know how to retard, stop, and even undo the aging process. Dr. Johan Bjorksten, the eminent and aging gerontologist, thinks he may *already* have a partly-effective "youth pill," and that it may be proved and improved in time to save *him,* not to mention thee and me.[115] A few other scholars also have some optimism about the near future.

My own view, for once, is conservative: I doubt that aging will be cured within a few years or even a few decades. For this reason, and because the heavy talent and the big money have not yet moved in, I feel the Societies must continue to emphasize freezing and build the program. Even so, we also do our best to support and encourage work in other directions, especially in gerontology. And if techniques of anabiosis or suspended animation more promising than freezing come along, we'll be delighted to encourage those. (So far, such alternatives as freeze-drying and hibernation seem to show only the faintest promise.)

Where the Buck Stops

The sense of the foregoing discussion, as the reader will perceive, is that cryonics is a going concern, that success is nearly inevitable, and that its development is only a matter of time. But there's the rub: some of us don't have much time, and almost all of us have less than we think.

This is why we find so infuriating the attitude of the typical citizen, who smiles in vague benediction, nods agreeably that science is wonderful, and mumbles something about making arrangements for himself and his family "when the process is perfected." He is so stupefied by the institutionalization of everything that he has no sense of personal responsibility; and he has no understanding of "lead time."

The latter concept is very easy to grasp, intellectually, but exceedingly difficult on an emotional level, somewhat as the danger of running into the street is easy for children to talk about, but requires long training—or a broken head—to *appreciate.* The cryonics program must be supported *now,* if it is to be scientifically and administratively advanced enough to maximize the chances of those dying *later.* We need fully-perfected freezing methods, and we need a vast network of hair-trigger emergency centers. (Eventually, it may be routine to wear an electronic pulse-watcher which will flash a coded distress signal whenever the heart falters, a little like the devices now used in the intensive-care wards of hospitals.) The methods and the network cannot bloom overnight; they must grow, bit by bit, and a later or slower start necessarily means a later maturity.

Those parents who imagine their children to be in no early danger, and think therefore cryonics has no urgency for them, are taking false comfort. Not only can death come without warning, but their chances fifty years hence may depend on actions taken now. We do not delude ourselves that the perfection of freezing methods will necessarily be easy; it is conceivable that, even with massive support, it will take another generation, although we hope not. If those dying now are to have any chance, and those dying later a maximum chance, the cryonics program must be implemented on a large scale—now!

Let us not deceive ourselves, either, that we can implement cryonic suspension on a selective basis—freeze only those who die under "good" conditions. We do not know where to draw the line, and a line-drawing attitude would effectively amount to paralysis. There must be no excuses and no exceptions. It must become habitual to freeze the "deceased," regardless of how unfavorable the circumstances may appear. Only thus can morale be maintained, and only thus can we make rapid progress.

After all, we are at war. The ancient enemy will take ruthless advantage of every weakness, every hesitation. He will give no quarter, and allow no second chances. We must not abandon our fallen, however grievous their wounds. Each time we do our duty, we strengthen the program, and gain confidence that those on whom we rely will, in turn, do their duty by us.

Governments and institutions protect our interests with reasonable efficiency much of the time, and we tend to rely on them. But by their nature they are sluggish, slow to react to new dangers or new opportunities. Just as the frontiersman of the Old West knew that only his own vigilance, courage, strength and skill stood between his family and mortal danger, so must we recognize our individual responsibility on the cryonics frontier.

When Harry Truman was President of the United States, he kept a reminder mounted on his office wall: *The Buck Stops Here.* I suggest that each of us look at the faces in his family and ask himself, where does the buck stop?

... And this might seem a good stopping point. But not everyone has a functional "duty button," and there is also a low road to the high place.

Greed & Jealousy to the Rescue

We have repeatedly pointed out that the main obstacle to our becoming superhuman is not technological, but psychological; it is a problem of morale, with some unusual kinks.

Ordinary political revolutions are also problems in morale; the question is not whether an oppressed majority *can* take control, but whether it *will* rise up, and sometimes all that is needed is a spark—a leader, a slogan, a dramatic event. Once the spark is struck, the flame is maintained by zealotry—idealism, militant enthusiasm, fanaticism.

The incipient cryonics revolution is under a severe handicap, viz., its supporters tend to repudiate zealotry and avoid mobs. To substitute for zealotry and mob action, individual rationalism is probably not enough; we need some emotional incitement. Perhaps *greed* and *jealousy* will help fill the bill. (Superman will not need them, but we still do.)

The aborigine who has never heard of a supermarket may be contented enough with roots, berries, and grubs. If he hears of a distant land where everybody gets fat on delicacies from the supermarket, he is still unlikely to attempt the journey. But if he hears of a supermarket being built in a nearby town, and if its delights are described in some detail, and if some of his clansmen decide actually to go there, *then* he may stir himself. He wants his share of the goodies, and he wants to keep up with his neighbors.

Likewise, citizens of a sleepy backwater town may be content with a very modest standard of living, and little intellectual challenge, whereas New Yorkers want more and ever *more*, both absolutely and relatively. The analogy is only partial, and to make it invites trite and superficial criticism; but the buttons are there, if we reach and press them.

At this point, presumably the reader is acquainted with some of the options of the immortal superman, and hopefully his appetite is whetted, his greed aroused. By now, too, he should be aware that some of us are determined to go the distance; we want it all, and intend to take it. To those who are slow on the uptake, then, we want to ask some nasty questions:

Won't you feel a fool if you are one of the last mortals to die? Won't you be ridiculous if you are one of the last humans thrown on the scrap-heap of history? Can you really settle for your worm's-eye view, your moment in a corner of the jungle, while some of us go onward and upward? Won't you be chagrined when we dance on your grave? Will you hold still for this? Will you hold still? Will you?

Appendix

The central theme of this book has been the indefinite improvability of mankind and of men, through eugenic and euthenics techniques. The crucial issue of credibility hinges on the scientific research to date, on which our projections depend. To supplement the previous discussion, we now offer the educated layman and beginning student some selected information of a slightly more detailed and technical nature. (The word "layman" refers to everyone—including almost all physicians and scientists—whose specialty is outside these fields; an "educated layman" is on who is familiar with the language of high school biology.)

Let me warn against over-diffidence on the part of the layman, who is apt to deprecate his ability to understand, let alone his competence to judge. While certain details and activities in a scientific discipline can be very difficult indeed, it is also true that intelligent and self-confident laymen can often quickly learn enough to participate in some policy decisions in a responsible manner; this happens every day, for example, in the Congress, which despite the jokes turns in some very impressive performances.

It may be worth a slight digression to point out that not only understanding, but even discovery and invention, may occasionally be within the scope of the amateur or beginner, if he is alert, perceptive and bold. (Not many people are. Very few college freshmen can even tell you whether the moon rises in the east or west, even though (a) they have seen it many times, and (b) they have enough information to infer it.) One of the most striking examples I know of invention deferred concerns the hot air balloon, which could have been built by anyone in a cloth-weaving society if he noticed that hot air rises; for *thousands of years* no one made the connection.

Cryobiology

People of our generation are not likely to become supermen unless they survive until a later era. The only promising technique for such survival involves cold storage of either live or legally "dead" patients. In this section we summarize some of the most pertinent research in low temperature biology.

1. Reaction rates and temperature.

It is well known that many types of reaction are slowed by cooling, typically by a factor of 2 for every 10 degrees Centigrade reduction. This exponential dependence implies that at liquid nitrogen temperature, —196°C, compared to body temperature, 37°C, reactions are slowed by a factor of roughly 8,000,000; at liquid helium temperature, just a few degrees above absolute zero, the factor would be about 2,000,000,000.[51]

Not all reactions behave exactly this way, and there are even some reactions that proceed faster (at least for a while, and in a certain relatively high temperature range) in ice than in liquid water. But many gross observations have verified the general effect; e.g., mammoths frozen for 30,000 years in the Arctic have retained much of their integrity.[137]

2. Instances of freeze-thaw survival.

Even the most extreme cold is not necessarily fatal to living tissue. Human conjunctival tissue and human sperm have survived freezing at less than 1° Kelvin (about —459°F).[83] A great many types of cell suspensions and tissues have survived freezing at liquid nitrogen temperature, and subsequent rewarming.[157]

Some types of cell, and most organs, require special

257

care to survive freezing, storage at cryogenic temperatures and thawing. With such special techniques, usually including a "cryoprotective agent" to perfuse the tissues, there has been notable (although limited) success in freezing such complex mammalian organs as the dog kidney [63] and the cat brain.[166]

3. Freeze-Store-Thaw damage.

There are many modes of freezing damage, not all of them well understood. The mode the layman thinks of first—mechanical stabbing or crushing by ice crystals—is not important in most cases, although in very fast freezing, where crystals form inside the cells, there may be such damage to organelles, membranes and other cellular infra-structure.[107]

The primary mode of damage, at moderate freezing rates, is thought to be chemical.[119] As the freezing proceeds, nearly pure water is drawn from the cells and crystallizes in the intercellular spaces as ice, leaving the intracellular medium hypertonic and otherwise unbalanced. Thus the cell is poisoned, and some of its proteins denatured. Prof. Armand M. Karow, Jr. and Dr. Watts R. Webb have developed a theory in terms of the biophysics of bound water lattices.[89]

Some deleterious changes may also occur in storage, even at cryogenic temperatures. If the temperature is above —130°C, the recrystallization point for ice, there may be a slow migration of molecules from small ice crystals to the larger ones, because there is an appreciable difference in the vapor pressure, depending on crystal size.[144]

Thawing damage may be as important as freezing damage, or more important.[157] In many cases of freeze-store-thaw experiments, it is not certain how much of the damage is attributable to which phase. Non-uniform thawing is obviously dangerous, since the life processes are resumed at different times and rates in different parts of the specimen. In some cases a very slow thaw seems to overcome this problem.[166] More often, a fast thaw is attempted, sometimes with microwave diathermy or induction heating, but this can produce irregular results, even to the extent of local boiling, which is bad for the health.[105]

When sizable organs are frozen and thawed, there may be apparent 100% survival of the cells, yet failure of the organ as a whole. This is often attributed to relatively minor failures in the resuscitation technique; e.g., certain small blood vessels may fail to open again completely, leading to ischemia of parts of the organ and gradual death.[144] But it must also be remembered that 100% survival of cells is not always essential; sometimes there is marked damage, yet the organ survives and gradually heals itself to recover fully. Thus, in at least one of the dog-kidney experiments, in spite of noticeable damage, there was long-time survival of the kidneys and of the dogs.[63]

4. Cryoprotective agents.

Many substances have been found to have a marked cryoprotective or cryophylactic action, beginning with Rostand's report of the effect of glycerine in protecting frog sperm against freezing damage.[147] Glycerine is still one of the most versatile and effective, but may be second to DMSO (dimethylsulfoxide), which has the additional virtue of great penetrating or diffusing power, as reported notably by Dr. Stanley W. Jacob and others. Another widely used agent is PVP, polyvinylpyrrolidone; still others include ethylene glycol and propylene glycol, and a variety of alcohols and sugars, as well as magnesium salts.[87] Their action is not well understood, but may include the prevention of freezing of small amounts of bound water necessary for membrane integrity in the cells.[89]

Recently Dr. Peter Gouras has suggested using much higher concentrations of DMSO than customary—perhaps as much as 65%, the eutectic proportion, for which the freezing point is much lower, which raises the possibility of low temperature storage in the liquid phase.[59]

5. Other alternatives.

Several workers are investigating the possibility of using very high pressures, in order (a) to prevent ice formation while the temperature is relatively high, and (b) to allow nearly instantaneous thawing. Results so far are inconclusive.

Although low temperature storage is by far the most

promising method of long-term preservation, there are others which just barely might work out. One is hibernation.[77] Another is freeze-drying, which just conceivably might be applicable to large organisms; and still another is the use of anti-metabolites or enzyme inhibitors.

To conclude, we note once more that while present methods of freezing are imperfect, the damage is sufficiently limited to warrant optimism about the eventual revival and repair of people frozen today, or at the very least, to make pessimism untenable.

Gerontology

To imagine that a "normal" life span can be satisfactory in any valid sense is almost certainly a delusion. Any proper superman will have to have greatly extended life, perhaps indefinitely extended.

A sharply limited life span has been so nearly universal in nature, and its acceptance so psychologically and sociologically necessary, that its inevitability has not been much questioned until recently, despite an occasional Gilgamesh, *hsien,* Condorcet, or Ponce de Leon. Among all the metazoons, only the sea-anemone is agreed to have an indefinite life span, and this lowly creature is more of a loose cell colony than a true metazoon.[97] (A very few species of fish and reptile, of a kind which never entirely stop growing, provide questionable cases with inconclusive data.) Among men, the increased life expectancy that civilization brings is almost entirely owing to reduction of infant mortality and infectious disease; in the last two hundred years the life expectancy of an American male after age 60 has scarcely changed.[8]

Nevertheless, many students of aging now agree that we shall learn not only to understand senile degeneration, but to prevent and even reverse it; some claim that, to a limited degree, we can do so already. Bernard Strehler: "It appears to me that there is no inherent contradiction, no inherent property of cells or of metazoa, which precludes their organization into perpetually functioning and self-replenishing individuals."[163] F. M. Sinex: "The present development of biochemistry and biology suggests the question, 'Why do we get old?' may be answered in the foreseeable future . . . preventative therapy is a possibility."[156] Johan Bjorksten: ". . . when the age problem itself has been solved, the age dependent diseases headed by cancer and circulatory diseases will automatically fall in line. The full benefit of all other medical research will only be realized when the process of aging can be braked."[14] I. N. Kugelmass: "(Man) may well become master of his own life and lifespan."[97] Seymour Bakerman: "The main objective in the study of aging is to obtain information that can be applied to humans for the prolongation of lifespan and, at the same time, for the maintenance of vitality."[8]

Some experimental and clinical results.

There have been some definite successes in increasing the life span of laboratory animals, and some apparent successes in improving the vitality of elderly human patients. We shall mention a few.

One type of therapy, effective with rats and mice, involves *restriction of diet*. In 1932 Clive McCay published results of experiments in which life spans of rats were increased about 50% by limiting caloric intake to slow down maturation; the rats remained healthy in most respects, and completed maturation when the diet was normalized. The deprived rats lived up to 1465 days, against a normal span of the control group of up to 969 days. These, and somewhat similar experiments, have been repeated by others; mice have had lifespan doubled by deprivation of a certain amino acid, tryptophan.[14] It is not at all clear whether a restricted diet in childhood would benefit humans.

Many clinical trials with human patients have involved *hormone therapy* of various kinds. Voronoff's early attemps to graft ape testicles to men had very little success, if any, despite his enthusiasm.[172] Gynecologist Robert A. Wilson, however, has claimed in recent years that hormone therapy has done wonders for some of his women patients, preventing most of the symptoms of menopause and producing, for example, ". . . supple breast contours, taut, smooth, skin, firm muscle tone . . . vigor and grace." In fact, he says some of them look, feel and act 20 years younger.[183] Many human glandular systems have been the subject of study and trial, with varying and unclear success.

The use of *cellular therapy* has been clouded by sensational stories, but seems to have a core of merit. (Cellular therapy involves injecting patients with foreign cells, typically intramuscular injection of the cells of young or embryonic animals.) The best known clinical practitioner is the Swiss Dr. Paul Niehans, who is rumored to have treated celebrities including W. Somerset Maugham and Pope Pius XII. Unfortunately, all the people named in the rumors have either continued to age or have died, and the clinical practice has not crossed the Atlantic to the U.S. Nevertheless, serious gerontologists here are impressed by some of the work. In one series of 471 patients, 53% showed long-lasting improvement in hardening of the arteries.[86]

Dr. Benjamin Frank, a New York physician, has a partly worked out theory of *nucleic acid therapy* for reversal of aging, and has applied it in clinical practice. He has been criticized for lack of well-controlled and quantitative experimental design, but says that patients have shown obvious and substantial benefit in remission of symptoms of aging—smoothing of wrinkles, improvement of skin tone, better heart function, and general increase in strength and vigor.[54] He also says that two dogs, nearly dead of old age and greatly debilitated at ages 14 and 16 respectively, after being given his treatment improved markedly and lived to 20 and 23 respectively, dying of accident and infectious disease.

Denham Harman, a physician and chemist at the Universities of California and Nebraska, like many others, was impressed by the similarity of radiation damage to senile degeneration, and consequently tried *antiradiation drugs* to combat senility; he believed he succeeded, in one series of experiments, in extending the lives of mice by 25%. The theoretical basis supposedly concerns the deleterious action of "free radicals"—active, short-lived molecular fragments—produced by radiation.[68] Other workers, however, think radiation damage cannot account for more than a small fraction of senile debility.[127]

Some theories.

Gerontology today is to some extent a matter of therapy without theory and theory without therapy. We shall now sketch a few of the theoretical views, without trying to make them systematic or mutually exclusive.

1. One of the oldest and most general theories is that of *depletion* of irreplaceable structures.[8] Contrary to popular notions, it is not true that our bodily material is all regularly replaced; it is untrue for many types of cells, including neurones, and it is untrue for some types of molecule within the cells, such as certain molecules in collagen. Loss of such elements may represent deterioration which is ordinarily irreversible. Of course the question remains why, and how the loss occurs, and how it can be prevented or repaired. Understanding of development, of ontogeny, might provide the answers, and this understanding is increasing.

2. More or less inverse to the depletion theory is another general kind of theory, that of *accumulation* of harmful elements. Some workers have noted apparent accumulation of "clinkers" of metabolism, inert residues interfering with normal physiology.[8] Strehler speaks of possible accumulation of ". . . a layer of varnish over various intra-cellular structures . . .", and says they may be related to unsaturated fats which, therefore, contrary to recent advertising, and despite the cholesterol danger, may be more harmful than saturated fats in the diet.[163] Still another example of this kind is the "calciphylaxis" theory of Hans Selye, which attributes a substantial portion of aging damage to calcium deposits or reactions.[152]

3. Genetic theories of aging are of several kinds. (Obviously, any aging process whatever is related to heredity in a broad sense.) One such general theory is that of *genetic instability,* the genes being somehow progressively damaged so they transmit erroneous information, fouling up the metabolism. Postulated causes of this instability are of many kinds, and one of the best known is that of *somatic mutation,* the idea that mutations occur in body cells through radiation.[8] But the radiation damage theory, as mentioned, has been pretty well ruled out as a major factor by the work of Muller and others.

4. Another genetic theory is that of *gene pleiotropy:* a gene which is valuable in terms of the survival of the species during development may eventually have deleterious effects during maturity.[156] A variation of this is the idea that genetic design is just imperfect in the sense that it does not take into account certain slow processes or changes in structural protein or lipid, for example. A somewhat similar but more brutal idea is that aging is directly programmed, that evolutionary forces created planned obsolescence because that somehow benefits the race, despite the cost to the individual.

5. Another slightly different view distinguishes *organismic aging* from *cellular aging*. In the former there may be disproportionate growth or imperfect repair—a lack of adequate coordination among the control processes of the body, resulting in cumulative insult and eventual death. In cellular death (occurring in cells which do not divide, or which do not divide rapidly or accurately enough) the basic cause or causes might be the same, on a small scale, as those mentioned above and below.

6. R. L. Walford and others have worked on an *autoimmunity* theory of aging; as age progresses, certain molecules may form or change in such a way that the body no longer recognizes them as "self", and the body is attacked by its own immunologic defenses.[173]

7. Finally we have the *cross-linkage* theory, associated with the names of Johan Bjorksten, Sinex, Bakerman and others. This is compatible with several of the aforementioned theories, and suggests that the main cause of aging is the cross-linking of certain large molecules, perhaps especially in collagen. This cross-linking more or less glues the molecules together at certain points, reducing their mobility and changing their properties in unacceptable ways.[14]

While aging may have several or many causes, the cross-linkage theory seems to be gaining favor, and this is hopeful, because cross-linkage suggests the possibility of relatively easy cure. Dr. Bjorksten believes there must be enzymes in the soil capable of breaking down the cross-linked aggregates—otherwise there would be much more fossil protein in soil. If we can isolate suitable enzymes, they might represent very nearly a "youth serum". (It would not matter if they also broke down non-crosslinked molecules, since normal anabolic processes would take care of replacement of normal molecules removed, if dosage is carefully controlled.)[15]

Genetic Engineering & Euthenics

Superman will be built in several ways: by manipulation of germ plasm before conception, which is genetic engineering in the most straightforward sense; by control of development, in both pre- and postnatal phases, to improve the phenotype, which is "euthenics" as narrowly defined; and by a variety of radical interventions to modify the individual, including the use of surgery, pharmacology, symbiotic organisms and many types of prosthetic appliances and auxiliary devices. Let us look at a few of the signposts and preliminary successes.

Despite differences of opinion there is no lack of bold, optimistic and authoritative predictions on the manipulation of human biology. Nobel laureate Joshua Lederberg has written, "... we should learn how to manipulate chromosome ploidy, homozygosis, gametic selection, full diagnosis of heterozygotes, to accomplish in one or two generations of eugenic practice what would now take ten or one hundred. ... The ultimate application of molecular biology would be the direct control of nucleotide sequences in human chromosomes, coupled with recognition, selection and integration of the desired genes ... it would be incredible if we did not soon have the basis of developmental engineering technique to regulate, for example, the size of the human brain by prenatal or early postnatal intervention ... When euthenics has worked itself out, we should have a catalogue of biochemically well-defined parameters for responses now describable only in vague functional terms. Then we shall more confidently design genotypically programmed reactions, in place of evolutionary pressures and search for further innovations."[100]

Another Nobel laureate, Arthur Kornberg—who has succeeded in synthesizing viruses—mentions a particular possible early application:

265

(Dr. Stanfield) Rogers has shown that the Shope papilloma virus, which is not pathogenic in man, is capable of inducing production of the enzyme arginase in rabbits ... (and) in the blood of laboratory investigators working with the virus there is a significant reduction of the amino acid arginine, which is destroyed by arginase. This is apparently an expression of enhanced arginase activity. Might it not be possible, then, to use similar nonpathogenic viruses to carry into man pieces of DNA capable of replacing or repairing defective genes?[96]

The above was published in 1968; in September of 1970 the newspapers reported clinical application of this idea. Twin girls in Germany suffered mental retardation and partial paralysis because of an excess of arginine, due to lack of arginase, owing to hereditary defect, an absence of the gene that normally directs the manufacture of arginase in the body. They were deliberately given a harmless form of the Shope virus in an attempt to change their heredity—possibly the first such attempt in humans. As of this writing, results are not yet known. (Even if successful in this instance, of course, the effect would probably not be to reverse brain damage already incurred, but only to prevent further damage.)

Still another Nobel laureate, James Watson—the co-discoverer of the double-helical structure of the DNA molecule—speaks of manipulation by "hybridization" of unlike DNA molecules:

If a heated DNA solution is slowly cooled, a single strand can often meet its complementary strand and form a regular double-helical molecule. This ability to renature DNA molecules permits us to show that artificial hybrid DNA molecules can be formed by slowly cooling mixtures of denatured DNA from two different species. For example, hybrid molecules can be formed containing one strand from a man and one from a mouse.[174]

This does not mean that we are going to grow mousy men, or manly mice, necessarily, but it indicates a possible way of patching in changes as desired.

The quotation from Watson, above, was published in

1965; in 1970 the newspapers have reported success in mixing genetic material from four mice—instead of the usual two, male and female—to produce real, live mice. A mouse with four parents! This is already achievement, not speculation, if the reports are accurate.

Eventually—as we have already noted, but not expressed in quite this way—we ourselves will have *no* parents; i.e., our heredity will be so thoroughly revised and improved that we will no longer, in any important biological sense, be any kin to our historical parents. Or rather, the kinship between ourselves and our historical parents—if they also survive to become supermen—will be fraternal instead of parental; they will share our new, improved characteristics, and none of us will have much in common with our former selves, except memory.

While major genetic engineering for humans is probably not in the immediate future, remarkable new powers of bodily control apparently are. Exceptional people have always shown ability to influence their bodies in ways beyond the "normal". In sporadic, spontaneous cases, there have been such manifestations as the well-known "stigmata of the cross", where religious hysterics ooze blood from the hands and feet. In more systematic cases, yogis and hypnotists have been able to induce trances, anaesthesia and changes in metabolic rates. Similar powers are now being studied by somewhat different techniques, including BFT—Bio-Feedback Training or "electronic Yoga". Using rather simple conditioning procedures, normal subjects have been taught to control their own heartbeat, blood pressure, and even brain waves, by such investigators as Joseph Kamiya at the University of California and Barbara Brown at the V. A. Hospital in Sepulveda, California.[88] It appears that, by a slightly different route, we may soon realize the long-deferred promise of hypnosis and self-hypnosis, possibly even to the extent, for example, of self-control of ovulation by women—the ultimate in birth control.

Intermediate between the relative simplicity of BFT and the great difficulty of full genetic engineering, there will be the broad spectrum of techniques including artificial body parts and brain extenders, electronic and chemical stimulation of the brain, ectogenesis or extra-uterine gestation, and partial control of development. We shall not go into detail here; one of the best recent lay surveys is Albert Rosenfeld's *The Second Genesis*.[145]

Repair of Damaged Neurons

Many of the foregoing considerations have been summarized and extrapolated by Jerome B. White as applied to a special area of great concern to our generation: the repair, especially in the brain, of frozen and resuscitated patients, who may have been considerably deteriorated at death and further damaged by crude freezing methods. The abstract of his paper follows:

An organic cell is a self-repairing automaton, but if environmental interference exceeds a certain limit, damage will become total. Freezing can be used to halt progressive damage along with all metabolism, but means are required to restore or augment the cellular genetic control program, or enrich the environment to enhance repair ability. It has been proposed that appropriate genetic information be introduced by means of artificially constructed virus particles into a congenitally defective cell for remedy; similar means may be used for the more general case of repair. Progress has been made in many relevant areas. The repair program must use means such as protein synthesis and metabolic pathways to diagnose and repair any damage. Applied to brain neurons, this might destroy long-term information content, which appears to be stored in molecular form, often suggested to be in a feedback cycle involving mRNA and protein. This information can be preserved by specifying that the repair program incorporate approriate RNA tapes into itself upon entry and release them on termination of repair.[180]

References and Notes

1. Allport, Gordon: PERSONALITY AND PSYCHOLOGICAL INTERPRETATION; Holt, New York, 1937.

2. Aquinas, St. Thomas: "Treatise on the Divine Government." From SUMMA THEOLOGICA *e.g.* in MAN AND SPIRIT, ed. S. Commins and R. N. Linscott, Random House, New York, 1947.

3. Ardrey, Robert: THE TERRITORIAL IMPERATIVE, Atheneum, New York, 1966.

4. ———— THE SOCIAL CONTRACT, Atheneum, New York, 1970.

5. Arnold, M. B.: "Psychological differentiation of emotional states." PSYCHO. REV. *52*, 35-48, 1945; quoted in Young below.

6. Asimov, Isaac: "The Price of Life." CAVALIER, January, 1967.

7. Associated Press (in DETROIT NEWS, Aug. 9, 1967): "Teen Swap Ad Leads to Youth Trade Agency."

8. Bakerman, Seymour, ed.: AGING LIFE PROCESSES, Charles C. Thomas, Springfield, Illinois, 1969.

9. Baller, W. R., ed.: READINGS IN THE PSYCHOLOGY OF HUMAN GROWTH AND DEVELOPMENT, Holt, Rinehart & Winston, New York, 1962.

10. Bedford, James: Last will and testament in Los Angeles County Probate File #518938, filed Feb. 14, 1967, Book 1819, p. 144.

11. ———— First publicized freezing; see *e.g.* LIFE, Feb. 3, 1967 (split edition).

12. Bester, Alfred: THE DEMOLISHED MAN. New American Library, New York, 1953.

13. Bevan, E. R.: "Syria and the Jews." CAMBRIDGE ANCIENT HISTORY, v. 8, ed. S. A. Cook *et al*, Cambridge University Press, 1923 and 1965.

14. Bjorksten, Johan: "Theories (of Aging)." In Bakerman, above.

15. ———— "The Crosslinkage Theory of Aging." JOURNAL OF THE AMERICAN GERIATRIC SOCIETY, v. 23, April, 1968.

16. Bromberger, Sylvain: "Why-Questions." MIND AND COSMOS, ed. Robert Colodny, University of Pittsburgh Press, 1966.

17. Brothwell, Don and Eric Haggs, ed.: SCIENCE IN ARCHEOLOGY, Thames & Hudson, Bristol, 1963.

18. Brown, R. W. and E. H. Lenneberg: "A Study in Language and Cognition." In Saporta below. Also see Carroll, below.

19. Burgess, E. W. and H. J. Locke: THE FAMILY. American Book Co., New York, 1945. Also see Shapiro, below.

20. Cameron, A. G. W., ed.: INTERSTELLAR COMMUNICATION. W. A. Benjamin, New York, 1963.

21. Cameron, Paul: "The 'Life Force' and Age." JOURNAL OF GERONTOLOGY, v. 24, No. 2, April, 1969. Also see Crovitz, below, and Dennis, below.

22. Carrel, Alexis: quoted in Rostand, CAN MAN BE MODIFIED, below.

23. Carroll, John B.: LANGUAGE AND THOUGHT, Prentice-Hall, Englewood Cliffs, N.J., 1964. Also see Saporta, below.

24. Clarke, Arthur C.: CHILDHOOD'S END. Ballantine Books, New York, 1953.

25. ———— THE CITY AND THE STARS. Harcourt, Brace & World, New York, 1956.

26. Cole, Dandridge and Roy G. Scarfo: BEYOND TOMORROW: THE NEXT 50 YEARS IN SPACE. Amherst Press, Wisconsin, 1965.

27. Cooper, Evan (writing as Nathan Duhring): IMMORTALITY: PHYSICALLY, SCIENTIFICALLY, NOW. Privately published, Washington, D.C., 1962.

28. Crovitz, Elaine: "Reversing a Learning Deficit in the Aged." JOURNAL OF GERONTOLOGY, v. 21, No. 2, April, 1966.

29. Cryonics Societies and related organizations:
    (Information as of November, 1971)
    Bay Area Cryonics Society, 1739 Oxford St., #6, Berkeley, Cal. 94709. Arthur Quaife, Chairman Jerome B. White, and others have been working with Dr. Peter Gouras and

other scientists to formalize an updated freezing protocol. Physical facilities planned.

British Cryogenics Society, 339 Eastwood Rd., Rayleigh, Essex SS6 7LG, England.

Continuelife Corp., c/o Forrest S. Walters, 1603 Millfair, Erie, Pa. 16505.

Cryo-Crypt Corp., c/o Edward Kuhrt, 5 Cornell Ct., Smithtown, N.Y. 11787. A permanent storage facility has been built, and is to be operated on a nonprofit basis, but is not yet operational.

Cryogenetics, Inc., c/o Frederik Horn, St. James Funeral Home, St. James, Long Island, New York. The company plans to store tissue samples for possible later use in growing organs in culture.

Cryonic Interment, Inc., c/o Cryonics Society of California, below. The firm operates two permanent storage facilities in cemeteries, in California and New Jersey.

Cryonics Society of Australia, nascent, c/o Dr. & Mrs. E. W. Walton, 19 Bindaga Street, Aranda A.C.T. 2614, Australia.

Cryonics Society of Austria, 11 Hauptplatz, 2620 Neunkirchen N-O, Austria.

Cryonics Society of California, 216 Pico Blvd., Suite 3, Santa Monica, Cal. 90405. One of the oldest, largest, and most active. A monthly newsletter, *Cryonics Review,* is published.

Cryonics Society of Colombia, Carrera 5a no. 16-14, Oficina 301, Bogota, Colombia.

Cryonics Society of South Florida, Box 693, North Miami, Fla. 33161.

Cryonics Society of France, 10 rue Thiboumery, Paris 15 France. This is the most active European society; it publishes a monthly bulletin and has some physical assets. Anatole Dolinoff, President.

Cryonics Society of Germany, Gruntenweg 2 - XI, 85 Nürnberg Langwasser, West Germany.

Cryonics Society of Illinois, 11138 S. Vernon, Chicago, Ill. 60628.

Cryonics Society of Kentucky, P.O. Box 7295, Louisville, Kentucky 40207.

Cryonics Society of Michigan, 24041 Stratford, Oak Park, Michigan 48237. The society has physical assets and capability and publishes a monthly newsletter, *The Outlook.*

Cryonics Society of New York, 9 Holmes Court, Sayville, Long Island, New York 11782. This is the oldest

Cryonics Society and one of the largest; it has physical assets and publishes a quarterly newsletter, *Immortality*.

Cryonics Society of Ontario, 2724 Huggins St., Niagara Falls, Ontario.

Cryonics Society of Spain, Calle Diputacion 464 Pral 4, Barcelona 13, Spain.

Cryonics Unlimited, Suite 818 Empire State Bldg., 350 Fifth Ave., New York, N.Y. 10001.

Cryo-Span Corp., c/o Cryonics Society of New York, above. The firm has storage facilities and, like Cryonic Interment Inc., also offers a full range of services.

Hope Knoll Cryogenic Cemetery Association, c/o Joseph Cannon, 2515 Gmeiner Rd., Appleton, Wis. 54911. A permanent storage facility has been built but is not yet operational. Mr. Cannon is also connected with Cryo-Era Corp., a firm planning to manufacture permanent storage units.

Manrise Corporation, P.O. Box 731, La Canada, California 91011. Fred and Linda Chamberlain publish *Manrise Technical Review*, which is expected near the end of 1971 to offer an annotated description of the latest freezing protocol.

Negative Entropy, Inc., c/o Paul Segall, 197 E. 4th St., New York, N.Y.

Northeast Cryonics Society, 29 Adams St., Lexington, Mass. 02173.

Northwest Cryonics Society, c/o C. C. Knight, 27128 S. E. Chase Rd., Gresham, Oregon 97030.

30. D'Andrade, Roy G.: "Sex Differences and Cultural Institutions." In Maccoby below. Also see Mischel, below.

31. De Bell, Garrett, ed.: THE ENVIRONMENTAL HANDBOOK, Ballantine Books, New York, 1970.

32. DeBlasio, Nicholas and Ann: See "Cryonic Suspension of Ann DeBlasio", by Curtis Henderson. CRYONICS REPORTS, v. 4, No. 9-10, Sep.-Oct., 1969.

33. Delgado, Jose M. R.: PHYSICAL CONTROL OF THE MIND. Harper & Row, New York, 1969.

34. Dennis, Wayne: "Creative Productivity Between Ages of 20 and 80 Years." JOURNAL OF GERONTOLOGY, v. 21, No. 1, January, 1966.

35. Dewey, John: "Morals and Conduct." From *Human Nature and Conduct*, in MAN AND MAN: THE SOCIAL PHILOSOPHERS, ed. S. Commins and R. N. Linscott, Random House, New York, 1947.

36. DeWitt, Bryce S.: "Quantum Mechanics and Reality." PHYSICS TODAY, Sep., 1970.

37. Doebbler, G. F.: "Cryoprotective Compounds." CRY-BIOLOGY, v. 3, No. 1, July-Aug., 1966.

38. Doyle, Sir Arthur Conan: "A Study in Scarlet." THE COMPLETE SHERLOCK HOLMES, Doubleday, Garden City, N.Y., 1905.

39. Dubos, Rene: "The Limits of Adaptability." In DeBell, above.

40. Durant, Will: THE LIFE OF GREECE. Simon & Schuster, New York, 1939.

41. ———— THE STORY OF PHILOSOPHY. Simon & Schuster, New York, 1953.

42. Dyson, Freeman J.: "Search for Artificial Stellar Sources of Infrared Radiation." SCIENCE, v. 131, p. 1667, 1959. Reprinted in Cameron, A. G. W., above.

43. Ehrlich, Paul. In DeBell, above.

44. Ephrussi, Boris and Mary C. Weiss: "Hybrid Somatic Cells." SCIENTIFIC AMERICAN, April, 1969. Also see Haldane, below, and Watson, below.

45. Ettinger, Robert C. W.: THE PROSPECT OF IMMORTAL-ITY. Privately published preliminary version, 1962; Doubleday & Co., 1964; Macfadden-Bartell, 1966 and 1969; Denoel, Paris, 1964 (as L'HOMME est-IL IMMORTEL?); Agon, Amster-dam, 1964 (as DE DIEPVRIESMENS); Sidgwick & Jackson Lon-don, 1965; Hyperion, Freiburg, 1965 (AUSSICHT AUF UNSTER-BLICHKEIT?); Rizzoli, Milan, 1967 (IBERNAZIONE NUOVA ERA).

46. ———— "The Penultimate Trump." STARTLING STORIES, March, 1948.

47. EXPRESS, London: "Dutch Men 'Married' by Priest." Reprinted in DETROIT FREE PRESS, July 6, 1967.

48. Eysenck, H. J. "Learning theory and behaviour therapy." In Lindzey below.

49. ———— "The Biological Basis of Personality." In Lindzey below.

Farrand, William R.; "Frozen Mammoths and Modern Geology." SCIENCE, March 17, 1961.

50. Fast, Julius: BODY LANGUAGE. Evans, New York, 1970.

51. Feinberg, Gerald: "Physics and Life Prolongation." PHYSICS TODAY, November, 1966.

52. ———— "Possibility of Faster-than-Light Particles." THE PHYSICAL REVIEW, July 25, 1967.

53. ———— THE PROMETHEUS PROJECT. Doubleday, Garden City, New York, 1968.

54. Frank, Benjamin: "Nucleic Acid Therapy and the Re-versal of Aging." Paper read at the Second National Cryonics Conference, Ann Arbor, Michigan, 1969. Reprints available

from the Cryonics Society of Michigan: see Cryonics Societies, above.

55. Freud, Sigmund: CIVILIZATION AND ITS DISCONTENTS. Hogarth Press, London, 1930.

56. Fromm, Erich: MAN FOR HIMSELF. Holt, Rinehart & Winston, New York, 1947; reprinted by Fawcett, 1969.

57. Good, I. J., ed.: THE SCIENTIST SPECULATES. Basic Books, New York, 1962.

58. Gordon, Theodore: IDEAS IN CONFLICT. St. Martin's Press, New York, 1966.

59. Gouras, Peter: See note under Bay Area Cryonics Society, under Cryonics Societies, above.

60. Gruman, Gerald J.: *A History of Ideas about the Prolongation of Life.* TRANS. AMER. PHIL. SOC., 56:9, 1966.

61. Guttman, F. M. and G. Berdnikoff: "Whole Organ Preservation II, A Study of the Protective Effect of Glycerol, Dimethyl Sulfoxide, and Both Combined While Freezing Canine Intestine Employing an *in vivo* Techique." CRYOBIOLOGY, v. 6, No. 4, Jan.-Feb., 1970.

62. Haber, David: "Cryonic Suspension—The Rule Against Perpetuities and Related Rules." (PROCEEDINGS OF THE) FIRST ANNUAL CRYONICS CONFERENCE. Published by the Cryonics Society of New York; see Cryonics Societies, above.

63. Halasz, Nicholas A., *et al*: "Whole organ preservation II. Freezing studies." SURGERY, v. 61, No. 3, March, 1967.

64. Haldane, J. B. S.; "Biological Possibilities for the Human Species in the Next Ten Thousand Years." In Wolstenholme, below.

65. Hamburg, David A. and D. T. Lunde: "Sex Hormones in the Development of Sex Differences in Human Behavior," In Maccoby, below.

66. Hamilton, R. W. and H. B. Lehr: "Survival of Small Intestine after Storage for 7 Days at −196°C." CRYOBIOLOGY, 3:375, 1967.

67. Hamilton, William and T. J. Altizer: "The Death of God and Theologies Today." In THE DEATH OF GOD, Thomas J. J. Altizer and William Hamilton, Bobbs-Merrill, New York, 1966.

68. Harman, Denham: "The free radical theory of aging: Effect of age on serum copper levels." JOURNAL OF GERONTOLOGY, v. 20, No. 2, p. 151, 1965.

69. Harrington, Alàn: THE IMMORTALIST. Random House, New York, 1969.

70. Harris, M. Coleman: "The Medical Profession and the Cryonics Movement." Paper read at the Second National Cry-

onics Conference, Ann Arbor, Michigan, 1969. Reprints available from the Cryonics Society of Michigan; see Cryonics Societies, above.

71. Hayakawa, S. I.: ETC., A REVIEW OF GENERAL SEMANTICS. Harper, New York, 1954.

72. Hayes, James S.: "Technological Routes to Immortality." In Good, above.

73. Heinlein, Robert A.: BEYOND THIS HORIZON. Fantasy Press, Reading, Pa., 1948.

74. —— STRANGER IN A STRANGE LAND. Putnam, New York, 1961.

75. —— "By His Bootstraps." (Writing as Anson MacDonald.) In FAMOUS SCIENCE FICTION STORIES, Modern Library, New York, 1946.

76. Henderson, Curtis and R. C. W. Ettinger: "Cryonic Suspension and the Law." UCLA LAW REVIEW, v. 15, No. 2, Feb., 1968.

77. Hock, R. J.: "The Potential Application of Hibernation to Space Travel." AEROSPACE MEDICINE, June, 1960.

78. von Hoerner, Sebastian: "The General Limits of Space Travel." SCIENCE 137, 18, 1962. Reprinted in Cameron, A. G. W., above.

79. Hoffer, A. and H. Osmond: THE CHEMICAL BASIS OF CLINICAL PSYCHIATRY. Charles C. Thomas, Springfield, Illinois, 1960.

80. Hossmann, K.-A. and K. Sato: "Recovery of Neuronal Function after Prolonged Cerebral Ischemia." SCIENCE, v. 168, April 17, 1970.

81. Irving, Laurence: "Adaptations to Cold." SCIENTIFIC AMERICAN, January, 1966.

82. James, William: ESSAYS IN PRAGMATISM. Ed. A. Castell; Hafner, New York, 1948.

83. Jacob, Stanley W. et al: "Survival of Normal Human Tissues Frozen to −272°C." TRANSPLANTATION BULLETIN, v. 5, p. 428.

84. Jensen, Lawrence N.: Professor and Chairman, Art Department, Castleton State College, Castleton, Vermont.

85. Johansen, Robert: "Cryonics and the Cross: Reflections on Immortality." Paper read at the Second National Cryonics Conference, Ann Arbor, Michigan, 1969; reprints available from the Cryonics Society of Michigan; see Cryonics Societies, above. Also see Montgomery, below.

86. Jussek, Eugene and Arno A. Roscher: "Critical Review of Contemporary Cellulartherapy (Cellutherapy)." JOURNAL OF GERONTOLOGY, v. 25, No. 2, April, 1970.

87. Kahn, Herman and Anthony J. Wiener: THE YEAR 2000. Macmillan, New York, 1967.

88. Kamiya, Joe: "Operant Control of the EEG Alpha Rhythm and Some of its Reported Effects on Consciousness." In ALTERED STATES OF CONSCIOUSNESS, ed. Charles Tart, Wiley, New York, 1969.

89. Karow, Armand M. Jr. and Watts R. Webb; "Tissue Freezing, a Theory for Injury and Survival," CRYOBIOLOGY, v. 2, No. 3, Nov.-Dec., 1965.

90. Kegley, C. W. and R. W. Bretall, eds.: THE THEOLOGY OF PAUL TILLICH. Macmillan, New York, 1952.

91. Keynes, John Maynard: "Economic Possibilities for our Grandchildren." In ESSAYS IN PERSUASION, W. W. Norton, New York, 1963.

92. Khorana, H. Gobind. See e.g., "New Clues on Makeup of the Gene and the Cell." NEW YORK TIMES, June 7, 1970, p. 8E.

93. Kinsey, Alfred C. et al: SEXUAL BEHAVIOR IN THE HUMAN MALE. W. B. Saunders, Philadelphia, 1948.

94. Kirk, Russell: "The Iceman Cometh." BOOK WEEK, May 22, 1966.

95. Koestler, Arthur: Interviewed by L'Express, published in translation in NEW YORK TIMES MAGAZINE, Aug. 30, 1970.

96. Kornberg, Arthur: "The Synthesis of DNA." SCIENTIFIC AMERICAN, 219, 4, 1968.

97. Kugelmass, I. N.: In Bakerman, above (Foreword).

98. LaFollette, Bronson C. (Attorney General of Wisconsin): Written opinion to the State Health Officer, Nov. 1, 1967.

99. Lederberg, Joshua: "Experimental Genetics and Human Evolution." BULLETIN OF THE ATOMIC SCIENTISTS, October, 1966.

100. ——— "The Biological Future of Man." In Wolstenholme, below.

101. Levi-Strauss, Claude: "The Family." In Shapiro, below.

102. LIFE, Aug. 19, 1966: "New Hands Muscled by Motors."

103. Lindzey, Gardner and Calvin S. Hall: THEORIES OF PERSONALITY: PRIMARY SOURCES AND RESEARCH. John Wiley & Sons, New York, 1965.

104. Lorenz, Konrad: ON AGGRESSION. Harcourt, Brace & World, New York, 1966.

105. Lovelock, J. E.: "Diathermy Apparatus for the Rapid Rewarming of Whole Animals from 0°C and Below." PROCEEDINGS OF THE ROYAL SOCIETY.

106. Lusted, L. B.: "Bio-Medical Electronics–2012 A.D." PROCEEDINGS OF THE IRE, v. 50, No. 5, May, 1962.

107. Luyet, B. G.: "An attempt at a systematic analysis of the notion of freezing rates and at evaluation of the main contributing factors." CRYOBIOLOGY, v. 2, p. 198, 1966.

108. Maccoby, Eleanor E., ed.: THE DEVELOPMENT OF SEX DIFFERENCES. Stanford University Press, 1966.

109. ——— "Sex Differences in Intellectual Functioning." In Maccoby, above.

110. Mandell, Pauline: Quoted e.g. in NEWSWEEK, Aug. 12, 1968, p. 29.

111. Maslow, Abraham H.: "Some basic propositions of a growth and self-actualization psychology." In Lindzey, above.

112. ——— MOTIVATION AND PERSONALITY. Harper, New York, 1954.

113. ——— "A Theory of Human Motivation." In Baller, above.

114. Masters, William H. and Virginia Johnson: HUMAN SEXUAL RESPONSE. Little, Brown, Boston, 1966.

115. McGrady, Patrick M. Jr.: "The Youth Pill." LADIES HOME JOURNAL, July, 1971. Also see Bjorksten, above.

116. McLuhan, H. M. and G. B. Leonard: "The Future of Sex." LOOK, July 25, 1967.

117. Mead, Margaret: NEW LIVES FOR OLD. William Morrow, New York, 1956.

118. Medawar, Peter B.: THE FUTURE OF MAN. Basic Books, New York, 1960.

119. Meryman, H. T.: "Mechanics of Freezing in Living Cells and Tissues." SCIENCE, v. 124, p. 515, 1956.

120. ——— Indirectly quoted in "Life in the Deep Freeze," THE SCIENCES, v. 4, No. 3, August, 1964.

121. Messenger, E. C.: "The Origin of Man in the Book of Genesis." In GOD, MAN AND THE UNIVERSE, ed. J. de Bivort de la Sandee, P. J. Kennedy & Sons, 1953.

122. Milne, Lorus and Margery: PATTERNS OF SURVIVAL. Prentice-Hall, Englewood Cliffs, N.J., 1967.

123. Mischel, Walter: "A Social-Learning View of Sex Differences in Behavior." In Maccoby, above. Also see D'Andrade, above.

124. Money, J.: "Influence of Hormones on Sexual Behavior." ANN. REV. OF MED., v. 16, pp. 67-82. Also see Hamburg, above.

125. ——— J. G. Hampson and J. L. Hampson: "Imprinting and the establishment of gender role." A.M.A., ARCH. NEUR. AND

PSYCH., v. 77, 333-36. Also see Mischel, above, and D'Andrade, above.

126. Montgomery, John Warwick: "Cryonics and Orthodoxy." CHRISTIANITY TODAY, v. XII, No. 16, May 10, 1968. Also see Johansen, above.

127. Muller, H. J.: "Mechanisms of Life-Span Shortening." CELLULAR BASIS AND AETIOLOGY OF LATE SOMATIC EFFECTS OF IONIZING RADIATION. Academic Press, New York, 1962.

128. Nakamura, Hajime: WAYS OF THINKING OF EASTERN PEOPLES. East-West Center Press, Honolulu, 1964.

129. Negovskii, V. A.: RESUSCITATION AND ARTIFICIAL HYPOTHERMIA, trans. Basil Haigh, Consultants Bureau, New York, 1962.

130. Nelson, Robert F. and Sandra Stanley: WE FROZE THE FIRST MAN. Dell, New York, 1968.

131. Nietzsche, Friedrich: In THE PORTABLE NIETZSCHE, ed. Walter Kaufman, Viking Press, New York, 1954. Or see THE STORY OF PHILOSOPHY, Durant, above.

132. Olds, James: "Pleasure Centers in the Brain." SCIENTIFIC AMERICAN, October, 1956. Also see Delgado, above.

133. Orwell, George: 1984. Harcourt, Brace, New York, 1949.

134. Otto, A. Stuart (writing as Friend Stuart): HOW TO CONQUER PHYSICAL DEATH. Dominion Press, San Marcos, California, 1968.

135. ———— ed.: THE IMMORTALITY NEWSLETTER, P.O. Box 696, San Marcos, California.

136. Parkinson, C. Northcote: EAST AND WEST. Houghton-Mifflin, Boston, 1963.

137. Pedersen, Alwin: POLAR ANIMALS. George G. Harrop, London, 1962.

138. Pei, Mario: THE STORY OF LANGUAGE. J. B. Lippincott, Philadelphia, 1965.

139. Pfungst, Oskar: CLEVER HANS (THE HORSE OF MR. VON OSTEN). Ed. Robert Rosenthal. Holt, Rinehart & Winston, New York, 1967.

140. Pohl, Frederik: "Day Million." In DAY MILLION, Ballantine, New York, 1970.

141. Polanyi, Michael: KNOWING AND BEING. (Essays edited by Marjorie Green.) University of Chicago Press, 1969.

142. Rahner, Karl: "Can Man Perfect Himself?" THE CATHOLIC WORLD, Oct. 2, 1965. (Translated from DE NIEUWE LINIE.)

143. Rhine, J. B.: THE REACH OF THE MIND. William Sloane Associates, New York, 1947.

144. Robertson, Ralph D. and Stanley W. Jacob: "The Preservation of Intact Organs." ADVANCES IN SURGERY, v. 3, ed. Claude E. Welch, Year Book Medical Publishers, Chicago, 1968.

145. Rosenfeld, Albert: THE SECOND GENESIS. Prentice-Hall, Englewood Cliffs, N.J., 1969. (Also see Sonneborn, below, and Wolstenholme, below.)

146. Rostand, Jean: CAN MAN BE MODIFIED? Basic Books, New York, 1959.

147. ———— "Glycerine et Resistance du Sperme aux Basses Temp." *C.R.*, Acad. Sci., Paris, v. 222, p. 1542, 1946.

148. ———— Quoted in "Revivre apres la Mart," SCIENCE ET VIE, May, 1963.

149. Rowe, Arthur W.: "Biochemical Aspects of Cryoprotective Agents in Freezing and Thawing." CRYOBIOLOGY, v. 3, No. 1, July-Aug., 1966.

150. Saporta, Sol, ed.: PSYCHOLINGUISTICS. Holt, Rinehart & Winston, New York, 1961. Also see Carroll, above.

151. Scholander, Per F.: "The Wonderful Net." SCIENTIFIC AMERICAN, April, 1957.

152. Selye, Hans: CALCIPHYLAXIS. University of Chicago Press, 1962.

153. Shapiro, Harry L. ed.: MAN, CULTURE AND SOCIETY. Oxford University Press, 1956. Also see Burgess, above.

154. Shaw, George B.: MAN AND SUPERMAN. In SEVEN PLAYS BY BERNARD SHAW, Dodd, Mead & Co., New York, 1951.

155. Shor, Murray: "How Embalmers Can Serve the Living." CASKET AND SUNNYSIDE, June, 1968.

156. Sinex, F. Marott: "Genetic Mechanisms of Aging." JOURNAL OF GERONOTOLOGY, v. 21, No. 3, July, 1966.

157. Smith, Audrey U.: BIOLOGICAL EFFECTS OF FREEZING AND SUPERCOOLING. Williams & Wilkins, Baltimore, 1961.

158. ———— "Frostbite, Hypothermia, and Resuscitation after Freezing." In CURRENT TRENDS IN CRYOBIOLOGY, ed. Audrey U. Smith, Plenum Press, New York and London, 1970.

159. Sonneborn, Tracy M. ed.: THE CONTROL OF HUMAN HEREDITY AND EVOLUTION. Macmillan, New York, 1965.

160. Spinoza, Baruch: "The Foundations of the Moral Life." In MAN AND SPIRIT, ed. S. Commins and R. N. Linscott, Random House, New York, 1947.

161. Stapledon, Olaf: TO THE END OF TIME (The Best of Olaf Stapledon), ed. Basil Davenport, Funk and Wagnalls, New York, 1953.

162. Stout, Rex: A RIGHT TO DIE. Viking Press, New York, 1964.

163. Strehler, Bernard L.: TIME, CELLS, AND AGING. Academic Press, New York, 1962.

164. Sturgeon, Theodore: VENUS PLUS X. Pyramid Books, New York, 1960.

165. ——— "The World Well Lost." STARSHINE, Pyramid Books, New York, 1966.

166. Suda, I., K. Kito and C. Adachi: "Viability of Long Term Frozen Cat Brain *in vitro*." NATURE, v. 212, Oct. 15, 1966.

167. Symonds, Percival M.: "Origins of Personality." In Baller, above.

168. Teilhard, Pierre ——— de Chardin: THE FUTURE OF MAN. Harper & Row, New York, 1964.

169. Tillich, Paul: THE COURAGE TO BE. Yale University Press, New Haven, 1959. Also see Kegley, above.

170. TIME, Aug. 11, 1967. "Technology: Stopping Bullets with Nylon."

171. Trevarthen, C. B.: "Double Vision Learning in Split-Brain Monkeys." NATIONAL ACADEMY OF SCIENCES, Autumn meeting, 1961.

172. Voronoff, S.: TESTICULAR GRAFTING FROM APE TO MAN. Brentano, London, 1929.

173. Walford, R. L.: "Further considerations toward an immunologic theory of aging." EXPERIMENTAL GERONTOLOGY, v. 1, p. 73, 1964.

174. Watson, James D.: MOLECULAR BIOLOGY OF THE GENE. W. A. Benjamin, New York, 1965.

175. Weinbaum, Stanley G.: THE NEW ADAM. Ziff-Davis, New York, 1939; Avon Books, New York, 1969.

176. Weinberg, George: THE ACTION APPROACH. World, New York, 1969.

177. Wells, H. G.: ANTICIPATION OF THE ACTION OF MECHANICAL AND SCIENTIFIC PROGRESS UPON HUMAN LIFE AND THOUGHT. Chapman and Hall, London, 1914. (Originally published in 1902.)

178. ——— STAR-BEGOTTEN. Viking Press, New York, 1937.

179. Wenk, Edward Jr.: "The Physical Resources of the Ocean." SCIENTIFIC AMERICAN, September, 1969.

180. White, Jerome B.: "Viral-Induced Repair of Damaged Neurons with Preservation of Long-Term Information Content." Paper read at the Second National Cryonics Conference, Ann Arbor, Michigan, 1969. Reprints available from the Cryonics Society of Michigan; see Cryonics Societies, above.

181. Whorf, Benjamin Lee: FOUR ARTICLES ON METALINGUISTICS. Foreign Service Institute, Washington, 1950.

182. Wigner, Eugen: "Remarks on the Mind-Body Question." In Good, above.

183. Wilson, Robert A.: FEMININE FOREVER. M. Evans, New York, 1966. (Distributed by J. B. Lippincott, Philadelphia.)

184. Wolstenholme, Gordon ed.: MAN AND HIS FUTURE. Little, Brown & Co., Boston, 1963. (See also Rosenfeld, Rostand, Sonneborn, above.)

185. Young, Paul T.: MOTIVATION AND EMOTION. John Wiley & Sons, New York, 1961.

Index

June 13, 1974